NOT QUITE AN ORDINARY LIFE

NOT QUITE AN ORDINARY LIFE

The Memories Of An Ordinary Man
Who Lived A Somewhat Extraordinary Life

J. David Joyce

iUniverse, Inc.
New York   Bloomington

Not Quite an Ordinary Life

The Memories Of An Ordinary Man Who Lived A Somewhat Extraordinary Life

iUniverse books may be ordered through booksellers or by contacting:

iUniverse
1663 Liberty Drive
Bloomington, IN 47403
www.iuniverse.com
1-800-Authors (1-800-288-4677)

Because of the dynamic nature of the Internet, any Web addresses or links contained in this book may have changed since publication and may no longer be valid. The views expressed in this work are solely those of the author and do not necessarily reflect the views of the publisher, and the publisher hereby disclaims any responsibility for them.

ISBN: 978-1-4401-1918-7 (pbk)
ISBN: 978-1-4401-1919-4 (ebk)

Printed in the United States of America

iUniverse rev. date: 1/26/2009

For my wife, children and grandchildren.

Contents

PART III - MARRIED IN THE MILITARY

PREFACE

I was born with wanderlust. Perhaps it filtered into my genes from my four grandparents; they were all immigrants to America. Two came from Ireland, one came from England and one came from Germany. Wanderlust can be a curse; it is counterproductive to amassing wealth. Robert Service alluded to this in his poem "*The Men That Don't Fit In*," when he wrote, "Could I find my proper groove, what a deep mark I would make!" Perhaps I could have fared financially better and made a deeper groove in life had I not such a strong desire to see what was over the next hill. As a young boy, I yearned to see places like Athens, Saigon, Istanbul, London, Tokyo and Rome. I wanted to explore the United States and Europe. I was able to do those things and more. Today, at age seventy-four, I feel that if told I had to stay in one place forever, I would choose to hasten the end my life, because I must have the freedom to move if the fancy strikes me.

This book describes my wandering and some of the effects it had on me. Part of the way through my travels, I met and married another wanderer. Until we met, Sylvia didn't know she had wanderlust. She was unknowingly infected with it when she was born on the back seat of a moving car on the causeway between mainland Texas and Galveston Island. No one else in her family has lived more than one hundred miles away from their place of birth, but Sylvia has traveled many hundreds of thousands of miles with me since we married.

Reminiscing can be dicey. Unless we are careful, every incident becomes better or worse when we talk or write about it; this is a natural tendency. In writing this memoir, I have made every effort not to exaggerate in either direction and to present incidents exactly as they occurred.

It's hard to have an open mind when we are young; we think we know everything and will live forever. Traveling in distant places tends to expand our outlook, and if we are lucky, we begin to learn and change as we travel our way through life. We begin to see the world through the eyes of others and it is enlightening. That's the way it was for me. What precious little I knew about life and how to live when I embarked on my journey, I learned from my father. More than a few bumps and bruises later, I have learned many things and matured a great deal.

Having been born into a family of very limited means and with only a high school education, there was no way I could explore the world on my own. I was, however, able to see part of it at the expense of American taxpayers as a member of the United States Air Force. Among the genes I received from my ancestors, some special ones must have flowed through to my brain. The career path personnel of the United States Air Force determined I had a relatively high IQ and selected me to work in foreign intelligence collection and analysis. The operative word here is "foreign." I spent almost fourteen years outside of the continental United States working in my career field. While in the Air Force, I served in San Antonio, Texas; Anchorage and Naknek Alaska; Trabzon, Turkey; Bremerhaven, Berlin, Darmstadt and Augsburg, Germany; Nha Trang, South Vietnam, and Brindisi, Italy; all before the age of forty. Since leaving the Air Force at the end of 1973, I have lived in San Antonio, Victoria, Kerrville, and New Braunfels, Texas. I have also resided in Albuquerque, Roswell and Rio Rancho, New Mexico.

Succumbing to my wanderlust, I have moved forty-two times in the past fifty-five years. Our financial position was improved by some moves and degraded by others, but almost all of them were voluntary and satisfied my intense desire never to be tied down to one place.

When I asked a writer friend to review the draft of a previous book, she suggested that I write a memoir. At the time, I didn't think many people would be interested in a memoir by a non-celebrity. Upon reflection, I concluded that perhaps the wacky characters and strange incidents in my past really might interest and even amuse others. After months of consideration, I decided to record some of the many interesting and sometimes funny things that have happened to me over these past seventy-four years. This lightly abridged story of my life, so far, is the result. My intention is to bring laughter, understanding and empathy to readers.

As is normally the case with a memoir, some of the photographs are very old and of poor quality. Rather than considering them as bad choices to include in this book, please think of them as authentic representations of history.

This book has undergone a formal, six month long security review by governmental intelligence organizations. The only criticism received from those agencies at the time of publication was my disclosure of unit locations around the world. My research has located unclassified, published documentation of USAFSS unit designations and locations in all parts of the world; thus, I have opted to publish the manuscript as originally written.

PART I – SURVIVING YOUTH

Chapter 1 - The Boy

Until I was in my mid-teens, I didn't know my first name was Jeremiah. Upon discovering that fact, I asked my father why everyone called me by my middle name. He told me he wanted to name me after his uncle Jeremiah, my mother wanted to name me David, and they compromised. They named me Jeremiah David but my mother never told anyone my first name was Jeremiah, and by default, everyone called me David. My father won the battle, but my mother won the war.

I was born in 1934, as the eighth child of nine, to parents of limited means. My father was a house painter and my mother did not work away from our home. Until I left home at the age of eighteen, I lived in a three bedroom, one bath house on Howard Street in North Tarrytown, New York. The town, originally called Sleepy Hollow, was small, about 14,000 residents.

In the seventeenth century, because Sleepy Hollow was one day's ride on horseback, about twenty-five miles, north of New York City, travelers found it to be a fine place to tarry for the night, and thus, they nicknamed it the tarry town. The name Sleepy Hollow faded away, and as more and more people settled into the area, the town grew and divided into Tarrytown and North Tarrytown. I was born in Tarrytown, as that was the location of our hospital, but I lived and grew up in North Tarrytown, the fictional home of the characters in *The Legend of Sleepy Hollow* written by Washington Irving.

In the following photograph, circa 1938, the characters are, from left to right, my mother, Helen, Marianne, yours truly, Patty, Danny, Alice, Bobby, Buddy, Betty, Kathleen and my father, George. Upon seeing this photograph for the first time, my wife remarked that it seemed to represent all the weight and responsibilities of being a wife and mother of nine children cascading downhill onto my mother.

Each of the children in the photograph was to have children of their own. They accounted for forty-seven grandchildren. Kathleen had seven children, Betty had ten, Buddy had four, Bobby had two, Alice had nine, Danny had two, Patty had four, I had two and Marianne had seven.

I'm already watching out for Marianne. (Courtesy: Kathleen Clark)

Our house on Howard Street was a block and a half from North Tarrytown High School; two blocks from Beekman Avenue, which was our main street; and three blocks from St. Teresa's Catholic Church and grammar school. That's right; we were Irish Catholic with all the baggage that goes along with that background. My father's parents were Irish immigrants. I have been unable to find out when my father's mother arrived, but based on a letter of recommendation carried by my father's father, he arrived in 1872. The letter states that he had been a hard working assistant groom, a stable hand, and could be trusted to be a good worker. When he arrived from Ireland, my grandfather's name was Richard Joice but he changed the "i" to "y" for unknown reasons. With his new name and his letter of recommendation, he started a new life that included his marriage to Miss Annie Sheehan in 1883. Richard Joyce became a skilled carpenter, and by the time of his death, he owned seven houses in North Tarrytown free and clear.

On my mother's side, there was a mixture. Her mother, Elizabeth Watkins, was an immigrant from London, England and her father, Ernest L. Conrad, was born in Hamburg, Germany. In 1874, to avoid military conscription, he worked his way to the United States as a seaman. He jumped ship in New York harbor and took up residence in Haworth, New Jersey. I've been told he eventually received his naturalization papers when an amnesty period for illegal aliens was declared. All I ever knew about my mother's father was that he was a mean, demanding person who made her early years very unhappy. With this mixture of blood in our veins, there is no wonder that most of us grew up hard-headed and quick-tempered. It's a good thing we had that little dab of English blood to temper us a bit.

According to my sister Kathleen, she pictures me in her memory as a happy, red-headed, freckled-faced child with a fishing pole over his shoulder with his dog Sheppy along side, leaving the house to visit a favorite fishing hole. My pole was not as you might find today. It was just a long branch from a tree, trimmed of twigs. It wasn't real fishing line either. I used whatever string I could find, a real fishing hook and a cork for a bobber. My bait would be night crawlers picked up from some neighbor's lawn late during the previous evening. For me, this all worked as well as the manufactured equipment some of the kids had.

Before my mother died at age one hundred and four, she sent some old photographs to her surviving children. In my case, she also sent a lock of red hair cut from my head that she had saved for well over sixty years. It is still silky smooth as it should be when taken from an eighteen month old child, and has retained its auburn color. It must be true about some physical traits skipping generations. I eventually married a young woman with deep auburn hair and yet none of our two children and five grandchildren was born with red hair.

My earliest memory is of the hurricane of 1938 that ravaged the northeast coast of the United States. I had just turned four years old, but can remember the talk of the impending storm and the fear that existed. My memory of the storm is only of the roaring winds that caused the branches of nearby trees to scratch the outside of our house as I lay in my bed in my parents' room. My little sister, Marianne, was only a year old but I don't remember where she was during the storm nor do I know anything about the rest of the family. It seems that I have strong memories of incidents in my life that I perceived as traumatic, but recollections of the mundane slip away from my memory. I do remember planting corn, string beans and carrots in our back yard as my mother explained the process of seeding, watering and growing. Other than that, my pre-school years must have been uneventful. My father was not an educated man; in fact, he told me he never got past the fourth grade. I don't know if that was a true story or not, but he had his own ways of teaching us about the realities of life. To help me understand a particular danger, he chose an unusual action.

On a cold, snowy evening, my father took me along with him to visit a funeral home. When we entered the viewing room, I quickly noticed the center of attraction. In the middle of the far end of the room, there was a white casket elevated a step above the floor. In the casket was the body of a boy of about my own age. He was dressed in a First Communion suit. The jacket and short pants were white; there was a large white bow on his left arm; and there was a set of rosary beads entwined in his fingers. There were other people in the room sitting in neatly arranged rows of folding chairs. They just sat there looking straight ahead without conversing. I really did not know what was going on, but I was with my father so the scene did not upset me.

I do not think I knew the boy; if I did, it must have been only a casual acquaintance. After viewing the body, we left the funeral home and returned to the car. On the way home, my father told me a car had killed the boy as he was hitching a ride on the back bumper with his sled. In those days, the bumpers on cars were straight. It was easy to slide the rope attached to the front of a sled on to the rear bumper and get pulled along over the snow. He told me it was important for me to see what can happen to a child who tries to hitch a ride on the back of a car. The visit to the funeral home made a strong impression on me concerning the danger of hitching my sled on to the back of cars, but I do not remember any sense of grief.

As we drove home, I must have asked something about dying because I can remember my father explaining how time has a way of taking care of grief. He told me that when someone dies, those left behind think of the dead person every day for a few weeks, but then a day soon comes and goes without a thought of the one who died. The first time this happens, people find themselves feeling guilty because they let a day go by without thinking of the dead person. He told me as more and more time goes by, the day without a thought turns into a week and then a month and then longer and longer periods between thoughts. He explained that it was all right to forget because it was a natural thing with people. All of this made as much sense as it could to a child and I kept the advice with me for life. Because he had not yet lost any of his children, my father did not know that the theory does not apply when you lose a child of your own.

Chapter 2 - Grammar School

Most of the Irish children in North Tarrytown attended Saint Teresa's elementary school, which was administered by Saint Teresa's Catholic Church and staffed with Franciscan nuns. There were also children of Italian, French Canadian and Polish descent who attended; however, the Slavic members of our community had their own Catholic Church and did not allow their children to attend our school; they attended the North Tarrytown public school. A perusal of the names in the eighth grade graduating class provides an insight into the ethnic diversity of our neighborhood. There were no black students in our class, nor were there any Hispanics. There were only Irish, Italian, Polish, French Canadian and traditional Anglo Saxon names. On the list, my name is David Joyce instead of Jeremiah or Jeremiah David. When my mother enrolled me in the school, she used her preferred name for me and no one asked any questions.

The school did not have a kindergarten level, as did the public school system; so on my first day in the first grade, at age six, I knew absolutely nothing about school. My mother told my sister Patty to teach me how to find the school. This was a questionable decision on her part as Patty, a third grade student, was only eighteen months older than I. It was to be an adventure and I anticipated it with glee. The glee was soon to dissipate. Patty walked along side of me and pointed out landmarks. At the corner of Pocantico and Howard Streets, my prior limit, Patty said that we would turn right, walk until we reached Elm Street, cross Elm Street and walk to Beekman Avenue. She told me it was easy because there were only two choices at Beekman Avenue and that we would turn right. She said that we would just walk two blocks until we saw the school and the play area on the left and we would be there. When we arrived, she took me to where the first graders lined up to enter the school when the bell rang. There were eight lines and the first graders were in the first line; so the concept was easy to understand. Before she left me, she asked if I would be able to find my way home for lunch and I told her that I would. That was it; I was in school.

My first day in the school was the first time I had seen a nun up close. She was scary. Sister Mary Francis stood in front of the class dressed in a black habit with what looked like white clothes line rope around her waist with a long piece of it hanging down almost to the floor. I couldn't see any hair on her head as the top of the habit covered her entire head and a piece of white cloth covered her forehead. Another piece of fabric ran under her chin. She stood there with her hands and forearms stuffed into the wide sleeves of her habit. Her face held piercing black eyes and jowls accentuated by the cloth stretched tightly under her chin. The jowls said, "Don't any of you dare say a word unless you are spoken to." My initial impression was one of fear. Sister Mary Francis laid down the laws I was supposed to follow throughout my eight years of elementary school. I can't remember anything else about that first morning, but I know I didn't speak a word.

Learning to find the school and find my way back home was the easy part. Dealing with the nuns and Father Fry, the Priest assigned to monitor the activities of the school, turned out to be a much larger challenge. Many years earlier, my brother Buddy apparently misbehaved at altar boy class and was slapped on the face by Father Fry, who supervised the altar boys. My father got his Irish up when he found out about the incident and went to the Rectory make his feelings known. When he encountered the housekeeper at the Rectory door, he insisted that he be able to speak with Father Fry. When Father Fry appeared at the door, my father invited him out to the lawn for a good old fashioned Irish whooping because, as he told Father Fry, "No one hits my children." Father Fry, who I now suspect to have been a pedophile, would not accept the invitation and my father would not invade the Rectory, so no fight ensued.

It was impossible to keep an incident such as this a secret in a town of fourteen thousand people, so Father Fry had to live with the shame of declining the invitation to fight for the rest of his life; but he found ways to get even. Every member of the Joyce family younger than Buddy had to deal with Father Fry's spiteful punishment through all of the eight years (nine, in my case) in Saint Teresa's elementary school.

When he started to take out his anger on me, I was unaware of the history between him and our family. His first retaliation was to deny me the right to serve as an altar boy, saying I did not know my Latin well enough. I knew my memorization of the Latin phrases as well as the other boys and could not figure out why he said it wasn't. My father expected me to be an altar boy and I didn't want to disappoint him. The situation was a quandary for me because I really didn't want to be an altar boy; it took time away from play and fishing.

Each Monday morning, Father Fry would come into my classroom and accuse me of not attending the nine o'clock Mass on the previous Sunday. I attended the nine o'clock Mass, although I had no idea why children were supposed to attend that particular Mass, so I didn't understand why he said I hadn't. The punishment for not attending the nine o'clock Mass was forty-five minutes of detention on Monday afternoon. I asked my sister Alice why Father Fry would do that, and she told me about the family history with him. As I recall his actions toward me, three things in particular come to mind.

Someone in my family said I should join the Boy Scout Troop sponsored by the Church. I dutifully attended a meeting, and although I felt a little out of place because I had no scout uniform as did the other boys, I paid attention and tried to learn about scouting. Near the end of the meeting, Father Fry announced that it was time for the "troop wrestle." With that, the lights went out and all of the boys started wrestling in the dark. I immediately sensed this as threatening and moved to a wall on one side of the room to keep the other boys away from me. When I returned home and related my experience to my father, he told me I didn't have to attend anymore meetings. At the time, I didn't even know the word pedophile much less the meaning; but now I am very suspicious of the intentions of Father Fry, who was the scout master. The incident soured me on scouting and I discouraged my children from participating in that endeavor because I worried about troop leaders I didn't know having an influence on their development.

The second incident occurred one Friday afternoon when the nun in charge of my class (I can't remember what grade, but a very early one) escorted us to the Church to participate in the ritual of confession. In the Catholic Church, members confess their sins to a priest each week to purify their souls before they participate in the ritual of Holy Communion at Mass on Sunday. The students sat side by side in the pews with about four empty pews between them and the confessional, ostensibly to provide privacy to the confessor. This idea was invalid, because the procedures also required three students to line up against the wall close to the confessional and await their turn. In addition, the confessional had entrances on each side, so while one person was confessing sins, there was another confessor waiting within a few feet. As I took my place as the third student in line that Friday afternoon, other students sat in pews and at the end of the first pew sat the nun who had taken us to the church. The door to the confessional flew open and Father Fry came out. He looked at me and said, "David Joyce, you were talking in church. That's a venial sin. Get out of my Church right now."

I was stunned. I hadn't been talking. I looked imploringly at the nun expecting her to defend me, as she was close enough to have known if I or anyone else had been talking in church. She only stared at me with a look of fear. There was nothing to do but to leave the Church and go home. When I told my mother about the incident, she suggested that Father Fry had probably heard someone else talking in church and mistakenly blamed me. She also told me not to tell my father about what had happened. It was at this early age that I began to question authority.

There was an attic above the second story of the school which contained meeting rooms and a recreation area. Two bowling lanes that utilized the smaller bowling balls and pins were on one side of the large room. One afternoon, Father Fry walked into the seventh grade class and invited all of the boys in the class to use the recreation facilities for the last hour and a half of the school day. When I entered the recreation room, he stopped me, said that the use of the facility was for all of the boys except "Joyce kids," and sent me home. The man just hated my entire family.

I think Father Fry developed a special dislike of me. When I realized I would have to stay after school on Mondays if I didn't attend the nine o'clock Mass on Sunday, my Irish stubbornness reared its wonderful head. I didn't think anyone should be able to tell me what Mass to attend, so to prove I wasn't lazy, I started attending the eight o'clock Mass. Each Monday when Father Fry accused me of missing the nine o'clock Mass, I responded with the statement that I had attended an earlier Mass. I stayed after school almost every Monday. Sometimes the nun in charge would let me leave after Father Fry left the area, but if she didn't, I simply used the time for homework.

Many of the nuns were as mean as Father Fry. I now know that, more than likely, they were sexually repressed women with extremely low self-esteem who vented their frustration by using physical punishment on students. Most of the time it was the boys who suffered the brunt of the nuns' internal anger with themselves. I also noticed that the nuns were careful not to pick on the students with wealthy parents. What I didn't know at the time was that the poor children were resented by Father Fry and some of the nuns. There was no specific amount of tuition charged for attendance at the school, but parents were expected to contribute extra funds to the Church as payment for the privilege of having their children receive a Catholic education. The wealthy families were able to contribute much more than the poor families. My family could contribute little or nothing, yet we attended Saint Teresa's elementary school. My father did donate his time and skills when something needed to be painted or repaired at the school. Although our parents felt a religious obligation to send us to a Catholic school, the church administrators would rather the non-contributing parents had sent their children to the public school.

I assume some of the nuns were deep into their religious beliefs and chose the convent as a way to ensure they would end up in heaven once they had outlived their bodies. Teaching children was just another assignment from the church which they accepted whether they were qualified or not. Some were really mean and had favorite ways to satisfy their needs to be cruel. One way was to have each student stand in front of the class to recite the multiplication tables. The student was made to stand with the palms of both hands facing upward while the nun stood there with a twelve-inch wooden ruler in her hand at the ready to use as a weapon should the recitation not go well. I once heard a comedian say he knew of a nun who could remove a kidney and a gall bladder with one swipe from a ruler like that. I never saw anything so brutal; but whenever I made a mistake in multiplication, down came come the ruler across my hands. After some of my turns in front of the class, I can remember my hands being so numb that I could not move my fingers. I credit my inability to recite the complete multiplication tables to this day to that horrible method of teaching.

Another favorite method of punishment for infractions of the rules that I endured was to stand at the rear of the classroom with arms outstretched to the side, parallel to the floor. After a while, my arm muscles would burn with pain. If I grimaced, the nun would say something like, "Stop making faces. Jesus hung on the cross for three hours and didn't complain." As the tiny muscles in my arms screamed out in pain, I could find a little relief if the nun turned her back to write something on the board. I would raise one arm high enough to get my shirtsleeve between my teeth to ease the strain on my arm muscles. A few seconds was all I would dare before switching to the other arm. This was a high-risk maneuver because, if caught, the penalty was another five minutes of torture.

It wasn't just the boys who suffered punishment from the nuns. I can remember a day when one of the girls in the class raised her hand with one finger up indicating she had to go to the girls' room to urinate. The nun, probably to punish her for some real or imagined infraction of the rules, denied her that privilege. Eventually, the inevitable occurred and the girl burst out in tears and placed her head on her desk. She was a sweet person who was badly treated by someone who should have known better. I can still feel her shame and embarrassment that was no fault of hers.

My experience in that school was the beginning of the poor education I received as a young person. It wasn't that the technical information was not available or presented; my objection is that the teachers did not see or nurture the independent thinking students. To them, there was only one way to teach; learn by memorization. They never encouraged individualism, which is both a curse and a gift, but nonetheless, does exist in some students. Once, I posed a question in geography class that caused some degree of consternation. I noticed the similarity in the coastlines of South America and Africa and how the two could fit together like pieces of a puzzle. I asked the nun if these continents had been together at one time and had moved apart. I even suggested that if we could look at the coastlines underwater, we might find evidence to support the idea. Her response suggested that I was either a heretic or had a wild imagination. She told the class there was no way what I suggested could have happened because God made the world the way it was and did it in seven days. This was in the days before the theory of plate tectonics was accepted as sound science. I do not know what they teach in that school today. I certainly hope things have improved.

My problems in grammar school were not all caused by Father Fry and the nuns. Being the eighth child, I got lost in the shuffle and received no encouragement to succeed in school or any academic help at home. There never was an expectation that any of us would aspire to higher education or become anything in life that required more than a high school education.

It took me nine years to get through eight years of elementary school. For all I know, part of the decision to require me to repeat the second grade was to bring some gratification to Father Fry. Maybe I was slow in reading or mathematics, or maybe I was just bored with the way they presented the material. I do remember staring through the windows of my classrooms thinking about fishing or playing baseball when I should have been paying attention to the nun teaching the class. I do know that my IQ has always been scored at between 126 and 130, and that, unlike most of those who did not have to repeat the second grade, I eventually earned both a Bachelor's and Master's degree. Maybe I was just a troublemaker. One time when I questioned something taught in religious instruction class, the nun teaching the subject told me that I should believe it as a matter of faith. When I asked what faith was, she hesitated for a few moments and then explained that to accept something on faith is to accept something that cannot be proved. This ridiculous request on her part has remained as vivid a memory as the day I was told I would repeat the second grade.

It was the last school day in the year. Father Fry came into the room with a piece of paper in his hand. He read my name and three others and told us to stand in front of the room. As we stood there, he told the others to report to the third grade next September and then told us to report to the second grade when we came back to school in the fall. That was it. We stood there in front of the class to receive their scorn or sympathy. It was a mean and unnecessary way to do things and only added to my objections to the Church. I am sure that if there is a Hell, the despicable Father Fry resides there. If there is no

Hell, which is more likely, Father Fry probably suffered mightily with his demons and died an unhappy, tired, old man, which also makes me happy.

Because I repeated the second grade, I was a year older than most of my classmates through the rest of my primary and secondary education. There was a side benefit to this. I spent a few of my years in high school as a friend of Amelia Zaicek. Amelia also had to repeat the second grade when she attended the local public elementary school. She was, and remains, a good Catholic but her family would not let her attend the "Irish" Catholic Church so she didn't attend Saint Teresa's elementary school with me. After reading some of my writing, she recently suggested to me that maybe it was a good thing she didn't have to deal with the nuns. Amelia had a plausible reason for her second grade failure; because her parents were immigrants from Czechoslovakia, she only spoke the Czech language when she started the first grade. She was never a sweetheart of mine, but was a friend and we continue to correspond these many years later.

This description of my days as a student at Saint Teresa's elementary school should not make you think my early years were all unhappy; there were good times too. I remember one particular nun, Sister Stanislaus, my third grade teacher, who was nice to me. I had resisted the Palmer method of cursive writing where each letter had a specific shape, height and width, preventing any individuality in handwriting. Even today, when I see handwriting from someone who attended a Catholic grammar school, I can detect vestiges of that teaching. In my rebellious manner, I decided to write at half the recommended height. When Sister Stanislaus saw my writing, she sat down with me and proposed a deal. She told me if would write at the preferred size in her class, I could write any way I wanted once I got through the third grade. That sounded good to me, so I went along with the deal. Four years later, when I walked into the seventh grade and saw Sister Stanislaus, who had been reassigned to teach the seventh grade, I knew I had the upper hand. She remembered our agreement and honored it. Sister Stanislaus was one of the few good nuns.

Chapter 3 - The Morphine Problem

I had another problem in grammar school which to me seemed important at the time, but in retrospect, was minor compared to my father's problem. As I attended the seventh and eighth grades, my father became severely addicted to morphine. For as long as I could remember, he had suffered from migraine headaches. He had been a house painter for his entire life, and some said that inhaling the fumes from the lead-based paints used in those days was the likely cause. The cause didn't matter. What mattered is that I remember him being on medication and the children being hushed when he was home sick. Whenever we saw the shades drawn down during daylight hours, we knew Dad was home sick and automatically followed the routine of silence.

Over the years, doctors of all kinds prescribed remedies for his headaches. He tried Chiropractic therapy, but that didn't work. There was a time when he followed the routine of eating only squab, because some doctor, probably a quack, said it would prevent headaches. There were over-the-counter medications all over the house. My mother tried every known home remedy to no avail. All of this was expensive to a large family subsisting on one tradesman's income and took a toll on all of us. The threshold for any of us to see a doctor was a wound that required stitches; otherwise, we depended on home remedies. If we did need stitches, it meant a trip to the emergency room at the county hospital. We paid property taxes, which supported that hospital, so we felt entitled to the service. However, the emergency room could not treat my father's problem, so many of the family's meager assets disappeared into the pockets of doctors and pharmacists.

One doctor prescribed Seconal, a barbiturate in use at the time as a sleeping pill. This kept my father drowsy or asleep much of the time. He became addicted to the medication and required higher and higher doses until the doctor refused to prescribe any more. The doctor switched him to Nembutal, another barbiturate, which was also addictive and worked the same way as Seconal. My father was in a daze most of the time and repeatedly had minor traffic accidents while trying to function in the world. Eventually, he required stronger doses of the Nembutal to a point that he was danger to himself and others and the doctor took him off of that drug. That was a good decision; my research suggests that such notables as Charles Boyer, Marilyn Monroe, Judy Garland, Carol Landis and Jimi Hendrix all succumbed to overdoses of Nembutal.

As a last resort, the doctor prescribed Morphine. The old country doctor had no idea of the power and addictiveness of morphine. The medication, which my mother injected with a hypodermic needle, completely blocked the pain of his headaches. The downside of morphine is that users become severely addicted and build up a tolerance, which requires more and more medication to block the pain of the headache, and to satisfy the physiological and psychological need for the drug. Although taking legal drugs, my father became little more than a street addict addicted to Heroin, a drug based on Morphine. During the two year period he was taking Morphine, there were incidents of overdoses that took him close to death. Those incidents, though very serious, were not as bad as the times when he ran out of Morphine. When overdosed, he simply went into a comatose state; but when he ran short of the drug, he turned into a needy person unrecognizable to me. Most of the time, he took the morphine on a regular schedule and functioned in a mental fog which caused him to make improper decisions.

One poor decision he made was to try to change the right rear tire of his car parked on a slight, snow covered incline. He was working at Marymount College that snowy day when he discovered the flat tire. He raised the rear of the car with a bumper jack even though the vehicle was not level. While reaching into the trunk for the spare tire, the jack slipped and the car moved rearward until the bumper pinned him against a snow bank. It was impossible for him to move and difficult for him to cry out because of the weight of the car on his chest. After about an hour in the freezing weather and with the pressure of the vehicle taking a toll on him, he began to fade in and out of consciousness. Fortunately, one of the young women attending the college decided to sneak a cigarette in the ladies room and opened a window to let out the smoke. She saw my father struggling under the weight of the car about forty yards from the building and sought help for him.

As my father described it to me, he had just about given up and decided to die when he saw three figures running toward him, their flowing black robes in stark contrast to the snow covered ground. He thought they were the devil's helpers coming to take him to hell. I don't know what he ever did to make him think he was going to hell, but that's the story he told to me. Once the nuns arrived at the car and he realized they were there to help, his thinking cleared and he tried to respond to their questions as to what they should do. Before he got the chance to tell them to call the fire department, one of the nuns opened the driver side door and announced she would put on the emergency brake. She didn't hear him shout not to get into the car; when she did, the vehicle pressed even harder on his chest with her added weight. This caused him to lose consciousness again. The fire department eventually reached the scene, pulled the car off my father and got him up on his feet. He told everyone he was fine and had one of the volunteer firefighters he knew take him home. When they arrived at our home, the man assisted my father up the front steps and into the house, helped him lie down on the couch and called for my mother.

My mother was used to unexpected arrivals by my father, either because he needed a fix or because he had overdosed. She just told the man to make sure he was comfortable and she would check on him later. The man insisted she come and check on him right away. Although that irked her, she responded anyway. The firefighter didn't know she was unaware of the accident and she couldn't understand why he was making such a fuss over something that frequently happened. Finally, after the man showed her the long, wide, ugly bruise across my father's chest, she realized it was not a routine situation. When she berated the firefighter for not taking him to the hospital, the poor man tried to explain that my father refused to go there. Eventually, they called an ambulance that took him to the hospital where he stayed for several days. Forever after, that firefighter viewed my mother as one tough wife, even though she did the right thing once she realized my father was injured.

When my father had depleted his daily allotment of morphine

and none was available, he morphed from being a parent into a junkie who would scream for a fix. Those are the times I remember most because I was an integral part of obtaining his medication. It fell to me to make visits to the doctor's office to pick up prescriptions. The doctor was so lax in his control of medications, that once a month he simply signed thirty or thirty-one blank prescription forms which I delivered to the pharmacy; then, each day, the pharmacist filled in the request for Morphine. I did this so often, I became very familiar with the two owners of the store and they allowed me to go behind the counter where the pharmacists worked. I watched as they counted out forty, one-quarter grain pills into a container before exchanging them for the money my mother gave to me to pay the bill. In those days, they measured Morphine in grains instead of milligrams which is the current standard of measure. To understand how strong the prescription was, consider this. During World War II, combat troops carried a Morphine injection container. It was a squeezable tube filled with one-quarter grain of liquefied Morphine with a needle attached to the end. Soldiers knew that an injection of the contents would dull the pain of wounds, up to and including the loss of a limb, for four hours. My father started out with an injection of one-quarter of a grain; by the time this phase of his life ended, my mother was injecting ten grains of Morphine into him every day. In terms of milligrams, the current recommended dose of Morphine for someone in severe pain is from 30 to 120 milligrams over a twenty-four hour period; my father was using 650 milligrams a day, every day.

I was the designated child to be at the drug store every morning when it opened at 8:00 A.M. to pick up my father's Morphine prescription. Since school started at 8:00 o'clock, I was late every day by the amount of time it took me to get the prescription, take it three blocks to where we lived and travel four blocks back to the schoolhouse. For several months while I was in the eighth grade, I walked into the classroom every day thirty minutes after instruction had started to the scowling look of a black-garbed nun who was incensed because she did not have control over the situation.

I can remember watching my mother dilute up to three of the one-quarter grain pills in water in a large spoon held over an open flame. She would then suck up the liquefied Morphine into a syringe through a twenty-five gauge hypodermic needle, push out any air in the syringe and inject the medication into my father's arm or leg or side, depending on which area was not over used. At his peak use of Morphine, he was receiving about fifteen injections a day. At the rate things were going, my father was going to die from an overdose of Morphine or kill himself while driving under the influence of the drug if something didn't change. Change came by way of a United States government's narcotics enforcement unit.

They showed up at Brunt and Brooks Pharmacy early one morning convinced that the druggists were engaged in the illicit distribution of Morphine. The pharmacists provided the proper paperwork, but the investigators were suspicious and insisted on meeting and interviewing my mother and father. They were finally convinced that one person was consuming the vast amount of morphine but said it could not continue. They agreed to allow the flow to continue at the rate in effect only if my father would commit himself to the federal government's narcotics addiction center, then known as "Narco," in Lexington, Kentucky. The agents arranged for my father's treatment, and in the summer of 1952, my mother and father, my brother-in-law, Ray Clark and I drove to Lexington. They admitted my father and two days later, we returned home. We had no idea what would happen to him, and I must rely on his description of what transpired.

He told us they let him know that the only treatment authorized was "cold turkey." They put him into a padded cell, offered him meals three times a day at specific times and did not administer morphine or any other drug to him. It took eleven days to "kick the habit." My father explained the derivation of the expression "kick the habit" to me. He described this severe withdrawal aspect narcotic addicts suffer. During the early stages of withdrawal, addicts cannot control their legs. Their legs will spontaneously jerk and no amount of mental strength can calm them. Eventually, the jerking ceases when the addict is on the road to recovery. In the eleven days it took my father to withdraw from his addiction, he lost twenty pounds, and in the subsequent two and a half months of confinement, he lost another fifteen pounds. Ironically, his doctor had been advising him to lose weight for quite some time.

During his recovery period, my father met other addicts at Narco. He told me of one addict who, after his padded cell period, constantly bothered other inmates to complain to the orderlies about having a headache and to ask for aspirin. His plan was to gather as many aspirin tablets as possible and take them all at once to see if he could get a "high." The most disturbing person he met was a very young man who had become addicted to avoid the military draft. The Korean War was raging and many draftees had died in combat. The young man was from a wealthy family that arranged with their doctor to have him prescription drug addicted when he showed up for his induction physical examination. He admitted to the examining physician that he was a drug addict and was declared unfit to serve. The family then arranged for his commitment to Narco to overcome his addiction. The young man told my father that he was more than willing to go through the addiction and the three months of confinement to keep from going to Korea where he might die in combat. He planned to resume his privileged life when released from Narco. This situation did not sit well with my father who had two sons in Korea at the time. As an impressionable teenager, I was shocked by the story. Now that I am older and more jaded, I feel certain that the addiction ploy was just one of many used to avoid the draft.

I left home in the summer of 1953 and until that time, my father had not stumbled in his addiction recovery. Recently I learned that later in his life, which was to end at age sixty-seven, he succumbed to the psychological need for pharmaceuticals. When my oldest sister, Kathleen, asked my mother how she could have resumed injecting him with drugs, she replied that the headaches came back so she had no choice. Kathleen then asked how she was able to find the morphine. My mother told her that they simply went to a doctor who was not aware of my father's history and obtained prescriptions. That is an example of an unsophisticated drug addict finding a way to obtain narcotics. My father died in his sleep on October 5, 1967. There was no autopsy and the coroner listed the cause of death as "natural." For all I know, his death was the result of yet another accidental overdose.

Drug addiction knows no social or economic boundaries. Our minds can thoroughly convince us we have an endless array of maladies that need pharmaceutical treatment just so we can receive a drug induced high. My mother and father were good people who found themselves caught up in the swirl of drug addiction. His addiction was no different from the street addict. Absent the intervention of the government and his stay at Narco, I hesitate to think of what might have happened as he required more and more Morphine to satisfy his need for the drug.

Chapter 4 - The Pony

When I was seven years old, my father's brother, Uncle Johnny, bought a pony. Johnny was an automobile mechanic and a lifelong bachelor. He showed great care and love for Snowball, who was a mixture of Shetland and Mexican pony strains. She was bigger than a Shetland and smaller than a standard Mexican pony. Johnny had no place to keep Snowball so he and my father turned half of our garage in to a pony stall and she remained there for most of her life. A few days after she arrived, Johnny put the bridal and saddle on her and put me on that diminutive beast. Upon settling down into the saddle, Snowball bucked for all she was worth and threw me off of her back. I can still see the space between her ears as I flew over her head. Everyone agreed that the only way to deal with the situation was to put me right back into the saddle because that is what everybody always said was the right thing to do. Oddly enough, it was the right thing to do. I learned how to hang on and ride that pony and never had any fear of ponies or horses for the rest of my life. I eventually learned to ride horses and have enjoyed many hours in the saddle.

Snowball became the mascot for the North Tarrytown High School as the mount for the headless horseman of Sleepy Hollow fame. The problem was, she was a small pony and had to have a small rider, so Johnny would teach the littlest girls in the neighborhood to ride. At the football games, the selected rider would wear a turtleneck sweater with the neck portion at the top of her head and carry a pumpkin in one hand as she rode out onto the field. It was a nice idea and people loved the show. As I got older, Johnny didn't want me to ride Snowball anymore because he thought I was getting too big, but I found ways to ride her while he was at work. Ponies by their nature are prone to be cantankerous. Add that trait to Snowball's dislike of the way I demanded to be in control of her and it was no wonder that she bit me one morning when I was putting on her bridle. It was wintertime and I had a sweater and winter coat over my shirt, yet she managed to bite through all of that and still break the skin on my arm. I couldn't tell anyone because I was not supposed to be riding her, so I just covered the bite with band-aids hoped for the best. I did give her a good smack but that just made her dislike me even more. All in all, it was a good experience to be around her; not many children had that opportunity.

Chapter 5 - Killing Sheppy

When I was six weeks old, my father brought home a white Collie puppy. My mother told me she remembered saying, "Oh, George, we've got all these kids, a new baby and you had to bring home a puppy!" Someone named the puppy Sheppy and he became part of the family. Sheppy and I grew up together and were inseparable until his death when we were both twelve years old. My parents took the photograph of Sheppy and me, below, in 1944 or 1945. In the photograph, it appears by the condition of his coat and lack of normal weight that he is in declining health.

Must be Sunday - I'm wearing a tie. (Courtesy: Helen Joyce)

My mother never feared to let me roam the neighborhood as a very little boy because that dog was with me whenever I left the confines of our yard. I never had to call him or urge him; he seemed to know it was his duty to protect me. There came a time, though, when he was just too old and lame keep up with me. He was suffering from rheumatism, which made it difficult to get up and down, and something they called, "the mange" that causes skin problems for dogs. Late in 1945 or early 1946, my mother and father made the decision that it was time to put Sheppy out of his misery.

He had been a fine pet for the entire family, so when the time to terminate his life arrived, all of the family members who were available attended the procedure. First, someone found an old steamer trunk for a coffin which my mother lined with a tattered comforter. We located a photograph of Sheppy and placed it into an eight by ten picture frame with a note explaining just whose remains they were, should they ever become unearthed. We had many Nembutal capsules left from when my father was using that drug instead of Morphine to control his migraine headaches and decided to kill the dog with an overdose of those. My mother inserted each of twenty capsules into a dollop of margarine and fed them to Sheppy; then, we sat and waited for him to die. Apparently, Nembutal has no effect on dogs, or at least not that dog. He didn't even appear groggy. After an hour of waiting, my father sent my brother-in-law Ray Clark to the drug store to buy some Chloroform.

When Ray returned with the Chloroform, a large kitchen strainer was located and lined with a baby's diaper. My mother poured Chloroform all over the diaper and the process began. Ray, one of my brothers and I held Sheppy down as my father forced the strainer over his face. The Chloroform smelled slightly sweet but was very strong and burned my eyes. The Nembutal didn't bother the dog, but Chloroform sure did. He fought us like a demon. Slipping and sliding all over the linoleum covered floor, the four of us ended up under the kitchen table, which finally came to rest when it collided with the refrigerator. By this time, Sheppy's struggling was almost contained. What the others didn't know, until I passed out, was that the Chloroform fumes had a strong effect on me. When I awoke, I found myself across the room with my mother attending to me. The three others were still holding down the lifeless body of the dog. They all looked a little groggy, too. Finally, my mother pronounced the dog dead and they let go of him;

he was out of his misery. If this process sounds barbaric, it wasn't; it is just the way things were done in those days. Money the family needed couldn't be paid to a Veterinarian to euthanize a pet.

The work wasn't finished yet; we needed a grave for the coffin. It was wintertime and the top of the ground was frozen. Because the Chloroform had knocked me out, my mother was upset and sent me to bed. I couldn't sleep for a long time that night. I could hear the sounds of the pick hitting the frozen ground in our back yard as my brother and brother-in-law dug the grave. Actually, as I write this, I can still recall those sounds.

My father tried to replace Sheppy with another white collie but it didn't work out very well. Sandy was a barker and displayed a touch of meanness toward children. My family could not tolerate either of those traits in a dog. One day, I came home from school and Sandy was gone. I never became attached to that dog so it didn't bother me. We were, however, to have another dog.

As I walked back from the local dairy where my mother had sent me to purchase a quart of milk, I came upon a man in his back yard with four or five puppies. I was a child, so I had to stop to pet them. One in particular caught my eye and the man told me I could have it if I wanted because he had plenty. My place in the pecking order of my family was very low. I knew if I asked to have a puppy the answer would be no. I told the man that there was no way my parents would let me have a puppy, and continued on my walk home. I never mentioned the offer of a free puppy to anyone.

The man, who remains unknown to me, must have known my father. The next day, when I returned from school, that very same puppy was in our house. I couldn't believe that I had received something I really wanted without asking. We named her Fatima, after an obscure brand of cigarettes on the market at that time. She was nothing but a mongrel, but turned out to be a great dog.

Chapter 6 - Work Ethic

A strong work ethic can be both a blessing and a curse. My father instilled a strong work ethic in me based on personal responsibility that affected all areas of my life. He told me that a man's good word was the most valuable thing he can possess, and not to live up to my word was the worst thing I could do. There came a time, after we built the stall for Snowball, that it was necessary to provide electricity to the garage. My father and I went to work one evening to dig a trench between the house and the garage for a galvanized pipe to hold the electric wires. As we dug with our picks and shovels, he gave me advice on several subjects. When I complained about how hard the work was, he took the opportunity to give me a lesson on meeting my commitments. He told me that digging the trench was a perfect example. He explained that if I had made a contract to dig a trench eighteen inches wide, two feet deep and thirty feet long for seventy-five cents a foot and then found that the ground was extra hard, I still had to fulfill the contract. As I recall, he said I should make sure that I completed the trench exactly as agreed to and the next time insist on a dollar per foot. I have never forgotten his lesson of that evening. The conversation changed when we suddenly discovered a hard spot that made a thumping noise when hit with the shovel. We had come upon the trunk that held Sheppy's remains. My father smiled and mentioned that we did good work together that night, too.

During that project and many others we worked on together, my father continued to give me advice on life. Because my personality traits include thinking in a linear manner most of the time, I have consistently thought back to his advice and used it in decision making. I am so linear in my thinking that I have often been accused of being inflexible. My response to that accusation has always been that some people are so flexible others can't tell where they stand on a subject, but everyone always knows where I stand.

My father taught me about prejudice. We did not have many black people in our town but we had some, and my father pointed out that many people wrongly thought blacks (we called then Negros in those days) were not as good as white people. As an example, he took me to the corner of Cortland Street and Beekman Avenue where the first and only, recently hired, black police officer was directing traffic. He pointed out the man's uniform was immaculate, that his shoes sported a perfect shine and that he directed traffic with polite and distinct sharpness. Then he told me if I compared him to other officers, I would find that they were not as sharp-looking nor would they display such a professional presence. He explained that black people had to do things better than white people just to get the job because of prejudice. Over my life time, I've told many people that I came from a white ghetto and did pretty well for myself, but have always been aware that it is easier to get out of a white ghetto than a black ghetto.

My father advised me that whenever I borrowed money from someone, I should agree to repay the loan two weeks after the date I knew I could. His theory was that, by repaying the loan two weeks earlier than the due date, I would improve my credibility in the world. I have religiously followed his advice on borrowing. He told me about the problems with being a liar. His theory was that you probably couldn't remember what you said if you lied, but if you told the truth it was easy to remember what you said. He acknowledged that telling the truth can be hard sometimes and can make enemies, but in the long run, it was the best thing to do.

My father was the foreman painter for Margotta Construction Company and was a member of the painters' union. More often than he should have, he would let me skip school on Friday afternoons and take me to job sites, where I would take water to the painters and help him clean up the work area. While giving assignments to the painters one afternoon, he told a man to take a window jack, a board designed to stick out of a window as a platform, and paint the outside of some sixth floor windows. This was before OSHA so there were no safety straps to prevent falls. The painter replied that he didn't use window jacks because they were dangerous and he was afraid of them. My father did not argue; he simply fired the man and told him to go to the main office and pick up any pay due him. I was shocked. My father had just removed a man's livelihood without any hesitation whatsoever.

I asked him about the incident and he explained that his responsibility was to his employer and that the fired painter's responsibility was to him. He said that arguing with the painter or allowing him to choose which jobs he would do would degrade his ability to supervise the other painters. This simple lesson went a long way in making me a successful supervisor later in my life.

Late one evening, a neighbor child came to our house to ask for help because he thought his father was going to kill his mother. My father called the police and then proceeded to teach me about wife beaters. First, he told me the most despicable thing a man can do is to hurt a child or a woman. Then he explained that, one hundred percent of the time, if a woman forgives a man who beat her, that man would beat her again. He told me of cases where women called the police for help, but then went to the jail the following morning with clean shirts for their husbands and refused to press charges. He was very adamant about this and I took him at his word. I have advised battered women based on his advice to me and have helped some of them.

He tried to teach me another lesson in life, but I'm not sure his advice resonated with me. The construction company's business office was only a block and a half from our home and on each Friday, which was payday, my father normally picked up the payroll at the office, had lunch at home, and then went to the job sites to pay the men. The company paid the men in cash contained in envelopes prepared at the office. One Friday noon, as he stopped at the corner of Pocantico and Howard Streets, only a hundred yards from home, he was car-jacked by two robbers. One man opened the driver's side door, pointed a gun, and told him to move over just as the other man with a gun in his hand opened the passenger side door and climbed into the vehicle. They took him to the woods a few blocks away, tied his hands and ankles with wire, took the money and drove off in his car to a point where they had parked their car. Eventually my father broke loose from his bonds and went to the nearest home to call for help. I asked him why he didn't pull the gun he was licensed to carry. He said it was one thing to carry a gun, but that discretion quickly comes into play when someone else pulls his gun first. He told me that he didn't think it was worth losing his life over the payroll. The owner of the company was quick to tell us he was happy to deal with the loss of $5,000 rather than have to deal with the loss of an employee. I so detest anyone who feels entitled to rob others, if it ever happens to me and I have any ability to retaliate, I fear I will risk my life to do so.

I remembered my father's advice about work ethics when I found my first job. I lied about my age when I was eleven; I said I was twelve, and obtained a newspaper delivery route. The newspaper company assigned one hundred and ten customers to me in a sub-division called Phillips Manor. Phillips Manor contained the homes of many affluent families where the houses were set back from the street and everyone had a large lot. I was so happy to find the job, I paid little attention to the contract as my father had advised me to do that evening as we dug the trench to the garage. For each paper I delivered, I received one-half of a cent. The paper was not published on Sunday, so I earned $3.30 per week for about fifteen hours of work. It wasn't much, and it wasn't really fair, but it was pretty good pay for an eleven year old kid from the poor side of town. To put it into perspective, a movie cost eleven cents and a quart of milk cost sixteen cents in those days. I delivered that paper on time in rain, snow, wind and cold, and I placed each paper in the paper holder underneath the mailbox attached to each house at the front door. I also had to account to the company for collections. Every Friday when I delivered the paper, I rang each customer's doorbell and requested the thirty cents payment for the week. Many customers, who were appreciative of my service, gave me a quarter and a dime and told me to keep the change. As much as I appreciated the tip, I began to develop disdain for those who gave me a quarter and a dime and waited for the nickel change. I didn't have a problem with those who handed me a quarter and a nickel; it was just the ones who waited for the nickel in change. It was a quirky position for me to take about people I did not know, but the disdain was there, nonetheless.

I kept my newspaper route until I was physically big enough to become a golf caddy. Once I could caddy, I quit the newspaper to let some other eleven-year-old lie about his age and take my route. One of my older brothers had organized a caddy strike at the local golf course some years earlier, so I was not welcome there. I had to work at the Fairview Country Club, which was about ten miles from my home. In those days, caddies carried two bags each. By doing this, I earned five dollars for a round of eighteen holes. I did that only on Saturdays because I had to go to church on Sundays. The trip around the golf course only took four to five hours, but I had to give up the entire day to make the money. I got up early, made two peanut butter and jelly sandwiches, and walked a mile to Tarrytown where the road to the country club area intersected Route Nine. From there, I hitchhiked to the area of the course. Often, I had to walk the last mile or two of the trip. Once at the caddy shack, I signed in and went to the caddy yard to wait for my "loop." Since I was younger and less experienced than most of the boys, I usually had to wait a long time to be called. The work was hard and the hours were long, but at the time, it was the best way for me to earn money.

Chapter 7 - The Marsh

The marsh area between where I lived and the Hudson River was a great place to ride the pony. When Uncle Johnny wasn't around, I'd find the current little girl rider, saddle Snowball and take her the half block to the edge of town where we would go down into a dried area of the marsh and take turns riding. As mentioned earlier, Snowball didn't like me much and had the typical poor disposition anyway, so it was usually a fight to stay in the saddle, but I mostly remember having a great time on those occasions.

The place we called "the marsh," wasn't really a marsh. It was a flood plain of the Hudson River from hundreds of years ago that had dried to a hard surface except for the area near Pocantico Creek that drained into the Hudson River . The river is close to three miles wide at that point and has a daily tide of about three feet, which includes the inflow of salt water. The Pocantico Creek, which was wider than some rivers I encountered throughout my world travels, traversed the marsh between Pocantico Lake and the Hudson River. It was a great place to fish in the summer, and when the lake froze in the winter, children would use it as an ice skating area. The marsh also held baseball fields for the local boys, and the high school football team practiced and played games there.

To reach the marsh, which was about forty or fifty feet below the level of the homes in the area, I only had to walk half of a residential block and descend a bank of sand. It was a large, adventurous area for a young boy. Because the river tides also caused a tide in the Pocantico Creek, a large portion of the marsh was covered with cattail reeds. I hated those reeds. Once they are dry, if you try to break them or pull them out of the ground, you will surely end up with cuts on your hands not unlike cuts from a razor blade. As late fall approached each year, the reeds would become dormant, dry out and turn into tinder just waiting for an ignition source. A year didn't go by when some pesky young boy didn't fulfill the urge to provide that source. It was almost like a rite of passage for some boys. There were no structures in the area, and if the fire department didn't extinguish the blazes, they would eventually burn out on their own, so the only real danger was to the arsonist. Yes, there came a year when I couldn't resist the temptation. It was the year that my father was the Chief of the five unit volunteer fire department. I was probably twelve or thirteen at the time and had become wise enough not to trust anyone with sensitive information, so no one ever found out that it was my year to be the arsonist. I learned from the older boys that it wasn't always easy to get a fire started in the reed field because the ground was usually moist there. Many attempts had failed over the years. They also told me that if I spent too much time getting the fire started, it made it more likely I'd be caught. I devised a unique system to ensure success.

I found two large pieces of cardboard. The pieces were large enough to ship a kitchen stove or perhaps a bathtub. I poked holes in the outer edges with my pocketknife and laced a piece of rope through the holes. I saturated the cardboard with some used engine oil and started it burning with a match. Once I had a good flame, I simply started running through the dry reeds with my left hand holding the rope and my right hand protecting my eyes from the sharp edges of the cattails; it worked like a charm. I had a raging fire going in seconds and had plenty of time to leave the area before anyone reported the fire. As I high-tailed it out of the area, I could hear the loud crackling of the fire, smell the distinctive scent of the smoke and feel the heat on my back. For a few seconds, I wondered if I had done something that might be more than could be controlled, but the thought didn't cause me to slowdown and look back; I was leaving the area as quickly as possible. When the fire whistle blew, everyone knew from the series of sounds that the marsh was burning. I joined the rest of the neighbors at the top of the sand bank above the marsh to watch the firefighters do their annual duty of containing the fire. Over the years, the firemen had learned it was better to let all of the reeds burn than to respond to several marsh fires, so they simply contained the inferno until all of the fuel was exhausted.

The Hudson River which bordered the marsh was another favorite haunt of mine. Along the shoreline there were water breaks constructed with huge blocks of granite that made great fishing areas. Before I learned to fish in the Hudson, the river had a profound effect on my personality. As a child, I had heard of people drowning there and of bodies surfacing at different levels of decomposition, so I knew it was a dangerous place. One summer day, when I was very young, I was at the river with a group of neighborhood boys of various ages at an area called "the barge." Many years before, a river barge broke loose from a line of barges being pulled by a tugboat and foundered on the shoreline. It had rotted away to not much more than a skeleton and had become a favorite area for swimming. A large tree grew on the river bank and someone had attached a rope to a branch to be used to swing out over the water and drop into the river. How or why I was with that bunch of boys, I'll never understand because I couldn't swim. Someone in the group realized that I was a non-swimmer and everyone decided that the best way to learn to swim was to be thrown into water that was over your head, so it would be "sink or swim." They threw me into the water.

I can still see in my mind's eye the wall of rocks in front of me through the air bubbles coming from my mouth as I sank below the surface. The water was probably only six or eight feet deep, but anything over my head was too much. When I hit the bottom, I pushed hard with my feet and broke through the top of the water, arms flailing, about eight feet from shore. I grabbed water as fast as I could and made it to shore with terror in my brain and pain in my chest as the others laughed and laughed at my plight. I learned two very important lessons that day: to have a healthy fear of the water and, what was more important, not to trust everyone. This incident may have been the genesis of my lifelong, intense desire to be a loner. From that day forward, I would fish in the Hudson River, Pocantico Creek, a small place called the Clay Pit, and Fremont's Pond, but always alone. I developed an ability to interact and get along with others when it was to my benefit or enjoyment, but always maintained the ability to survive happily on my own.

Chapter 8 - A Calf in the Cellar

My mother spent many years living on a farm, albeit as little more than an indentured servant who had to do all of the cooking and house work for her family and the farm hands. She learned many things, including how to milk a cow. We were a very large, poor family and could not afford to buy a lot of real milk, so we depended on dried milk, a commodity developed during the Second World War. My mother often commented on how nice it would be to have a cow. As it happened, my sister Betty was dating a man who worked for a gentleman farmer. That's someone with a regular job who maintains a small farm outside of the city that is not necessarily profitable and is really a hobby. The farmer bred horses and Jersey cows. He kept all of the colts and the female calves, but instructed the farm hands to sell male calves on the veal wholesale market after six weeks. After the birth of one calf, Betty's boyfriend, Rusty, told the farmer that a male calf had been born. The farmer never checked, and after six weeks, my father gave Rusty the money a calf would bring on the market to give to the farmer. We became the proud owners of a pure bred Jersey calf.

I went with my father and mother to the farm one evening to pick up the calf. Rusty put one gunnysack into another and placed the calf into them with her head sticking out. I was only eleven or twelve and not a very big kid, yet the calf was small enough to fit on my lap as I sat on the back seat of our old car. Before we got home, I could smell the reason Rusty used two gunnysacks. Over the years, I discovered that the smell of cow manure or horse manure is not such a bad thing.

Not enough planning went into this venture; we had no place to put the calf once we arrived home. Someone suggested the cellar and that is where she went. A calf in the cellar of a home within the town limits? That must have been a violation of some ordinance. Barriers were put up, some straw bedding from Snowball's stall in the garage was laid down on the dirt floor and the calf, we named her Penelope, had a new home. Penelope wanted her mother and started bawling. That was another new experience for me. Fortunately, my mother was prepared for the problem. She went up stairs to the kitchen and mixed some dried milk with water using our electric mix-master. Then she brought the reconstituted milk down to the cellar in a galvanized bucket. The calf didn't know what to do with the bucket of milk because her last drink of milk she had came from her mother's teats. My mother knew that was going to happen and laughed as she taught me to convince the calf to drink from the bucket. She had me stick my hand into the milk with one finger facing toward the top as she pushed the calf's snout down into the bucket. I stuck my finger into Penelope's mouth and she started sucking. She continued to suck the milk after I removed my finger. This started the weaning process, and in a matter of days, I didn't have to trick her to drink.

As she learned to drink from a bucket, Penelope also learned that the sound of the mix-master operating in the kitchen above her improvised stall meant that milk was on the way. This resulted in her incessant bawling whenever she heard the mix-master. It didn't matter if my mother was preparing batter for a cake or mixing some other concoction; to Penelope, the sound meant milk and she would bawl and bawl until I took some to her.

After some weeks, someone noticed that the calf was growing and could end up being too large to get out of the cellar if we didn't get her out soon. My father got to work and built a stall for her next to Snowball's stall in the barn that had once been our garage. That poor calf hadn't seen natural light in some time and didn't quite know what to do when she was let loose in the yard. The stall was nice but she couldn't live there for her entire life. It fell to me to clean out her stall and to take her to the marsh area to graze once she had teeth. At first the neighborhood children made fun of me as I walked the half block to the marsh with Penelope in tow, but they quit doing that after a while.

We had Penelope bred when she was about fourteen months old; it was quite an eye-opening event for me. She had been bellowing from the early morning hours and my mother knew she was in estrus. We loaded her into the pony trailer and took her to a nearby farm. The farmer locked her into a stanchion in the bull yard and let the bull loose. That huge beast had been inside detecting the smell of a cow in heat and did not hesitate for a second once he was in the yard. There was no foreplay; it was over in a matter of seconds. Eleven months later she produced a male calf, which we sold for veal. Along with the calf came milk. Penelope had to be milked twice a day, seven days a week no matter what. Not only that, she would start bawling from the pain of a full udder if the milk wasn't taken on time and that would bring the neighbors down on us. I was a good barn hand but I drew the line at milking; my mother did all of that. We had heavy cream on our oatmeal every morning and there was always plenty of milk in the refrigerator. According to my mother, we didn't have to pasteurize the milk as long as Penelope had her shots and wasn't around any other cows. I guess she was right because none of us ever got sick from the milk.

As more and more children left home, the need for Penelope's milk became less and less. Eventually, we sold her to a farmer who had plenty of pasture for her. My farming days were over and I was glad. It was time for me to start high school and I didn't want to go to school every morning smelling like cow manure.

Chapter 9 - The Woods and Guns

I don't remember the first time I fired a gun. I do remember my brothers teaching me to shoot our .22 caliber, single shot rifle in the basement of our home. My father smoked Lucky Strike cigarettes and the package had a red circle on each side that we used for practice. We nailed an empty cigarette pack to a plank of wood and leaned it against the brick wall at one end of the cellar as a target. My brothers taught me to shoot well enough to hit the red circle every time I fired. The low velocity, .22 caliber short bullet is the smallest and weakest you can buy. It makes very little noise and has very little power. Although there are instances when this type of a weapon and bullet caused fatalities, normally any wound would be non-fatal. I used this little weapon to hunt rabbits and squirrels.

At ten or eleven years of age, I often stuck that Stevens rifle down the leg of my trousers with the butt end under my shirt and headed off to the woods to hunt. The woods ran right up to the edge of a residential section of our town and I was doing something that would raise serious alarm today, but I thought it was an innocent activity. I learned that once you flushed a rabbit, all you had to do was keep an eye on it until it stopped running. At that point, the rabbit would go into the, "If I don't move he can't see me" mode. They were simple to shoot at that point, and after killing a few, I found it wasn't fun to shoot them unless they were on the run.

I learned about the Poison Ivy bush while tramping around those woods. I was no different from any other little boy who likes to roam in the woods; the whole area was my latrine. On one of my hunting trips, I apparently touched a Poison Ivy bush sometime before I had to urinate. The poison transferred from my hand to my penis, and a few days later, I was in big trouble. I was bed bound with a swollen scrotum and a penis covered with oozing pustules. I can't begin to describe the itching which cannot be alleviated without making matters much worse. Every day when my father came home from work he came to see how I was doing. Each time he checked, he told me if I didn't get better soon, he was going to call the Rabbi. I didn't know what he was talking about but everyone else got a good laugh. As I matured and found out what the word circumcision means and that a Rabbi normally performs the procedure on male infants, I concluded he was implying that the Rabbi would cut the whole thing off. No wonder they all laughed.

One day, while in the woods scaring up rabbits, one of them took off running. I ran down the trail after it and took a shot while on the run. I could only see the rear end of the rabbit, which didn't present much of a target, and I missed. He went over a rise and I followed him. As I topped the rise, I didn't see the rabbit but I did see a man sitting at the edge of a pond holding a fishing rod. He shouted, "Holy mackerel, I thought I heard a shot. You could've killed me." I was surprised and tried to explain that if I couldn't see him because he was below the rise, there was no way my bullet could have hit him. He wasn't interested in my explanation, and insisted I shouldn't be in those woods with a rifle. He didn't call the police and I learned that I shouldn't be shooting in those woods. I voluntarily gave up hunting there. As I look back at the incident, I know I wasn't sneaking out of the house with the gun. No one in the family seemed to mind and my parents knew I was shooting in the woods because I would come home with squirrel tails and rabbits' feet. I only hid the gun in my trousers when I was in a residential area to keep from alarming people. Today people might say it was poor parenting; I think it was just a case of so many children that there wasn't much close supervision.

There were always guns in our home. My father had a small collection of handguns that he would take out from time to time. They were of different types and calibers and were very interesting to me. Beside the single shot Stevens caliber .22, we had a Remington caliber .22 that I would take to the woods and a military issue caliber .30, carbine. Among the collection, I can remember a Smith and Wesson .38 caliber police special, an Iver Johnson .32 caliber and a breech-loading .38 caliber that was unusual. Two of my brothers, Buddy and Bobby, had served in the Marine Corps by that time and they taught me how to field strip the carbine for cleaning. By the time I had finished my training with that gun, I could disassemble and assemble it blindfolded.

Even though my father and brothers had drilled me in gun safety, an incident did occur. I had been out hunting in the woods with the .22 caliber Remington that was a slide action, repeating rifle. That is, after firing the gun, one had only to pull back the sliding mechanism with the left hand to eject the empty shell and insert a new bullet into the breech. The magazine that held the bullets was a long tube located below the barrel. I always made sure that my guns were empty whenever I returned home. In the case of the Remington repeater, I followed my normal procedure; I unloaded the tube magazine, looked into the breech to make sure the firing chamber was empty and then worked the slide backward and forward three times to make triple sure there were no bullets in the gun. I placed the rifle in a corner of the kitchen and went out to visit some neighborhood friends. The rifle wasn't empty.

Robert, my sister Kathleen's first born and about four years old at the time, grabbed the rifle and dragged it behind him as he walked across the kitchen. My brother Bobby, who was sitting at the kitchen table, took the rifle away from him. As Bobby pointed the weapon toward the ceiling, he told his nephew the rule about never pointing a gun at someone unless you intended to shoot him and pulled the trigger. Bam! The gun fired a round into the old fashioned, tin covered ceiling. With all my carefulness, somehow a bullet had hung up in the magazine and on my third and final pull of the slide mechanism, it dislodged and went into the firing chamber. When I returned later in the evening and they told me of the incident, I couldn't believe it had happened. Kathleen told me to keep my guns where little kids couldn't reach them and to be more careful in the future. The hole stayed in the kitchen ceiling for as long as I lived at home as an example to encourage gun safety.

Chapter 10 - The Soapbox Derby

With the end of World War II in 1945, the annual soapbox derby races resumed around the country in the summer of 1946. The village leaders in Tarrytown and North Tarrytown dusted off the rulebook and went to work to organize a race. Hanging from the rafters in our cellar was a dusty old soapbox derby car used by one of my older brothers many years before. My father became energized about the race and told me we were going to enter. Theoretically, a young boy, with some help from his father, is supposed to be the racecar builder; that is rarely, if ever, the case. One look at the cars in the races, and the ages of the boys driving them, would indicate a great deal of adult engineering and mechanical work was required to reach the technical level displayed. The reality of this was no different in my case.

We took the car from the storage area and went to work. For the most part, my contribution was unskilled labor; my father and brothers did all of the technical and skilled work. We bought new wheels and my father taught me how to break them in on the workbench. I also did the painting under his tutelage. In a matter of weeks, the car was ready.

While we were refurbishing the car, I heard the stories of when my brothers drove in soapbox derbies. They told me of the year they caught one of the entrants cheating. After the weigh in, the father and son had placed a bread pan filled with lead into the nose of the car. The added weight allowed the car to win the race, but when officials noticed the bread pan during the post race inspection, they disqualified the driver. My father even had a photograph of my brothers Buddy and Bobby holding the lead filled pan.

Among the old family photographs that I remember was one of my sister Betty standing next to her soapbox derby car. In 1936, my father was yet to have a son old enough to enter the derby and girls were not allowed to enter, so he had Betty's hair cut in a boy's style, dressed her in boy's clothing and entered her into the derby disguised as a boy.

Betty didn't win anything, but I think she may hold the title of the first girl to drive in a soapbox derby.

I couldn't drive in a race without any experience, so we hatched a plan to get some driving time for me. On three Sunday mornings, we arose very early and took the racecar to a hill located in one of the more affluent areas of town which had little traffic. At daybreak, my brothers positioned vehicles to block traffic from entering the street from either side, then, with me behind the wheel, my father released the car at the top of the hill. I drove the gravity powered car down the hill, past the cross streets blocked off by my brothers and rolled slowly to a halt with minimum use of the brake to reduce brake pad wear. That home designed brake was to come back to haunt me. My father had taken an emergency brake handle from an old car and attached it to a steel bar which ran through the solid plank that formed the floor of my racecar. The brake shoe with a brake pad attached to the steel bar was to make contact with the road surface on the right side of the car when I pulled back on the brake handle. The idea of using an automobile's modified braking system was sound on paper, but in application, was far less than sound engineering. None of us realized that applying a brake to only one side of a racecar could be disastrous.

On race day, there was a huge crowd lining both sides of the "track," from the top of the hill to the bottom. Town vehicles blocked side streets and there were fire trucks and an emergency medical vehicle on hand at the finish line. The mood was festive and there were many wishes of good luck from strangers and friends. When it came time for my heat, I had no fear and little, if any, anxiety. The red car I was to race against was a little larger than mine was and the boy was a year older, but I wasn't intimidated. I was confident I had the fastest car and was ready to race. When the barrier fell, I threw the weight of my small body forward and started down the ramp. I focused on the track in front of me, yet I could sense the red car alongside keeping pace with me. As we passed the finish line side by side, I couldn't tell who had won the race; I was focused on the vehicles and crowd in front of me in the runoff area. I grabbed the brake handle with my right hand and gave it a mighty pull. We learned right then that breaking the inertia on only one side of a racecar will quickly cause it to spin. I didn't, and couldn't, count the spins, but I stopped just short of the crowd that was dispersing in panic. The red car had beaten me by a fraction of a foot. I learned how to handle disappointment that day, just as I learned about brake dynamics.

At age twelve, I was still young enough to drive in the soapbox derby in 1947. We used the same car with a new paint job and a revised braking system. Because of my spin during the race of 1946, the organizers changed the rules to eliminate the use of an outside brake handle, which required the driver to take a hand off the steering wheel. This year, we hooked up a foot activated braking system that caused a piece of steel with a brake pad attached to drop down from under the center of the base plank. We learned about brake dynamics the previous year, but we didn't learn about brake testing. We followed our procedure of practice runs for three weeks before the race and felt we were ready to go. The atmosphere on race day was as festive as the year before and my confidence had not withered. One difference was the addition of a mobile unit from the local radio station located at the finish line.

The start was much the same as the previous year except that I never saw the car on my right because I was ahead of it on the track. I flew across the finish line with a grin on my face and my feet pressing with all my might on the metal brake actuator. The car did not want to stop. The brake pad was rubbing on the pavement but we had miscalculated the distance from the bottom of the base plank and the road surface. No matter how hard I pressed, I could not increase the stopping rate. A fire truck blocked the end of the run off area and knew I did not want to hit that, so I pulled the wheel to the left hoping to put the car into a spin. Spin I did - right into the mobile radio station equipment and announcer. My mother, listening to the race from home, only had to wait a few minutes for the station to come back on the air and report that I, the announcer and his equipment had survived the crash. I won the heat but the officials disqualified my car for having faulty brakes.

My racing career ended with that crash in 1947, but I have been a fan of open wheel racing ever since. Until this day, I will arise early in the morning to watch televised Formula One racing, the pinnacle of open wheel racing, from cities all over the world. I still wonder, if given another chance, how good of a race driver I might have become.

Chapter 11 - The Stephentown Adventure

Sometime in the spring of 1949, my mother and father purchased 140 acres of land near the small town of Stephentown, New York. Stephentown is twenty-six miles east southeast of Albany, New York, about three miles west of the Massachusetts border and a hundred and twenty miles north of North Tarrytown. I was with them the day they found the property. To reach the land, we had to travel two miles down a dirt road after leaving the main highway to Stephentown. Once there, we found over grown farm fields, a two-stall barn and an old farmhouse with no electricity or running water. Ash, Oak and Hemlock trees covered much of the land and a year round, twenty foot wide creek, locally called the Black River, flowed through part of the property. My mother fell in love with the place and convinced my father to find some way make the purchase. The seller wanted $2,000, which was huge amount for our family. My father offered the real estate agent $40 dollars, all he had, as a down payment to hold the land until he could borrow the rest from our hometown bank. The agent accepted the offer and the purchase agreement papers were signed.

I will never know how my father arranged the loan, but he did. For ten years they made monthly payments on that land until it was theirs. We made weekend trips to Stephentown whenever possible to improve the place, cut timber to sell and farm the fields. I learned how to tack draft horses with collars and drafting equipment, clean downed trees of limbs, use horses to pull large tree trunks from the forest and use a horse to plow fields. We even had a horse-drawn buckboard that I used just for fun. These were great accomplishments for a skinny little kid who probably weighed no more than one hundred and ten pounds soaking wet.

We had two draft horses, Daisy and Jerry. Daisy was a big, thick, brown and white Belgium plow horse and Jerry was a tall, skinny, grey gelding good for work in the forest. These were gentle giants and we worked together with a minimum of disagreements. We arranged for a neighbor to water and feed our horses during the week in exchange for his use of them when needed. As I look back at those times, I wonder why the other children in the family had so little interest in the farm. Perhaps the others were too old and busy with other things and Marianne was too young. Whatever the case, I spent a lot of time with my parents on the farm.

My brother-in-law Ray, my father and one of my older brothers did all of the tree felling with a thirty-six inch long, two man chain saw; I just wasn't big enough to handle either end of that monster. Our lumbering endeavor probably only made enough money to cover the cost of the equipment purchased to pursue the business. The farming didn't amount to anything either. I helped my father make the old house habitable and can remember evenings with only kerosene fueled oil lamps for light and the wood burning kitchen stove for heat. It was life at a simple level, including an outhouse for toilet facilities. It wouldn't be until I served in Vietnam that I got to enjoy an outhouse again. I loved wandering around in the woods, and the work with the horses was more fun than work. There is one incident with the horses that I will never forget.

I went up the hill behind the house one morning with Jerry to pull out a forty-foot long Hemlock log. At the same time, my father was digging a well down to the water table, which was only about twelve feet below the surface. Near the hole he had placed three, thirty-six inch diameter, four foot high sections of ceramic pipe to line the new well. Just as I finished hooking the log up to Jerry's harness, Daisy, who was in heat, let out a loud whinny. This was not supposed to bother Jerry, who was a gelding, but it did. He was what they call in horse parlance as "proud cut." That is, although he was neutered, he didn't know he was neutered. Jerry bolted for the barn, which was almost a mile away from where we were working, to answer Daisy's call. He galloped down the hill toward the house, but had to negotiate a double width gate in the fence to reach the barn. The gate was right where my father was working and he either saw or heard Jerry coming and climbed out of the well to stop him. There was no stopping Jerry that morning. As he made the turn toward the barn after running through the gate, the Hemlock log streaming behind him smashed into the fence, my father and the three ceramic pipes. The log tore a fence post out of the ground, smashed the pipes into thousands of pieces and shoved the nail on my father's big toe into flesh on his left foot, which caused severe pain. By the time I reached the disaster area, my father was limping from the house toward the barn with a rifle in his hand. My mother was behind him shouting that it wasn't Jerry's fault. I didn't say anything. I had never heard my father swear or seen him angry, but right then, I thought he was going to shoot Jerry. My mother's pleas prevailed and he stopped short of shooting the horse. I think it was the economic factor of replacing Jerry rather than my mother's pleas that stopped him, but he always credited her with saving the horse's life.

My father gave up on the well digging project for a while and we just used the hand cranked water pump in the kitchen to obtain whatever water we needed. I left home in the summer of 1953 and was no longer available to help on the farm. It was a wonderful experience for me and helped me to learn that it was all right to try anything rather than be afraid of failure.

After my father died in 1968, a real estate company constantly pressured my mother to sell the land in Stephentown. She finally caved in and sold it sometime in 1969. Depending on which sibling I speak to, my mother sold the land for some amount between $14,000 and $42,000. I suspect it was closer to $14,000 because she had very little money for the remainder of her life.

Chapter 12 - High School Years

Being fourteen years old in those days was much different than it is today. I was completely unsophisticated, obeyed my parents and did not complain. A new Catholic high school had opened two years earlier named after Archbishop Aloysius Stepinac, a Croatian Cardinal falsely imprisoned by the Communist Yugoslavian government in power at that time. Someone decided I should attend the boys only school, so in the fall of 1949, I enrolled as a freshman. My parents didn't appreciate the fact that it was an upscale school and we were a down scale family. My brother-in-law Ray went with me to the enrollment session and sensed the situation. The following week, he took me to a clothing store and we purchased shirts, ties, trousers and two jackets to help me fit in with the more affluent students. I don't know where the money came from; Ray probably took it from his own assets. Attending Stepinac High School was a challenge.

The first challenge came in getting to the school. At the time, there were so many family members living in our small home, I occupied a space in the unfinished, unheated attic. I had two old alarm clocks; one displayed the proper time but did not ring, the other would ring but had no hands. I could see the stubs where the hands had been broken off the ringing clock and was able to set the alarm. As I did not have a watch, I used the other clock to keep track of time. My daily routine was to get up at 5:30 AM, before everyone else, and perform some chores before leaving for school. I had to go to the cellar and start a fire in the pot-bellied stove we used to heat water. The routine included inserting wadded newspaper pages into the firebox, then kindling I prepared with a hatchet, and after the wood caught fire, a shovel full of coal completed the process. Next, I prepared enough oatmeal cereal for the family in a large pot on the kitchen stove and then made sure others were awake.

After breakfast, which I ate alone, I used my few minutes in the one bathroom in the house to prepare for school. I made my own lunch and left the house as early as possible to walk the one-mile route to the bus station in Tarrytown. From there, it was a thirty-minute bus ride to the town of White Plaines. At the bus terminal in White Plaines, I transferred to another bus that included the high school on its route. I reversed this procedure at the end of the school day. Unlike the public schools, every student attended seven forty-five minute classes each day, including, of course, a class on Religion. We had only thirty minutes for lunch and could not leave the campus. The courses, taught by Catholic Brothers (a position in the Catholic clergy below that of a Priest), were difficult, but not more than I could handle. I followed this routine for a year and a half with little or no time left for anything after school but homework.

I was not necessarily happy attending Stepinac High School. The days were long; the schoolwork was time consuming; I didn't feel like I fit in with the other students who mostly came from wealthy families; and there were no girls enrolled. One day early in January of 1951, I received a notice to report to the school administrator's office. I can't remember his name, but the red piping on his cassock identified him as a Monsignor, which is a level above a Priest but below a Bishop. The Monsignor told me that my parents had fallen behind on the $15 per month minimum monthly tuition charge. In fact, they were ten months behind and he wanted me to tell them the bill had to be paid. My lack of sophistication did not diminish my fierce independent streak. I thought about his words for a very few moments and replied that I would have to quit Stepinac High School and enroll in my local public school, because I knew my family could not afford to satisfy the tuition debt. He marveled at the quickness of my decision and suggested I discuss the problem with my parents. When I told him a discussion would be fruitless, he suggested I contact the school's liaison at my local church to obtain financial aid. After scrolling through his rolodex to find the name of the representative, he told me to contact Father Fry at Saint Teresa's Church. I laughed and told him that was impossible because of a long-standing feud between Father Fry and my family. The consternated Monsignor resorted to his final and most revealing tactic. He told me that my parents had a responsibility to send me to a Catholic school and that they risked eternal damnation of their souls if they didn't find some way to keep me enrolled. That point in the conversation marked another step in my flight from Catholicism, and eventually, Christianity. I stood up, told him that what he had said was wrong and left his office. I went to my locker, picked up my belongings and made my way to the bus stop. I never visited the school again. That man must have truly believed what he said to me; it is the only way he could have found the audacity to make such a completely stupid statement. I did notice on the Stepinac High School web site today that tuition has increased to $7,000 per year over the past fifty-six years. I suspect poor children don't attend that school anymore.

That same afternoon, I visited the North Tarrytown High School and asked to speak with the Principal, Mr. Carl Neiman. Mr. Neiman listened to my story as related above, and with a wry smile, told me he would be happy to have me as a student at his school. He arranged for me to work with a counselor to have my records transferred from Stepinac High School and to schedule my classes at my new school. When I related my experience that day to my parents, they had no disagreement with my actions. The next day, I joined a sophomore class of about sixty-five students and a new adventure began. I knew the students who lived in my neighborhood, but not many of the others. Until they got to know me, some of the guys were a little wary of me because, as the "new guy" in school, many of the girls were interested in me and that made me a threat. After all, I was a handsome kid with a devilish smile.

Yearbook photograph – 1953

I dropped Latin and Spanish, which were required at Stepinac High School; and without the long bus trips every day, I had a lot more time to be a normal high school kid.

I met a girl named Eleanor Hatzman one evening and asked her for a date. She told me she would have to ask her father. The next day she told me that when she asked her father, he said that if I were George Joyce's son, it would be fine. I had no idea that her father and mine had been friends for many years and served in the same volunteer fire department company. Eleanor and I had an on again, off again, love affair throughout the remaining two and a half years of my high school life. We did the normal things teenaged kids did in those days and immensely enjoyed each other's company. Our romance would eventually end when I left town in the summer of 1953 to start my military career.

In 1952, one of my older brothers was getting ready to leave town and had a vehicle to sell. It was a beat up, bare bones 1933 Chevrolet coupe with a rumble seat. I made a deal to buy it from him for $100. I earned the money to pay him by caddying on weekends and working in an automobile body shop one day a week. A man who lived in our town owned a body shop in New York City. Almost every Friday, if he had the work for me to do, I would skip school, ride to work with him and hand-sand repaired automobiles in preparation for the painting process. For the work, he paid me $1.00 per hour. Between the two jobs I was able to pay for the car and quickly leaned I had to keep working to purchase gasoline and to maintain and repair it when necessary. Whenever the high school truant officer called my mother to report my absences on Fridays, she acknowledged her awareness and no further action was ever taken. The authorities were understanding of the economic situations of families and looked the other way in many cases.

I worked on that car during any free time I had. John Martin, a friend of mine from school, who came from a wealthy family, helped me do repair jobs in his underground garage from time to time. Otherwise, I worked outside in all kinds of weather. I recall one night when John and I were replacing the muffler on my car. The work required a significant amount of banging and loud exchanges between us, which normally wouldn't bother anyone, but that evening, when we weren't making a racket, I could hear notes from a piano in the room above us. I asked John if we were bothering whoever was playing the piano. He told me not to worry because it was only the piano tuner. I was impressed. I knew what a piano tuner was but I had never known anyone wealthy enough to hire one. Many years later in my life, we purchased a piano, and to make sure it was ready for use, we hired a piano tuner. As he sat on the piano bench hitting keys and making adjustments, I thought to myself that I had come a long way from that night in John Martin's garage.

During my high school years, I developed a fascination with airplanes. I made models powered by rubber bands when I could afford the kit and the glue. I couldn't stop myself from looking skyward whenever I heard an aircraft. I decided it was time to fly. I worked at the golf course every weekend on Saturdays for quite a while to save the money to pay for an airplane ride. On a Saturday morning in June of 1952, I drove to the municipal airfield in White Planes and sought out a private pilot. I found a small office with one man inside and inquired as to how a person could buy a ride in an airplane. The man smiled and asked me if I had ever flown in an airplane. When I told him my story about wanting to fly and working at the golf course to raise the money, he took a liking to me. He asked if I had $15, which I did. He agreed to take me up in his plane for the $15. He put the money in his pocket, locked the door to the office and we headed for the two-seat Piper Cub on the runway apron.

We were airborne in no time and I was thrilled. When I told him where I lived, he banked the little airplane and told me we could fly right over my house. I really fell in love with flying that day. We flew over all of the local landmarks I had only ever seen from the ground. I saw Sing Sing penitentiary as we flew over Ossining, the local reservoirs, the lakes where I fished and the wide Hudson River. The pilot pointed out on the instrument panel that we were traveling at a ground speed of one hundred and twenty miles per hour, but it seemed like we were just barely moving forward. In less than an hour, we returned to the airfield and landed. The pilot told me then that he had given me a big break on the cost of the flight because I was the first kid that ever walked into his office with an, "I just have see what it is like to fly" look on his face. He must have been a nice person; perhaps I reminded him of himself when he was a youngster. Eventually, after enlisting in the United States Air Force, I tried many times to be accepted into pilot training but was unsuccessful. I had the brains and physical attributes but lacked the ability to know where I was when upside down in a turn while flying a simulator. There are things one just can't do without certain natural talents.

About midway through my junior year in high school, a job became available at Bev Rodman's ESSO service station at the corner of Broadway and Pocantico Hill. I raced up there as soon as I heard the news and filled out an application. My reputation as a hard working, honest, responsible person landed the job for me. I worked alone every weekday evening from 6:00 P.M. until 10:00 PM., and on Sunday, I worked from 8:00 A.M. until 6:00 P.M. My starting wage was $0.75 per hour, and after a three month probation period, I received a raise to $1.00 per hour. Working thirty hours a week left little time for dating and high school activities but I was happy to have a steady income. I think Mr. Rodman only kept the station open on weekday nights to keep his regular customers happy. I arrived every evening at 5:45 P.M. and was in uniform and ready for work early every day I worked there. Each evening at 6:00 P.M. when he left for his home, Mr. Rodman gave me thirty dollars in bills and change; most nights I would only take in thirty dollars in sales over the four-hour period. With gasoline at $0.24 per gallon, and oil at $0.60 per quart, I think we barely made enough profit to pay my salary and the electric bill, but it kept his regular customers happy. My responsibilities were limited to dispensing gasoline, cleaning windshields, selling a quart of oil from time to time, repairing flat tires and performing grease jobs and oil changes. I remember installing a new fan belt a few times, but I was not a certified mechanic and knew my limitations.

On weekday evenings, in between waiting on customers, I was able to do school homework and even maintain the spit shine on my U. S. Marine Corps Reserve uniform shoes. I enjoyed the work and the work schedule, and kept busy at all times. The only time the work got hard was in the winter when the snowstorms came. The station was located on a level area between two hills. Drivers who had problems getting up the snow covered hill and some of those who had trouble stopping coming down the snow covered hill would slide into the station and ask me to install their snow chains. I wasn't paid extra for the work and seldom received a tip for my effort. It meant cold hands and wet shoes and uniforms that made my evening unpleasant at best and downright miserable at worst.

I recall another unpleasant incident. One summer evening, as I cleaned the windshield of a car as the fuel flowed into the tank, I looked through the glass on the passenger's side and saw my old girlfriend, Eleanor Hatzman. She was out on a date with the driver of the vehicle I was servicing. We were at an off again point in our on again, off again romance, but it really was a very awkward moment. I remember feeling hurt that she let the incident occur; when actually, she probably had no control over the situation.

On the advice of my oldest brother Buddy, I had enlisted in the United States Marine Corps Reserve. I was a member of the Corps for a little over one year during my high school years. I participated in two days of drills each month and attended a shortened Boot Camp training session for reservists at the Paris Island training facility at Beaufort, South Carolina. I didn't really buy into the one hundred percent blind obedience to those of higher rank, but I survived the training and became a fully trained rifleman and light machine gun (.30 caliber) operator. They issued me the best pair of dress shoes I ever owned, work shoes I could use and uniforms for the winter and summer. Because the Marine Corps allowed me to have the uniforms tailored, I quickly realized they were mine to keep, so I took advantage of the opportunity to use the trousers in everyday life. I had a job and belonged to the USMCR, where I made friends and obtained extra clothing; life was good. Near the end of my final school year, my second oldest brother, Bobby, thought I needed some advice.

As I approached graduation from high school, I had every intention to transfer from the reserve to the active duty Marine Corps. All of the children in the family internalized the idea that our responsibility was to get through high school, leave home and no longer be an expense to our parents. In April of 1953, Bobby approached me on a Saturday afternoon and invited me to have a beer or two with him at Tommy Lamasney's bar. Tommy was a diminutive man with a thick shock of white hair, an engaging smile and a quick wit. Everyone called him "The Silver Fox." Tommy's catered to clientele of Irish heritage and the bar was decorated in that vein. Every selection on the jukebox had an Irish theme. He did have an unwritten rule that said only two of the four Joyce brothers could drink there at the same time. Experience told him that if three or four of us tried to get along without a ruckus in a bar, the attempt usually failed.

Tommy wasn't working that afternoon; the bartender was a man called "Bumpy" Gallagher. We were the only customers there and settled on stools at the far end of the bar. When Bumpy placed a beer in front of each of us and picked up thirty cents from the hand full of coins Bobby had placed on the bar, Bobby asked Bumpy to stay a moment. "Tell my brother David why we call you Bumpy, okay?" Bumpy smiled and agreed to tell the story; he had told it many times before. During World War II, he was a light machine gunner in the Marine Corps. He told me that whenever a machine gun opened fire in combat, everyone on the other side responded with whatever they had, including mortars, to silence the weapon. A mortar shell had taken off his leg in a firefight and he picked up the nickname, Bumpy, because of how he walked with his imitation leg.

Bobby then told me that he had been a radio operator during his six years of active duty in the Marine Corps. He explained that, while being in combat in Korea was no fun, he was safer as a radio operator than as a riflemen or machine gunner because he was normally located with the unit commander. He went on to say that he thought I was the brightest kid in the family and could do better than being a machine gunner. He recommended I enlist in the Navy and request training as a radio operator because it was a much safer profession. I valued Bobby's advice on many things; he was my favorite brother. He looked out for me when I was a young child and I never forgot that. He went into the Marine Corps in 1945, just before the end of the war. His first assignment was in China assisting the Nationalist Chinese government as they fought the advancing Chinese Communist revolutionaries. Conflicts between the Marines and the Communists were rarely publicly reported, but they did occur. The Marine Corps troops and the Nationalist Chinese government eventually left mainland China and retreated to Taiwan, then known as Formosa. After he completed his four years of active duty, he returned home in 1949 to start a new life. He was only home a few days when he had a serious accident while driving my father's 1948 Dodge sedan. He was driving too fast, lost control going downhill and wrapped the car around a very large tree. It took many months for him to recover from a broken leg, broken pelvis and several internal injuries. He had so many steel screws and plates placed into his body he could never get through the current airport screening process.

Not long after he completely healed, the Marine Corps changed Bobby's Ready Reserve category to Active Duty status because of the Korean conflict. The day he left for his physical exam with copies of his x-rays under his arm, he told me they would never accept him once they knew of his internal repair work. The screws and plates in his body did not bother the Marine Corps at all; he passed his physical exam and they inducted him that day. As mentioned earlier, Bobby went on to serve as a radio operator for over a year in combat in Korea. After the conversation in Tommy's, I took Bobby's advice; however, being a poor swimmer and having no fear of flying, I opted to enlist in the United States Air Force rather than the Navy.

Chapter 13 - Sibling Dynamics

As the eighth child of nine, my view of the family was unique and I assume that each of the other children felt the same way. In her later years, my mother told me she was sorry I had not known my father when he was a young man before the onset of the migraine headaches. She said he was a completely different father to the first children than he was to the later ones. I contemplated that information and accepted that what she said was probably valid, but I never thought my father was a bad person nor did I think he favored one child over another. I am certain that his advice and example as an honorable, hard working man had a significant effect on my success and happiness in life. It would be impossible for me to fathom how the other children viewed their upbringing, but I can make some observations about my siblings from my perspective.

Kathleen May Clark

I called her Katie. The oldest of the nine, she was far away from me in years and association. Katie was born in April of 1923, which made her eleven years old when I was born. During World War II, she attended nursing school and became a Registered Nurse, a profession she followed for her entire life. I was proud that my sister was a nurse and felt I could go to her for medical advice or care whenever she was near. She married Ray Clark who served in combat as a radio operator in the U. S. Army Air Corps during the war. Ray was always nice to me and I considered him the same as a brother. Katie, now a widow, is still as mentally sharp as ever and lives with my little sister, Marianne, in North Carolina. We remain on good terms.

Helen Elizabeth Burton

We called her Betty. She was born in March of 1925. As with Katie, I can recall very little interaction. My most significant memory is her part in my rescue from a childless couple into whose care Marianne and I were entrusted when my mother entered the hospital for an appendectomy. Marianne was three and I was six and we were very unhappy about our situation. Betty told my father of our unhappiness and he retrieved us from our predicament. He told Betty to stay home from school and take care of us until our mother came home from the hospital. Other than that incident, I can only recall her marriage to Bill (Rusty) Burton and leaving home. Betty and Bill are still married and live in Florida.

George Edward Joyce

We called him, Buddy. I guess that is a nickname for a son named after his father, or at least it was in June of 1926 when he was born. I honestly do not remember much about Buddy at all before 1946. I knew he was my brother and that he had quit high school to join the United States Marine Corps when he was seventeen and went off to war, but I do not remember any interaction before that time. I can recall the notifications of the combat deaths of at least two neighbors, one who lived next door to us, Anthony Lombardi, and another who lived across the street, but I can't recall anyone returning from the war. In my undeveloped, unsophisticated mind, I had accepted the fact that Buddy would not be coming home and relegated his relationship to me as a memory in the back of my mind. When he did come home, it was a shock to me.

I was eleven years old when I walked into the house at lunch time and found him sitting at the dining room table talking with my mother. When I saw him and realized he was alive, a tear came to my left eye. I think the tear must have had something to do with having to acknowledge I was wrong about his death rather than happiness that he had returned. We were not close brothers in any sense of the word. When Buddy asked what was wrong with me as I stood there staring at him, I simply said that I thought he had been killed and it was hard to believe that he had come home. I'm sure Buddy and my mother thought the scene was funny, but I didn't, or I wouldn't be able to remember it so well today.

Buddy was only eighteen when he was part of the second wave of Marines to land on the beach during the invasion of Iwo Jima. He also served in combat during the Korean War. I'd like to think that being forced into killing other humans on Iwo Jima at such an impressionable age caused the mean streak I eventually found in Buddy, but maybe it was there all the time. I remember some advice he gave me either before he left for the war or afterward; I can't be sure when. He told me that it appeared that I would never be a large, strong man, so I needed to learn how to take care of myself. He advised me to consider a threat of physical violence as an actual assault and to strike first to gain the advantage. He gave me advice as to how to take down a larger boy and strongly suggested I aim for the other guy's head to immobilize him as soon as possible. As Buddy put it, "If you let him get up, he is going to be really mad and give you a good beating if he is bigger than you, so you can't let that happen." He also told me that if I did get whipped by a bully or a bigger boy, there was always a way to get back at him even if I had to resort to putting a pound of sugar into his gas tank. The whole point of the advice was to gain a reputation that to attack me was a bad idea. Although Buddy and I were never to become close brothers and were estranged at the time of his death from cancer in December of 1999, his advice served me well throughout my life.

Robert Charles Joyce

We called him Bobby. He was born in April of 1928 and was only six years my senior. Bobby was an intelligent, gentle person. I remember him watching over me as a young boy. He wasn't so much a protector as he was someone I sensed was always keeping an eye on me to make sure I was safe. He often had kind words for me when I felt I was being lost in the shuffle. Bobby joined the Marine Corps right after high school, too late to participate in World War II. He was sent to China and fought alongside of the Chinese Nationalist as they tried to keep the Chinese Communists from overwhelming the country. The Nationalists eventually lost that war and Bobby ended up on Formosa (Taiwan) before his four year enlistment was completed. He also served in combat in Korea during that war.

After his return from Korea and his discharge from the Marine Corps, Bobby attended a local Junior College and received an Associate Degree. He was successful in several endeavors during the remainder of his life. We kept in touch as well as we could, considering my frequent relocations. He obtained great pleasure in questioning me as to whom it was I was trying to avoid with my many changes of address over the years. Even today, in conversations with the surviving siblings, it is often mentioned that Bobby might well have been the nicest of all of us. Sylvia and I visited him not long before his painful death from prostate cancer in July of 1995. He was my favorite brother.

Alice Marie Hanback

Alice, the middle child, was born in February of 1930. As a middle child, she really had a unique view of the family. A great deal was asked of her with regard to the care of the younger children. I can recall at least as much care giving from Alice as I received from my mother. She learned to sew and did a lot of that to make clothes for us. Alice was dyslexic and struggled to complete her school work. She conquered her handicap and was eventually certified as a Registered Practical Nurse. If Bobby was the nicest of the boys, Alice had to be the nicest of the girls. She seldom complained, worked hard and always had a kind word for everyone.

Alice married Burt Hanback, a merchant seaman who, beyond any doubt was a unique human being. He could be as gentle as a lamb or as rough as a bear, depending on the circumstances. I have to believe he was gentle with Alice as their marriage lasted until his death a few years ago. Alice left us in April of this year. She had overcome many serious health challenges in her 78 years and seemed to be healthy and happy when she checked into a hospital for what was deemed to be a minor setback in her recovery. To the surprise of everyone, heart failure claimed her life, and all of her discomfort ended in a moment.

Daniel Thomas Joyce

We called him Danny. He was born in July of 1931, almost three years to the day before my birth. Danny was another sibling with whom I was not close. When one of the "Joyce kids" was in trouble with the law, it almost always was Danny. I don't think he was led astray; trouble just seemed to follow him. He was instrumental in arranging a strike by the caddies at the Sleepy Hollow Country Club to demand better pay. The strike was successful, but he was *persona non grata* there forever. When World War II ended and the local automobile factory switched from manufacturing airplanes to Chevrolet vehicles, General Motors crossed swords with Danny and his friends. The factory manufactured an over abundance of vehicles and proceeded to store them on the athletic field area of the Marsh. There was no place for the high school athletes to practice or play sports and they became angry. Danny was behind the decision for the students to participate in a school strike until the situation was rectified. The local and national newspapers published photos and stories about the strike that presented General Motors in a poor light. GM moved the vehicles to another area and developed an updated set of athletic fields for the town. I don't know if it was his desire to be treated fairly or if he had a troublemaking personality that drove him to organize the strike; it certainly was not his love of school.

Danny quit high school at age sixteen. When my mother told him he would have earn his keep if he no longer attended school, he worked around the house and at odd jobs in town until he turned seventeen and could enlist in the U. S. Army. In the Army, he grew up, obtained his GED (General Educational Development) certificate that roughly equates to a high school diploma, and did well as a Combat Engineer. After his three years in the Army, he enlisted in the Marine Corps. Perhaps he wanted to emulate his older brothers; whatever the case, he did well in the Marine Corps and was a Gunnery Sergeant, the third highest enlisted rank, when he was killed in combat in Vietnam. His death was not a surprise to me; he was on his third tour of duty in that war and his presence there when he was killed was voluntary.

Patricia Ann Reeves

We call her Patty. She was born in September of 1932 and was one of the brightest children. My earliest memories of Patty are of hearing her read stories to the rest of the children at bedtime. There was no television and we only had one radio, so story reading was a big thing in our family. I am a poor reader, which makes me a good proof reader because I pronounce each word as I read, but Patty was an excellent reader and entertained us for hours. I can still visualize the wolves chasing a sleigh in one of the Zane Grey novels she read to us.

Patty married a man named Roy Reeves but they eventually divorced and she became a single parent. She did an excellent job of raising her children and pursued a successful career with the Internal Revenue Service. She resides in Saratoga Springs, New York, her long time residence.

Marianne Connolly

Born in July of 1937, Marianne is my little sister. Both of us still look back with anger at the time we were farmed out to Agnes and Charlie Delade, a childless couple, when our mother had to enter the hospital for an appendectomy. Charlie was okay, but Agnes had no clue how to care for a three and a six year old. Marianne was intensely unhappy there. I can remember being locked out in the back yard when Marianne had to urinate and Agnes told her she would just have to "hold it" until later. I talked back enough to her until she relented and let Marianne use the bathroom, but it made her dislike me even more. When Betty came to visit and we told our story, she told our father and he came and took us home where Betty baby sat us until our mother came home. Agnes Delade had many lilac bushes in her yard and they were in bloom at the time. The scent of those blooms still has a dampening effect on my mood whenever I encounter them. Marianne considered me her protector, and I guess I did look after her, but she wasn't always happy with me.

When she was a freshman in high school and I was a senior, she had a boyfriend named Louis Connolly. That sounds Irish, but Lew was half Italian and I think my parents may not have approved of him. They told me to keep them apart if I saw them together at school. Those instructions led to a fight with Lew near the back entrance of the school which included a little pounding on me from Marianne while Lew and I were going at it. My interference didn't change things; they continued to see each other. While I was serving in Alaska, I received a letter from someone in the family that told of my father chasing Lew down Howard Street with a hatchet in his hand; I laughed and told myself I was glad I wasn't there then. Marianne recently told me that the story was not true; it was only a claw hammer he had in his hand. It seems they had skipped the two hour a week session the Catholic students attending the public schools were allowed to attend for religious instructions at Saint Teresa's Church and someone had told on them. Marianne says they weren't doing anything wrong, but my parents did not believe them.

Apparently, my parents got over their dislike of Lew because eventually he and Marianne married and all was forgiven. My parents became so fond of Lew that some of the other siblings and in-laws used to refer to him as Saint Lew. They had a long, successful marriage until Lew's recent death from cancer. Marianne and Kathleen, I call them the two old widows, live together in North Carolina and seem to be hale and hardy. As I type this paragraph, they are visiting our ancestral home in Ireland.

PART II – SINGLE IN THE U. S. AIR FORCE

Chapter 1 - Enlistment

I drove to White Plaines, the nearest town large enough to have enlistment offices, and volunteered to serve four years in the United States Air Force. They wouldn't accept me because I failed the dental portion of the physical examination. I never had a tooth brush as a child and we simply cleaned our teeth with salt poured onto a finger and rubbed over our teeth. Obviously, this was poor dental hygiene, but we were poor and that's the way it was. The family gathered enough money for me to go to a local dentist where the teeth with cavities were removed. On my second attempt, I passed the preliminary physical examination and was scheduled for induction a few weeks after graduation from high school. My trip to the induction center was the first of many adventures as a member of the military establishment. Although I lived and grew up a scant twenty-five miles north of New York City, I had never traveled there on my own and had never been on a train. The recruiter told me to report to an address on Water Street in New York City for my final physical examination and the swearing in procedure. I boarded the train early on a July morning in 1953 and started a new life. When the train trip ended at Grand Central Station, I found my way to an information booth and asked how to get to Water Street. The attendant told me to go to the subway just outside of the terminal and to check the map to figure which train to take. I left the station and emerged into the hustle and bustle of a large, vibrant city. People and vehicles were traveling in all directions with an air of urgency. I didn't know what a subway station looked like, so I couldn't find one. Finally, I stopped a man who wasn't walking as fast as most and asked for directions to the subway. He suspected he was speaking with a country bumpkin and asked me if I wanted the IND, the BMT or the IRT, all different subway companies. His question was almost like listening to Chinese; I didn't know what he was trying to ask. He smiled, now convinced he was speaking to a hayseed, and pointed to the nearest subway entrance and said I could get information there to find out which train to take. I thanked him and went down the steps to the subway platform. It was a good thing I wasn't shy about asking for directions or I might never have found my destination.

After asking for help from several people and finally a Transportation Police Officer, I boarded the correct train to Water Street. I paid close attention to everything around me to ensure I could find my way home; a technique I would use many times in the years to come. The government building on Water Street was stark on the outside and as plain as could be on the inside. I showed a clerk my instructions from the recruiter and he directed me to a briefing room. The "briefing" consisted of someone telling us that when enough of us had arrived, processing would begin. We were to be processed like animals.

We were each issued a keyed locker and a small cloth bag with a drawstring. Then the herder told us to place any valuables into the bag, hang it around our neck and place every bit of clothing into the locker. Questions about what he meant by everything were answered with "Everything! That means shoes, socks, underwear!" It was not a pretty sight. There were naked men of many sizes and shades of color standing in line, each with a little white cloth bag containing wallets, rings and watches hanging from his neck. They measured, weighed, poked and prodded us. Someone asked about health history and someone, who may have just been posing as a doctor, examined me. After redressing and returning to the briefing room, another clerk handed me two pieces of paper. One had a serial number typed on it and the other was a military order that contained instructions written in strange, military style language. I was sworn in and told to go home and memorize my serial number, which was AF 12436782 (my USMCR serial number, 1132161, is also tattooed onto my brain). The orders told me to report to the New York City Port Authority terminal the next day and board the Greyhound bus to Sampson Air Force Base near Syracuse, New York. I was instructed to bring nothing but the clothes on my back and shaving material. The orders also said that officials would seize all cigarettes, candy and any other non-authorized items. My brothers had given me advice before I started out on this adventure. It boiled down to: do what you are told, don't talk back and try to fade into the group. I was ready to go.

With all of my experience from the day before, I had no trouble finding the Port Authority building, which was a hub for buses. I boarded the bus for Sampson AFB and waited for departure. We soon left on the long ride to the Air Force training base on the shores of Seneca Lake in northwestern New York State. The bus arrived at the base by mid afternoon. As we stepped off, an enlisted man looked at our orders, directed each of us to a specific area of bleachers in the base gymnasium, and told us to sit and be quiet. One by one, with inquisitive looks on their faces, the members of my training flight filled the spaces around me in the bleachers. At 8:00 P.M., our Tactical Instructor (TI) arrived and told us to follow him to the floor of the gymnasium. He formed us up according to size and marched us out into the parking lot where he started screaming at us for our sloppy marching. I knew what I was doing but the other recruits didn't have a clue.

As I reflect on that day, I now realize that the trainers had factored in all of the waiting and delays to make us as uncomfortable as possible. The TI herded us to the supply office where we were issued a pillowcase, two sheets, a mattress cover and two olive drab blankets. There was more shouting from the TI and the personnel in the supply section to make us more uncomfortable. It was midnight by the time we were settled into our open bay barracks, assigned a bunk and a footlocker and learned how to make up a bunk in accordance with Air Force Regulations. The lights in the barracks had only been out for a few hours when, at four o'clock in the morning, the TI turned them on and threw an empty, 39-gallon, galvanized steel trash receptacle known in the services simply as a "GI can" down the middle of the barracks to wake up his charges. This was the beginning of 12 weeks of harassment euphemistically called Basic Training.

Seven days a week, at least 14 hours a day, for the next eight weeks, we were taught close order drill; how to keep ourselves, our clothing, equipment and living quarters immaculately clean; Air Force history and organization; and how to wear the uniform. Training was interrupted from time to time with 16 hour stints of KP[1] at the dining

---

1   KP is military shorthand for Kitchen Police or working at the Chow Hall.

hall or 12 hour stints on the garbage trucks. As could be expected, most of the guys complained all of the time; I thought it was a good deal. I had more clothes than I ever owned before and they gave me three pairs of shoes. When growing up, all I had were hand-me-downs until I joined the Marine Corps Reserve. One rather strange routine, which was to continue in the Air Force until the very late 1960s, was the procedure followed on paydays. Automatic pay deposits had yet to be invented and military personnel made so little that very few had checking accounts anyway, so we were paid in cash. Once a month, squadron personnel lined up in alphabetical order and when their name was called, reported for pay. It was a formal drill and required the wearing of the Class A uniform[2]. The payee walked smartly up to the paying officer's desk, snapped to attention, saluted, stated his rank and name, and announced he was reporting for pay. The payee would then sign for the amount indicated on the pay list; the officer would count out the money and push it toward the payee. As part of the routine, there was always a loaded .45 automatic handgun on the desk within reach of the pay officer. It didn't bother me at all when the formal pay routine eventually ended.

We were given a break after the first eight weeks. Our TI told us if we gave a pint of blood, we could get a three-day pass. Just about everyone jumped on the offer. One of the guys who came from Massachusetts arranged for his parents to pick him up on the first day and bring him back to the base at the prescribed hour. He offered to give me a ride to Route Nine in eastern New York, where I could hitchhike home to North Tarrytown, and then pick me up at the same spot on the way back. I needed a break from the regimen and wanted to see my girlfriend, so I accepted the offer.

Darkness had fallen by the time they dropped me off on the highway to home. It was a far more innocent time in history and hitchhikers had little to fear. Feeling the chill of an early September evening, I began to wonder what I would do if no one stopped to offer a ride. I was in the middle of nowhere thumbing a ride when a dark sedan pulled off the road in front of me and stopped. I wasn't too surprised when I opened the passenger side door and saw only a woman driver and no one else in the vehicle. Citizens felt little or no

2   This is a formal uniform including a tie rather than the more relaxed Class B uniform.

fear in picking up a man in uniform; some even felt it was a duty to help a GI looking for a ride. Before I could get in, she spoke up and asked, "Wait a minute, do you smoke?" I told her I did and she said, "I just want to make it clear that I would never stop for a hitchhiker but I'm out of cigarettes. I'll give you a ride, but all I want is a cigarette. Do you understand?" I couldn't believe that the woman would think I would be interested in her. I was just nineteen, and although she was very attractive, she must have been at least thirty. That was an old woman in my view. I assured her she had nothing to fear and climbed into the vehicle. She was on her way to New York City and had to pass right through my hometown to get there, so the ride was perfect. We shared my cigarettes and conversation in the warm car, and she never once pulled into a rest stop to attempt to have her way with me. I still wonder what I would have done if she had.

Chapter 2 - Assignment Mississippi

The few days at home were enjoyable and my parents drove me to the arranged pickup point where we met the family from Massachusetts. I didn't look forward to returning to the base, but the next four weeks of basic training were much easier. They involved testing of all sorts so the Air Force would be able to make an informed decision with regard to the technical training I was to receive. Of course, no one told us anything until it came time to receive our orders. My orders were to report to Radio Operator School at Keesler Air Force Base in Biloxi, Mississippi. Dressed in my winter uniform in October, I boarded an aircraft in northwest New York State that took me to Biloxi where it was still summer. I had a rude awakening when the warm, damp air of southern Mississippi hit me as I deplaned at Keesler Air Force Base.

A clerk assigned a bunk in a student barracks to me and told me where and when to be for my induction into the technical school system; a new phase of my life started. With the harsh discipline of basic training behind me, life was a lot better. We attended school for six hours each day. The first part of our routine included getting up early, eating breakfast at the chow hall and preparing the barracks for inspection. Once that was done, we fell into formation and marched to the classrooms which were in huge aircraft hangars that bordered the flight line. Our classes started at 6:00 A.M. For three hours, an instructor taught us Morse code and supervised our practice sessions. For the first phase of the training, we copied the code with a pencil on paper. After the code class, we attended a three-hour typing class. At the end of the typing class, we formed up and marched back to the barracks area where the First Sergeant stood on a high platform to read the names of men assigned to various squadron and base details before dismissing us for the day. Evenings and weekends were free and I enjoyed going to town for a beer now and then. I even proved I was nineteen and naive when I decided to have panther tattooed onto my upper right arm. He still keeps me company today.

During this assignment, I came to realize the depth of racial discrimination in parts of the country. The military services had only recently been desegregated, so there were very few black men in our class and those that were there easily assimilated into the group because we came from all over the country. At the close of one of our many poker games on a Saturday afternoon, someone suggested we go down town and take in a movie. A black kid in the group, his name was Cooper, said we should go ahead without him because he couldn't. When I asked him why, he told me he wouldn't be allowed in the theater because of his color. I had been to Biloxi several times, but because I wasn't looking for them, I never noticed any "white only" signs. Cooper quickly assured me they were there and again encouraged us to go without him. I can still recall the complex look of anger and acceptance on his face.

In those days, and probably still, there were unwritten regulations governing life in military barracks. There wasn't any privacy and very little security for personal items so we had to have our own rules. The worst thing a man could do was to be a barracks thief; when caught, he would be severely dealt with by barracks mates. The second worst thing was to touch another man's personal items that were left on his shelf. Items like shaving gear, a girl friend's photograph, a soap tray or laundry soap. Everyone knew the rules, yet there were always pranksters among us.

One evening, as I pulled down the blanket from my bunk, which was an upper, I noticed that granules of laundry detergent had been poured on to my sheet. It was not an uncommon prank but it had never been done to me. I knew that everyone else in the area must have been aware of the prank and that if I asked who had done it, no one would tell me because that was another unwritten rule of barracks life. After a few seconds, I said, "Okay! One of you guys had enough nerve to pour soap into my bed. The question is, does whoever did it have enough nerve to admit it?" Questioning a barracks mate's manhood is about the most challenging thing you can do in a barracks. If he doesn't admit to the prank, the other guys will think of him as a coward; if he does admit to the prank, he has to deal with the victim.

Yet another unwritten rule of barracks life is that if you don't fight back when someone picks on you, you will be fair game for anyone else who is in the mood to torment someone. When Will Finley, a man who outweighed me by about thirty pounds and was two inches taller, said, "I did it! What are you going to do about it?" I knew I had to retaliate or my life would be miserable for months.

Between each set of bunks was a large metal coffee can, one third filled with water, used as a receptacle for cigarettes. I picked up the butt can and poured the nicotine stained water and wet cigarette butts on to Finley's bed, which was a bottom bunk across from mine. My retaliation was many times worse than the original prank and Finley went ballistic. He quickly shoved the upper bunk into the air so he could remove one of the bed adapters, which were two foot long pieces of pipe with a jagged end that connected upper bunks to lower bunks. I recognized that he was reaching for a weapon and took off down the open bay toward the entry to the building as I contemplated my next move.

When I reached the entry way, I could hear him coming after me and was desperate until I saw the cases of empty Coke bottles next to the Coke machine. I snatched a bottle from a case and with the same movement smashed it over the edge of the GI can next to the machine. Fortunately, the bottom broke off with my first attempt. Holding it by the neck I had a deadly weapon to protect myself. Finley came through the door with the bed adapter raised over his head but stopped when he saw the broken coke bottle in my hand. He knew by the look in my eyes that as soon as his hand started down, I was going to jam the sharp end of the bottle into his stomach, so he hesitated. Standing there in our underwear, we stared at each other for a few seconds and then he said, "Damn! There's no sense in one of us getting killed over this. I guess I had it coming." No one ever messed with either of us the rest of the time we lived there.

The biggest bump in the road during my training was when I had reached the ability to copy Morse code at ten words a minute and was able to type twenty words a minute. That was the point where they took our pencils away and we had to type the code coming into our ears through headsets. It was like running into a hard wall. I had just barely learned two distinctly different mechanical skills and now I had to meld them. At first it just wouldn't work, but after some setbacks, which the instructors had seen many time before, I eventually reached the point where I could type the code I heard. The typing practice went on for three hours each day and the code practice continued until we could copy press releases at sixteen words per minute and what was called "psycho" by the instructors, mixed letters and numbers in five character groups, at twenty words per minute. We never knew when a test was in progress. We sat there copying what was being transmitted and from time to time an instructor would stop by to let a student know what level he had reached.

One day, an instructor came to me and told me that I had passed all the requirements and that the following week I was to report to the "spook" outfit that was located behind a barbed wire fence at a remote part of the base. I had no idea what was going on, but in the military, you don't ask questions, you just do as you are told. The following Monday morning, I reported to an organization that I would remain a member of for almost twenty years. It was the United States Air Force Security Service, commonly referred to as the USAFSS. In 1953, the USAFSS was on the cutting edge of foreign intelligence gathering and analysis. The Air Force has changed the name a few times since then[3], but to us old timers, it was simply, Security Service. By typing USAFSS into an Internet search engine, one can find many entries about the command including histories of USAFSS and many of its subunits. A succinct statement found in the Wikipedia encyclopedia states, "USAFSS was composed primarily of airmen culled from the cream of the Air Force's enlisted recruits. USAFSS was a secretive and tight-knit branch of the Air force cold war warriors charged with monitoring and interpreting military voice and electronic signals of countries of interest (which often were East Bloc countries). USAFSS intelligence was often analyzed in the field, and the results transmitted to the National Security Agency for further analysis and distribution to other intelligence recipients.

"Individual airmen – stationed at locations scattered across the globe, did a variety of jobs, almost all of them related to listening to, interpreting, and analyzing East Bloc, Communist Chinese and North Vietnamese military communications. Some were linguists who listened to voice communications. Others monitored Morse code

---

3   Electronic Security Command (ESC), Air Intelligence Agency (AIA) and Air Force Intelligence Surveillance and Reconnaissance Agency (AFISRA).

broadcasts. Some were engaged in monitoring other types of radio signal transmissions.

"These jobs, which required a Top Secret Codeword clearance, were extremely high pressure and were considered essential to U. S. cold war efforts. Members of the USAFSS were not allowed to discuss their jobs with outsiders – in fact, USAFSS members could not talk amongst themselves about their jobs unless they were in a secure location. Because of their value as targets (in cold war Berlin, the capture of a USAFSS member was worth several thousand dollars), while stationed overseas their off base travel was severely restricted" I didn't know the mission of the USAFSS when selected to be a member, but I sensed it was something significant.

I was one of about twenty-five who reported to the USAFSS facility on a characteristically warm, humid Mississippi morning. A security police officer with a clipboard listing the names of the new students met us at the guard shack outside of the facility. He checked identification cards and escorted us to a training room where we met our new instructors. An instructor told us that tests we took at basic training indicated we had high IQ levels and were therefore selected by Security Service for this training. None of us had ever heard of Security Service or knew what its mission was. We didn't know that the Form 1098 we filled out that asked for every possible bit of information about us had been used by the FBI to check our backgrounds to certify us to work on Top Secret projects. Because the results of our background checks had not been received, we couldn't be told just what we were going to do. The instructors sat each of us down at what is called an intercept position. There was a chair, a desk modified to hold two Super Heterodyne high frequency radio receivers, and an MC-88 typewriter. An MC-88 is a manual typewriter that types only in capital letters, standard numbers and special characters. It was designed specifically to type messages received through Morse code transmissions. The instructors assigned each of us a frequency to monitor and told us at what time we could expect a transmission. While waiting for the transmission, our job was to search the airways with the second receiver to find other transmissions. Again, with only limited access to classified material, they didn't tell us that the receivers were hooked up to an antenna farm that targeted Central and South America.

When we heard Morse code and started to copy it, we were all in for a shock. The code sounded nothing like what we had become accustomed to at the first school. In our previous training, we copied Morse code using tapes created by the best Morse code key operators that could be found, and there was no background noise. What we heard in our new facility was almost amateurish keying of Morse code enveloped in static with other Morse code signals in the background. My first day as an Intercept Radio Operator was genuinely inauspicious. I didn't know what I was copying, who was sending the code or what the messages said. I wasn't sure they had picked the right guy for the job. All of the instructors got a kick out of our consternation. A few days later, after our clearances arrived, they told us we were intercepting Honduran, Columbian and Panamanian fishing boat transmissions. The exercise was to condition us to the real world of international Morse code. They told us about Security Service and its mission of intercepting Morse code around the globe to obtain information on enemy strength and activities. For the following six weeks, we copied code from many countries and found that each operator had his own way of keying code and some could be recognized by their sending characteristics. The intercepts were not really to obtain information; they were just to familiarize us with what to expect at our next assignment.

Chapter 3 - Assignment Alaska

When our assignments arrived, I found that I was to report to the 3rd Radio Squadron Mobile at Anchorage, Alaska. When comparing assignments, I noticed that men received orders for organizations all over the world. Alaska sounded like an adventure to me, so I wasn't dissatisfied.

During the nine months at Keesler Air Force Base, I made several acquaintances; some of which would last a lifetime. Four of us who hailed from the east coast, Pete "Zinger" Zimmerman, Charlie Wilson, "Snake" Holderman, and I arranged to take turns driving Pete's 1949 Mercury to New Jersey. There we would split up and go on leave before reporting to our next assignments. The Air Force paid each of us enough travel money to reach our ports of debarkation so pooling our funds allowed us a net gain. It was sleep, eat and drive regardless of time of day or weather conditions; paying for a motel would have been wasted funds for us. All went fine until we entered Virginia.

It was very late in the evening, around 10:00 P.M., and I was driving on a dark, two lane, black-top road in a rainstorm. Zinger and Charlie were dozing off in the front seat and Snake was sleeping on the back seat. I hit a spot on the road where the rain had washed dirt from the shoulder into a slippery, muddy mess and the car started to fish tail. I turned into the skid but over corrected and the car skidded in the opposite direction. When I turned into that skid, the front wheels went off the road into the mud on the left side and all control was lost. We rolled over at least once, sheared off a power pole and then the vehicle came to rest on its right side. There were no seatbelts in automobiles in those days, so forces of the accident tossed us around in a blur. When I regained my senses, I was unhurt and holding on to the steering wheel, but the two guys who had been sitting next to me were not there. I looked over my shoulder and saw Snake crumbled up against the right rear window of the car. The thought struck me that he was dead. The right side passenger door had a huge bulge toward

73

the inside that I thought was caused by the bodies of Pete and Charlie. A dreadful feeling of responsibility for the deaths of these three friends came over me just as steam from the broken radiator began rising from the engine compartment. I thought the steam was smoke and having the deaths of three people crushing my conscience, I decided to stay where I was and burn to death rather than live with what I had done. It was the darkest day in my short life; then I heard Pete's voice.

I couldn't see him, but I heard Pete asking "Is anyone alive in there?" At the sound of his voice, fatal depression switched to hope and I looked for a way out of a vehicle I thought was burning. I climbed through the broken, driver's side window to find both Pete and Charlie, covered with mud but on their feet. The bump I had noticed on the passenger side door was from the car coming to rest on a tree stump. Then we heard Snake asking what had happened as he came crawling out of the broken window. Beyond a few bruises, none of us was injured, even though Pete and Charlie were ejected from the car during the rollover. That 1949 Mercury two door sedan was built like a tank. As we stood there in the rain surveying the scene, we saw a great deal of our personal belongings from the trunk lying in the mud. Pete noticed a farmhouse about a half mile up the road and off he went to ask for help. When he returned, he said the people called the state police to report the accident and invited us into their home. He also told us that when the farmer opened the door he was holding a loaded shotgun, which startled him a bit.

The state trooper arrived and recorded all pertinent information while a tow truck hauled the destroyed Mercury out of the mud and to a junk yard in Orange, Virginia, the nearest town. The farmer and his wife could not have been nicer people. They gave us a snack, provided sleeping arrangements for the four of us and prepared a huge country breakfast the next morning. Just when I was thinking that these two people had to be the nicest I ever met, Pete asked the farmer why he answered the doorbell with a shotgun in his hands the night before. The farmer replied, "I heard the crash and though it might be some niggers. They're always crashing on that curve, but I never let them in my house." I was jolted back to the realization that I was still in the south.

The farmer gave us a ride to town where we examined the wreckage of the car in the daylight and wondered how we had survived. Pete had insurance on the Mercury and didn't seem at all perturbed that it had been destroyed. We arranged for transportation to our hometowns and said good-bye. Eventually, I saw Snake again because he also served in Alaska, but I never saw Pete or Charlie again. The accident did come back to haunt me for many years in my dreams and once in my real life. Pete never reported the destroyed power pole to his insurance company and because I was listed as the driver, the state of Virginia sent a bill for $115, about two month's pay, to me at my address in Alaska. I didn't think I had to pay for the pole because Pete had insurance, so I ignored their request. Some months later, I received a letter from the state of Virginia, which said they had tried me in absentia and found me guilty of the destruction of public property. The letter also said they had issued a bench warrant for my arrest. The bench warrant got my attention. I didn't know what to do, so I went to my First Sergeant who in the eyes of a young inexperienced trooper was all knowing. He looked at the paper work and told me the best thing I could do was to avoid visiting the state of Virginia for the rest of my life. I have never been back to Virginia and I don't think I will ever go there; at a conservative, compounded interest rate of five percent, that $115 would amount to about $1,650, not to mention any jail time.

The time I spent in Alaska was not very memorable. My first assignment, the 3rd Radio Squadron Mobile, was located at a remote part of Elmendorf Air Force Base near Anchorage. The economy in Alaska, which was a Territory at that time, was much different from that in the lower forty-eight states. Everything was grossly overpriced and our pay scale, which was reasonable in Mississippi, did not allow us to spend much time in town. The job was also somewhat boring. I copied Russian radio operators eight hours a day with no knowledge of what was done with the information. Every hour, someone collected the intercepted messages and took them to a room where Radio Traffic Analysts analyzed the information. That was the routine for each of my eight hour shifts.

It was necessary to have Intercept Operators on the job twenty-four hours a day, seven days a week. To this end, the operators and analysts were broken down into four units called Tricks. The Tricks were Able, Baker, Charlie and Dog. Three Tricks were always on duty and one was always off duty. To accomplish this, a work schedule was devised whereby a Trick worked six swing shifts (4:00 P.M. until Midnight), off duty for a day and a half; six mid shifts (Midnight until 8:00 A.M.), off duty for two days; and six day shifts (8:00 A.M. until 4:00 P.M.) and then off for two and a half days. Weekends and holidays had no meaning in our lives; they were just workdays.

Part of our off duty time was allocated to unit details that were required, barracks inspections and anything else the First Sergeant could come up with to make our lives miserable. Many of the married men and those not assigned to shift work loved the assignment; I hated being there. On one of my break periods, I had to attend an arctic survival class. That exercise included learning how to survive if lost in the arctic winter. The night I spent outdoors in a self-made lean to, bundled up in my sleeping bag, the temperature dropped to 36 below zero. To ensure our safety, there were experienced instructors standing by to make sure none of us died out there.

I toiled along until the day my supervisor told me to pack my gear because I was to be transferred to a detached unit at Naknek, a remote village at the beginning of the Aleutian Island chain. Actually, the village of Naknek was a few miles from the Security Service unit. Our outfit was located near a small airstrip known as King Salmon Airport. Because it was a remote assignment, that is, family members could not accompany the military member, each day there counted as two when a trooper's return date to the lower forty eight was calculated. This meant that my Alaskan tour was cut to about eighteen months instead of the originally scheduled thirty months. Conditions at the detachment were the same as at Anchorage, except there was no civilization nearby. Unheated wooden passageways, that kept some of the cold out, connected all of the buildings. There was a small movie theater, a chow hall and a few day rooms where a person could go to escape the confinement of our four man rooms that were crammed with bunks and footlockers. We could also check out .22 caliber rifles from the armory and go out to hunt snowshoe rabbits and ptarmigan, a partridge like bird that inhabited the area.

Two other significant things about Naknek stick in my mind: the large, black mosquitoes that live in the tundra and salmon fishing. The mosquitoes were absolutely ferocious. When we played softball, the gloves we wore were not to protect our hands from the ball - they were to protect them from the mosquitoes. We also tucked our trousers into our socks, wore netting over our faces that we tucked into our long sleeve shirts and covered each other with insect repellant.

The year I was there, the return of the red salmon from the ocean was one of the best years ever. You couldn't walk across the Naknek River on the backs of the fish, but almost. To catch a salmon, all one had to do was to throw out a line with a hook attached and pull – no bait was required. A sharp knife to cut salmon steaks from the catch, the minor theft of a pound of butter from the chow hall, a frying pan and a hot plate was all that was needed for a feast. We cooked our fish in the unit laundry room to keep the fried fish smell out of our living quarters. Like most GIs, we were adaptive and inventive.

From time to time, we would wander into the town of Naknek just to get away from the military life. Following is a photo of George Murphy and me when we befriended some of the local children on one of those trips. I'm the one with the widow's peak.

George Murphy, me and unidentified Aleut children.
(Courtesy: Ben Pennell)

At Naknek, we followed the same six-day rotating shift we had at Anchorage, but my assignment there was a little different. They assigned me as a direction finding (DF) operator. I worked alone in a little hut about three quarters of a mile from the operations building, which itself was already located in a remote area. Upon the request of the Non Commissioned Officer (NCO) in charge of the Trick, I operated equipment that could determine the exact direction from which a Morse signal emanated. Analysts at higher echelons of the intelligence community would eventually combine my input with the input of other direction finding stations to isolate the location of a target. To analysts in today's world, our work would be considered as Stone Age technology, but back then it was relatively new. Aside from the boredom, the cold and the lousy food, the six-day shift schedule was the hardest thing to handle. In the winter, I arrived at my DF hut in the dark on a day shift and departed the hut in the dark. Add to this the darkness of the evening and night shifts and sleeping in the day time, there were many long periods when I did not see the light of day.

At the end of my tour, I received a promotion to Airman First Class (three stripes) and orders to attend the Radio Traffic Analyst school at March Air Force Base at Riverside, California, to begin in January of 1956. On a cold, rainy December morning, I reported to King Salmon Airport with all of my belongings to board an Air Force C-119 transport aircraft. As a few other passengers and I climbed on board, the Loadmaster handed each of us a parachute harness with a parachute and helped us don the equipment. I asked him why we needed parachutes because we didn't need them when we flew into the airport on a C-47. With a smile, he told me that the C-119 was such an untrustworthy aircraft, everyone on them had to wear parachutes all of the time. If that didn't bother me much, the answer to my next question did. I noticed the Loadmaster had a red handkerchief sticking out of his parachute pack and asked why it was there. With an even bigger smile, he told me that he always packed his own parachute to be sure it would open if needed and the red handkerchief was there to indicate which chute was his. Thankfully, the flight to Anchorage was uneventful. Soon after that time, the Air Force grounded all C-119 aircraft, derisively called the flying coffin by crewmembers, to perform an extensive study to determine the cause of frequent crashes. Later I would see a few of them flying in Vietnam, so the problem must have been corrected.

Chapter 4 - Assignment March and Kelly AFBs

I had previously met several of the men assigned to the March Air Force Base Radio Intercept Analyst school while at Keesler AFB or during my tour in Alaska. One of the guys, Richard B. "Zak" Zakrzewski, knew a young lady from his home town of Oswego, Michigan, who was a member of the United States Marine Corps stationed at El Toro Naval Air Station. El Toro was not very far from Riverside and a few of us associated with some of the lady Marines stationed there. One of the men in our group, Bill Chapman, eventually married one of those women and they enjoyed a long, happy relationship until his recent death from a stroke. Being around an abundance of the opposite sex after my remote assignment to Alaska, where women were almost non-existent, was heady stuff for me. The schoolwork was challenging but nothing we couldn't handle, even with the distraction of Southern California in the springtime and the beautiful, friendly women in the area. We all enjoyed the assignment and I have good memories of those days. The good times in paradise ended when we completed the school and were shipped us off to the USAFSS Headquarters on Kelly Air Force Base in hot, humid San Antonio, Texas in May of 1956.

At age twenty-two, just finding out about life, little did I know that across town from the base there was a cute little fourteen-year-old, red haired girl who would eventually become my lifelong partner; but that is a story for later. For the next fourteen months, I sharpened my skills as an Intelligence Analyst by working on copies of intercepted radio transmissions from around the world. I also discovered I had a bourgeoning skill with words and my supervisor selected me to write reports based on the analysis of others. I enjoyed the writing assignments and concentrated on improving my skill. The assignment didn't seem too bad once I had a routine.

We didn't have much money in those days, but somehow, a couple of the guys could afford vehicles. My Friend, Herb Dennison, was able to buy a 1954 Ford, two door coupe. Those who didn't own a vehicle always willingly paid what they could for fuel and food to try to even out the costs of our trips around the area. Zak met and married a cute little blond who worked in our unit and Herb and I did our thing until our separation dates arrived. Herb got out of the Air Force in May of 1957 and I separated the following July. As previously arranged, we met in Los Angeles and enrolled in a business college in September of 1957. We planned on earning degrees in Accounting and finding work in the Los Angeles area. The work was not difficult, but I had a hard time fitting in with such a young crowd; just about everyone had recently graduated from high school and seemed very immature. Rather than spend my days unhappily, I decided to reenlist in the Air Force. When I left the Air Force, I was a Staff Sergeant and I knew I could retain my rank if I signed up for four more years within a specific period. I went to the recruitment office and did the deed before telling Herb. I didn't want my decision to have any effect on his life. When I told him what I had done, his response was that he had been thinking about doing the same thing but didn't want to affect my view of the future. A few days later, he quit school and reenlisted for four more years.

My chosen assignment was Trabzon, Turkey, a town in the northeast corner of the country. There was no base there and troops assigned to the unit received double pay to enable them to live on the Turkish economy during a one-year tour of duty. The extra money and the opportunity to visit the mysterious Middle East drew me to the assignment. Herb went back to San Antonio, married Pat, his lifelong partner to be, and took her with him to an assignment in Germany. It was good to be young, not tied down and able to make spontaneous decisions. This decision started me on the path to another sixteen years of interesting Air Force service.

Chapter 5 - Assignment Turkey

It was the fall of 1957 and the first Russian earth satellite, Sputnik, had been placed into orbit; the technical revolution had begun. My participation in that revolution was to start with my assignment to Turkey. The reenlistment office provided me with military orders, the necessary travel money and sent me on my way. I flew by commercial airline from Los Angeles to New York City. From there, I made my way to McGuire Air Force base in New Jersey where I presented my orders to the operations section of the Military Air Transport Service (MATS). The orders simply said to proceed to Trabzon, Turkey using any military transport facilities available. After a few days lying around the transient NCO quarters waiting to hear from MATS, I finally got the word that they could send me to Wheelus Air Base at Tripoli, Libya. That seemed to be on the way to Turkey, so I accepted the flight.

Over the years, I've wondered if anyone in USAFSS ever notified the personnel section at the 6933 RSM, the parent organization of the detachment at Trabzon that I was on the way. It took me two weeks to get to Libya and I hadn't encountered any search parties looking for me. There was no MATS desk at Wheelus, so I just showed up at Air Operations every day looking for a flight to any place in Turkey. I hadn't even bothered to check and see just where Trabzon was located in Turkey, but I knew I had to find the parent organization, which I thought was near Istanbul. Finally, after two weeks, the clerk in operations told me I had just gotten lucky. Someone in the Air Force had been killed in an accident in Turkey and they had to send an aircraft to pick up his body. I caught a ride on that aircraft to the Istanbul International Airport.

As I entered the terminal, it was as if I had entered a different world. The garb of the travelers was distinctly different and I stood out like a sore thumb in my Air Force blue uniform. I scanned the walls looking for a language I could understand and finally saw a familiar word; it was TUSLOG. My orders instructed me to report to TUSLOG

Detachment 3-1 at Trabzon, Turkey. No one told me that using the USAFSS designation of 6933 RSM would mean little or nothing in Turkey. To reduce the visibility of our organization in Turkey, it went by the name Turkish United States Logistics Group or TUSLOG in military shorthand. The United States government found it useful to hire and assign to TUSLOG a large number of American and Turkish civilians to provide much of the maintenance and support needed to operate our facilities in Turkey so on the surface, it appeared to be a civilian organization. I found an Air Force two striper manning the office and told him I was trying to get to Trabzon but didn't know where to go from where I was. He laughed and said it happened all of the time and that was the reason they maintained an office at the airport. He told me that the TUSLOG office in Istanbul was on the fifth floor of the building right next to the Hilton hotel and gave me the address. He then wrote down the information I needed to find a Turkish bus from the airport to Istanbul and headed me in the right direction. When the bus reached Istanbul, I stayed on it until the last stop because I hadn't seen the Hilton hotel. The bus driver spoke no English at all but finally made it clear to me that he was at the last stop and I had take my bags and leave. Fortunately, I was in an area where taxis were abundant; I climbed into one and told the driver in English to take me to the Hilton hotel. He didn't have any problem with that, nor did he have any problem accepting a twenty dollar bill for the fare. In those days, American money was accepted as legal tender in almost any city in the world. I still don't have any idea if he over charged or short changed me in the deal, but I got to where I had to be.

The best thing that could be said of the TUSLOG office in Istanbul was that it was between the Hilton hotel and a great international restaurant called the Corte en Bleu. It contained the standard military steel furniture and had a large adjacent room with about twenty double deck bunks for use by military personnel stuck in Istanbul waiting for transportation. I asked the clerk there if he knew how to get to Trabzon. He told me to take a cab in the morning to the Galata Bridge where I would find a ferryboat to Karamursel, the location of TUSLOG Detachment 3 (the 6933 RSM). The clerk was an inconsiderate moron, an ignorant malcontent or, as a private joke, made the instructions sound simple.

I expected to see a bridge and a ferryboat when my taxi reached the Galata Bridge. What I found was a bridge that was a third of a mile long over the famous Golden Horn area of the Bosporus Strait. The bridge was eighty yards wide, lined on both sides with large ferryboats destined for a myriad of ports, and alive with the constant hustle and bustle of a drably clad working class population. I looked around to find a place to buy a ticket and found a long row of kiosks. Although it was obvious I was a stranger as I stood there looking confused, dressed in my Air Force blue uniform, no one seemed to take special notice of me. When I reached the front of the line at one of the kiosks, I said, "Karamursel," and shoved a hundred lira note toward the clerk.

The clerk took the bank note and said, "Yolava." I responded with Karamursel and he replied with "Yolava" again. Realizing I was at an impasse, I took back my money, stepped out of line and went back up to the bridge. I looked around for someone who was well dressed and each time I saw one, I asked if they spoke English. After a number of failures, a Turkish man acknowledged that he spoke some English and offered to help. When I explained my problem, he laughed and told me that Karamursel was an inland town and to get there I would have to travel first to Yolava. He went with me back to the ticket kiosks and figured out which ferry I should take and told me how much to pay for the ticket. He was the rare nice Turk I was to meet during my fourteen months in the country. I thanked him and proudly said "Yolava" as I pushed the lira toward the ticket seller. I found my ferry, a large ship filled with people, vehicles and animals. I climbed aboard for my trip across the Sea of Marmara, a link between the Mediterranean Sea and the Black Sea, and headed to the next stop on my odyssey.

As the ferry bumped into the dock at Yolava and the crew started to secure the vessel, people began jumping onto the dock with their belongings to hurry on their way as others jumped from the dock to the deck. Suddenly, a little boy about half my size, who had jumped onto the ferry, grabbed my bags and took off down the gangway to the dock. I struggled through the mass of humanity trying to catch what I thought was a thief. When I finally reached the little urchin, he smiled at me and said, "Okay GI, Okay GI. Karamursel" and pointed to a parking lot filled with about thirty buses. He had outrun his competition to carry my bags to the bus for a tip. When we reached the proper vehicle, he pointed to the sign above the front windows that indicated its destination was Karamursel and stuck out his hand. I gave him a five-lira note and he scurried off to find another job.

I must digress a moment to explain the use of Turkish lira. I had been using twenty-dollar bills since arriving and only received Turkish lira in change. Guessing at the value of food and services, I made a rough calculation that a dollar was worth about nine or ten lira on the street. The official exchange rate was 1.8 lira to a dollar but there was a flourishing black market for currency of all types in that part of the world at that time. To purchase currency at other than the official exchange rate was punishable by arrest and jail time, but the Turkish government ignored the activity and let the market set the unofficial rate.

The bus driver could see by my uniform that I was headed for the American base and stopped at the gate which was at the outskirts of Karamursel. I dragged my bags off the bus and entered a little bit of America built in this strange, ancient country. The guard at the gate called for transportation for me and a pickup truck came to the gate and took me to the personnel office. The First Sergeant directed me to a clerk to have a room in the barracks assigned and gave me instructions to return to the Personnel Office the next day. I told the clerk that I was only there to catch a ride to Trabzon and would only need transit quarters; he told me he had instructions to assign me to the Operations Section at Karamursel and that was what he was going to do. Apparently, someone really had passed the word that Staff Sergeant Joyce was en route to Turkey. I was too tired to argue and figured I would straighten out things in the morning.

I checked in with the personnel section the next morning and explained my situation. It was the middle of November in 1957 and I had been on the road to my new unit for over six weeks by this time and still hadn't reached my destination. The personnel officer didn't want to hear my story. He told me I was assigned to the day group of analysts in the Operations Section and that I should take up my problem with the Operations Officer, Captain Mock. I went through the process of clearing onto the base and showed up for work the next morning at Operations. My new roommate, Mike Everson, an Aleut Indian from Alaska, had already clued me in to the fact that it was a poorly run organization with no real leadership. The Non Commissioned Officer In Charge (NCOIC) of the analytical section pointed to the room where I was to work and told me to find a work space. When I walked in, it seemed apparent the organization did not need another analyst. Someone occupied every chair and desk. The next thing I noticed was that the place looked like a pigsty; it hadn't been kept at the normal level of military order and cleanliness. That NCOIC was a poor excuse for a Non Commissioned Officer. I do not, nor do I want to, remember his name. I wasn't assigned any mission and had no place to work. Rather than wander around like a dunce, I introduced myself to the other analysts and asked if anyone needed help. A couple of guys said they had more than they could handle so I went to work at the edge of a desk using fully packed burn bags, thick paper bags that contained classified information to be burned, as a chair. I realized right away that if I were going to go to war with Captain Mock, he didn't have a chance given the way he ran the Operations Section.

I went through all the channels available to try to get orders that would send me on my way to Trabzon but ran into a brick wall everywhere I turned. No one wanted to hear my story or offer any solutions. I made some new friends in the outfit and we made several trips to Istanbul on weekends to get away from the base. On one of the trips, I was with Mike Everson and he told me about a small Post Exchange in the city. I needed cigarettes so we made our way there. As we entered, the Turkish guard, hired to ensure that only Americans entered, waved me through the door but stopped Mike. We were in civilian clothes and to the guard it was obvious I was American, but Mike had dark skin and looked like he came from the Middle or Near East. The guard thought he was trying to sneak into the Exchange. After Mike had his military identification card thoroughly inspected by the guard and his supervisor, he was allowed to enter. Mike and I got a kick out of the incident, but then I began to wonder if Mike felt insulted and asked him if he had been bothered by what had happened. He gave me his big, friendly smile and told me it was nothing compared to the old days. When I asked what he meant, he explained that when he entered the Army in 1950, the services were still segregated and he was assigned to a black unit because of his heritage and dark skin. He also served in the Korean War with a black unit led by white officers. Our conversation that day added to my education about our country. Through the wonder of the Internet, Mike and I still correspond. I had been enjoying my weekend trips to Istanbul to see the sights and learn about a new culture, but I wanted the extra money that went with the Trabzon assignment and the work at Karamursel was miserable. By late December I got the feeling that if I didn't do something soon, nothing would ever be done and I'd be stuck at Karamursel for the full twenty-four month tour of duty.

On the following Monday morning, I sought and received an appointment with Captain Mock. He struck me as an angry man who was unhappy to be where he was and didn't want to spend any time listening to my problem. He must have been asleep in the Officers Training School on the day they taught the students the famous lesson that "All enlisted men are stupid but some are crafty and bear watching." He told me he was short of Analysts so he had changed my assignment from Trabzon to Karamursel. I told him that I had been given a guaranteed reenlistment assignment to Trabzon and that he wasn't authorized to make the change. He accused me of being insolent and insubordinate and dismissed me. I think it was at that point I began to realize that just because someone is a military officer, it doesn't mean he is more intelligent than I am.

I told the NCOIC of the Analysis Section that I had some matters to take care of at the Personnel Office and walked over to the headquarters building. When I got there, I told the First Sergeant that I had a serious personal matter I needed to discuss with the Squadron Commander. Normally, it is difficult to take a personnel problem directly to a unit commander, but when it is couched in terms of a personal problem, First Sergeants will acquiesce and make the interview happen. When the Commander, a Lieutenant Colonel, asked about my problem, I turned it around by telling him that he had a problem with one of his officers. "Oh! What's that?" he asked me with a glowering look. I told him that it had become apparent to me that his Operations Officer, Captain Mock, had concluded that the success or failure of the entire operations section depended on me, a lowly Staff Sergeant, who had only been in the unit for a few weeks. I didn't say anything about the poor conditions I had witnessed in operations; I simply explained that I wanted my guaranteed assignment to Trabzon but that Captain Mock felt my absence from Karamursel would lead to a disaster. The Commander leaned back in his chair and stared at me for several moments; I waited for him to blow up and jump down my throat for wasting his time. To his credit and my relief, that didn't happen. He leaned forward, stared at me even harder and slowly said, "No organization of mine will ever depend on one person, no matter his job or rank. Go back to the barracks and pack your bags. Report to the Personnel Office in the morning to pick up your orders and arrange transportation to Trabzon. You are dismissed." I stood up, saluted, thanked him for his decision and left his office. I have to assume that he must have had unpleasant dealings with Captain Mock in the past, because he never once questioned the details of my story and made his decision on the spot. Although I remained in the USAFSS Command for the following sixteen years, I never dealt with, or heard of, Captain Mock again.

My trip to Trabzon was aboard a Turk Hava Yollari (THY) Airlines aircraft. I can't say for sure, but I think the aircraft was a very old, eighteen passenger Lockheed L-18 Loadstar. In aviation, there are Instrument Flight Rules (IFR) and Visual Flight Rules (VFR). IFR procedures are used in foul weather or when the pilot can't see the terrain and VFR procedures are used when the weather is clear and the pilot can determine his location by viewing the terrain. On the day I flew to Trabzon, I don't think the pilot was instrument rated or perhaps, in that backward country, there were no IFR aids available to help him. It was seriously overcast and raining when we departed the international airport at Istanbul. The pilot turned the aircraft eastward and located the coastline of the Black Sea and mainland Turkey. He couldn't fly much higher than fifteen hundred feet above the surface of the water or he would lose sight of the coastline in the overcast. While the pilot tried to keep us airborne in the unstable air by countering the up and down and sideway bounces, the copilot, sitting at his right, kept him informed of their estimated position by comparing the coast line to a map on his lap. I concluded the pilot had come up with a new rule. He was flying IFCL; I Follow Coast Lines.

We finally completed the approximately 450-mile flight with a smooth landing in the rain at Trabzon. One look around told me I was in the middle of nowhere. We ran through the rain from the aircraft to the rundown terminal and waited for the bags to be unloaded. Before my bags reached the terminal, a taxi driver approached me and asked, "Hotel?" I knew there was no base in the city and quickly realized that I would need a hotel until I found a place to live so I said, "Okay," a term understood everywhere in the world. He stood next to me to ensure some other driver didn't poach his fare as we waited for my bags. When they arrived, he snatched them and put them into the trunk of his cab. The cabbie took me to a hotel in downtown Trabzon which was third or fourth class by our standards, but one of the best in that town.

As I arranged for a room, an American in civilian clothes who had been on the plane with me, and turned out to be a newly assigned radio operator, asked if I knew where the American unit's orderly room was. When I told him I didn't know anything, the hotel clerk asked, "American Office?" We both said yes and the clerk shouted something in Turkish to a cab driver parked outside. The driver came into the hotel, and through international sign language and broken English, we arranged for him to take us to the orderly room. We found one person at the orderly room, an administrative clerk assigned to handle personnel matters for the unit. Fortunately, he had the time and inclination to brief us on the operation of the detachment. I began to feel welcome.

The unit had fewer than a hundred men assigned. There were no barracks so everyone lived on the economy with the Turkish residents of the city. He told us he was sure there were a few openings at some of the apartments that had historically been rented to Americans since the unit opened in 1953. He said he would pass along the word that new guys were in the hotel looking for quarters. The clerk told us the detachment Commander, Captain Carl J. Carlson, and First Lieutenant James J. Easley, the Operations Officer, were good men and smart officers. The unit used the standard four Trick schedule and the men worked at a compound on the top of a hill that overlooked the city. According to the clerk, every trip up or down the hill via a dirt road in one of the unit's trucks was an adventure. He took our orders and told us to report back the next morning to meet the Commander and the Operations Officer.

Our meeting with Captain Carlson and Lieutenant Easley soon confirmed the opinion of the orderly room clerk. Both of these officers came across as men who would not put up with any nonsense from their troops, yet were officers who had the welfare of the men in their organization as a paramount concern. Jim Easley told me there was a Sergeant on duty in operations waiting to brief me on my job because I was his replacement and he was more than ready to go home. He also told me to find quarters before reporting to work. Carl Carlson told us that whereas there hadn't been any trouble with the locals, danger did lurk in the alleys of the town and recommended that troops never walk around the town alone. The Turkish government did not allow us to have regular military weapons, but he recommended each man carry a hunting knife or an oversized "church key," GI slang for a beer can opener. This advice, of course, was informal. These were my kind of officers.

In the few days it took for me to find a place to live, I had a crash course in living in a remote Muslim town far removed from the secular area of the country. Based on the local garb, there seemed to be two distinct tribes. One wore traditional clothing in black and the other wore black and orange striped clothing. The women wore the customary chador,[4] and carefully avoided eye contact with men. Although some local men wore traditional Islamic clothing, most wore western clothing in town. Unlike the women, men constantly sought out eye contact to the point of seeming rude by staring with their universally dark eyes. Women always walked behind their husband or male family member but were allowed to walk in front of any male hired to carry purchases from the market. There were many tea houses where men sat, drank tea and discussed the politics of the day. Women were not allowed in tea houses, nor were they allowed in the few restaurants in town.

With one exception, the only cars in the town of about thirty to forty thousand citizens were taxis. The Italian government maintained a consulate in Trabzon and the Counselor had a black Mercedes assigned to him. Other than the main thoroughfares, streets were unpaved and were little more than alleys. Even on the main thoroughfares, pedestrian traffic had the right of way. When moving on city streets, our trucks

---

4   This is an ankle length garment with long sleeves which also covers the head but not the face. A veil that covers the nose and mouth is added when a woman is in public.

carefully avoided conflict with foot traffic. Ninety-six American men in a Muslim community constituted an oddity and the local people viewed us with interest. They knew we were sanctioned by the Turkish military, so we received tacit acceptance.

I got lucky and found a one-person unit on the top floor of a four-story apartment building. It was known as the "penthouse," but that was an exaggeration. The room was about forty feet long and fifteen feet wide. There was room for a bed, a table and a few chairs. One end, with a door to the flat roof of the building where maids hung laundry, was dedicated to the kitchen facilities: a kitchen sink, a hot plate and a pantry. There was another sink with a mirror across from the bed, which I used for shaving. Just off the entry door on the opposite end of the long room was a small bathroom. It had a shower at one side of the room, and the other side, in lieu of a commode, contained what we jokingly called a bombsight. The bombsight was a slightly depressed tiled area in the floor with two raised footprints. Behind the footprints was an open four-inch diameter pipe to facilitate urination and defecation. A few inches above the floor, there was a water spigot.

I purchased the existing furniture and remaining canned goods from the man who was leaving and felt fortunate to have a place of my own. As he handed me the key when he was leaving, he said, "Oh, one more thing; before you go into the bathroom, make sure you kick the bottom of the door to scare the rats down the pipe." He was not joking. The rats were so big in Trabzon, they had a mutual non-aggression pact with the cats in town. I can remember seeing a cat walking down one side of the street while a rat walked in the same direction across the street without either acknowledging the existence of the other. I didn't have the presence of mind to take a photograph of the bombsight area for posterity but I do have a photograph of a modern one I recently took in Southern Spain while on vacation. I assume the strong North African and Muslim influence in that area accounts for the existence of this type of facility found in an up-scale restaurant in the city of Tarifa at the southernmost point of Europe.

No foot prints in this version. (Photo by Author)

Using the accepted black market rate for the Turkish lira, the accommodations cost me twenty dollars a month. I inherited a maid, an old, bent over Russian lady named Anna, who came in a few days a week to clean the place and do my laundry. I paid her ten dollars a month. We seldom spoke but we had an established routine. Clothing to be washed was to be left on the floor; it was important not to leave anything on the floor that I did not want washed. Anna would iron my clothes, but only if I inserted the plug into the electrical outlet; she thought electricity was magic and refused to touch the plug. If I placed any rock hard, stale bread in the trash, she would remove it and tell me Allah would make me go blind if I threw away bread. I learned to give her any bread I did not want. Anna would remove her veil while in my apartment but would replace it if anyone came to the door. Overall, living in Trabzon was somewhere between miserable and tolerable, but the mission of the organization made it worthwhile.

The trip up to the top of Boztepe, the hill at the edge of town, was indeed an adventure. The road was dirt and gravel and had three switchbacks so sharp that trucks had to stop, back up several feet and then start forward again in order to make the turns. To run off the road was certain death. We used the standard military two and a half ton trucks nicknamed "six bys" because power can be applied to all six wheels. I soon realized it was safer to walk down the hill on the well worn path when I left work; the ride down in a truck was just too scary.

My work at Trabzon prepared me for future assignments as a Surveillance and Warning Center Supervisor, the most important position in any operational Security Service unit. Our job was to monitor the communications used by the Soviet missile development program. At that time, the Soviet Union operated three major missile test ranges. They used Kapustin Yar Missile Test Range (KYMTR) to develop short-range missiles; Vladimirovka Lake Balkhash Missile Test Range (VLBMTR) was dedicated to intermediate range missiles; and Tyura Tam Missile Test Range (TTMTR) tested intercontinental ballistic missiles (ICBMs). Although we had a non-Morse intercept operation on the site that worked in concert with the Morse intercept operation, the Morse intercept mission was the prime reason for the existence of the detachment.

Our operations building consisted of three, forty-foot long trailers, with rear doors removed, connected by a wooden frame passageway. One trailer held three Morse intercept positions; the middle trailer held a communications center and an office for the operations officer; and the Intelligence Analysts used the third. There was also a desk in the third trailer for the one Cryptanalyst assigned to the organization. I received a wonderful briefing from my predecessor that was as good as a training class; his forte was probably teaching. Each Trick had three intercept operators and a Morse supervisor who was responsible for their activities and the operation of the Morse link with our units at Samsun and Karamursel. Each Trick also had one Intelligence Analyst assigned who reported to the Morse supervisor while on duty but formally worked for me. In addition to the analysts working shift work, I was also responsible for the Cryptanalyst who worked the day shift only. I reported directly to the Operations Officer and formally worked the day shift, but was available for duty twenty-four hours a day, seven days a week.

The non-Morse intercept operation was in a building a few steps away from the Morse area. They had a similar structure to ours and reported to the Operations Officer. This was my first experience as an operational supervisor and I effortlessly transitioned into the position. I had an extremely strong work ethic and expected everyone under my command to work as hard as I did. This style of supervision does not always sit well with people but it leaves no room for misinterpretation. In Trabzon, and throughout my career, everyone under my supervision knew exactly what I expected from them. They also knew I would do everything possible for their well-being if they performed their duties as I directed. In two incidents during my Air Force career, I even allowed myself to be arrested while defending men under my command; those are stories to be treated later. Many men came to me over the years to confess that they really didn't like me when we first met but eventually came to appreciate me and my style.

My participation in the mission of the unit was tremendously gratifying. Our job was to locate and intercept Russian Morse transmissions emanating from launch facilities at the three missile test ranges when they notified down range stations and Moscow of impending operations. It was a cat and mouse game. Each operator had one receiver tuned to the frequency last used by the Russian control station and one to search for missile related transmissions on other frequencies. The Russians knew we were listening so they changed frequencies and call signs from time to time to make our job more difficult. Although their transmissions of regular traffic, administrative messages and radio checks only took a few minutes to complete, our experienced intercept operators could recognize the sounds of specific transmitters and operator sending techniques and were able to identify our targets when they did change call signs and frequencies. Countdowns to missile launches were a little different; the transmissions lasted only seconds. The Russian control operator would transmit: CQ CQ CQ (I am trying to get your attention) DE (this is – and transmit his call sign) BT (beginning text). At this point, he would transmit a three number group we interpreted as "X minus," followed by a second group of numbers to indicate the number of minutes left until launch and then sign off. The number 120 would indicate two hours, 090 was 90 minutes and so forth. An example of the transmission would be, CQ CQ CQ DE ABCD BT 543 120 K (message finished) SK (signing off). This way of informing everyone that a launch would take place in two hours took very few seconds. It was not very sophisticated when compared to the present era of digital communications, but it was all they had in the 1950s. As a countdown got closer to launch, they would transmit at the 20, 15, 10 and single digit minute intervals. At launch, the transmission was NW NW NW which is international Morse code jargon for "Now."

Besides having to locate the enemy on the bandwidth and identify him, we also had to determine if the operator was practicing or if the transmissions were valid. We accomplished this through coordination with the non-Morse people and other units. We reported each countdown, as it progressed, to our headquarters in the United States and associated units throughout the world through secure teletype communications with very high priority status messages. Our one Cryptanalyst and I were on call for all countdowns to make decisions as to the validity of the activity and to edit and approve outgoing reports. There were many times when I spent several days and nights at operations with only catnaps to sustain me when technical problems interrupted major launches from the Tyura Tam launch site. The ICBM launches, which included a thirty-minute flight to an impact site on the Kamchatka Peninsula in the Far East Soviet Union, were complicated and could often take several days to accomplish.

As mentioned earlier, the Russians knew why we were at Trabzon and they liked to toy with us. Whenever our teletype operators told us they had a suspicious attempt at communications with our unit, we could check the signal with our direction finding equipment. It invariably came from a station across the Black Sea on the Crimean Peninsula. As far as I know, they never fooled any of our communications personnel.

They would also try to contact us through our Morse net by using the call signs from our units at Samsun and Karamursel but they were never successful because of the sophisticated identification procedures we used. Even without the identification procedures, the poor sound quality of their transmitters gave away their attempts to fool us. It was interesting to know that there were guys just like us across the Black Sea and the Turkish/Russian border working for the other side.

I absolutely loved every moment I was involved in the daily operations of the unit but there was more to Trabzon than the job. Surviving on the local economy had its challenges, as did living in a GI community of slightly less than one hundred men. Finding entertainment in such a remote area was difficult and there were the inevitable, surprise problems that were bound to occur. I'll describe a few of the incidents that stick in my mind as either funny or scary.

Food and Drink:

To help us survive our remote assignment, the Air Force assigned what they called an Independent Medic to our unit. "Doc" was a special guy. Real doctors enter the Air Force as Captains and nurses enter the Air Force as Lieutenants. Our "Doc" was a lowly Staff Sergeant, certified to perform many of the procedures assigned to doctors and nurses under normal conditions. He could sew up wounds, pull teeth, apply casts and prescribe medications. He even performed as a Veterinarian whenever one of our pet dogs got ill or puppies needed to have tails removed. "Doc" had the authorization of the Commander to lay down the law with regard to his areas of expertise. The city-provided water was not potable so he advised us to use iodine pills in any water we consumed. Some of us did and some of us didn't. He told us not to purchase any meat from the local butchers because they didn't have refrigeration in their shops. Some of us did and some of us didn't. At one point, so many men had received ankle and knee injuries walking down from the top of Boztepe rather than risking the ride, he convinced the Commander to forbid that action. Some of us listened and some of us didn't. Everyone got sick at one time or another. Many men contracted hepatitis-A and were shipped out and replaced on a regular basis. When I contracted some type of stomach ailment, "Doc" gave me a bottle of paregoric, an opium based medication. He told me to take it at specific intervals and not to drive. I did as he said and was in a fog for several days but recovered. After living there for a few months and having been acclimated, I can remember buying ground meat from a butcher in spite of the thousands of flies in his shop. It was better to watch him cut the meat from a fly covered carcass hanging from a hook and grind it in his grinder than to purchase an already ground package; there was no way of knowing what went into that grinder when no one was around.

Every so often, the Commander would send a truck to the American base at Ankara in Central Turkey to purchase supplies for us. Paramount during cold weather was the availability of kerosene for our space heaters. We could also order canned goods. I pretty much lived on a diet of canned crabmeat or tuna fish mixed with concentrated tomato soup heated on my hot plate. I never noticed the word "concentrated" on the soup can, so without dilution, my special recipe invariably caused heartburn. Sometimes, Anna would make a Turkish meal for me; I was never impressed with the flavor but ate to survive. Fresh bread from the local bakeries smeared with an imitation butter found in the grocery stores was always a treat. Although Turkey had a secular government, the consumption of alcoholic beverages was frowned upon in the provinces. With a little effort, we were occasionally able obtain small amounts of beer on the black market. We also had American beer illegally shipped in via military aircraft from Germany.

I don't know if it was the food, the water, the remoteness of our small unit or some other cause, but there came a time when one of our men crossed over into some level of insanity. I was playing poker with some of the men in an apartment not far from the orderly room when they told me that one of the guys who lived there had been acting strange. He told them that when he was attending technical school he had been drugged by the government and taken to a dentist where a miniature radio was installed in one of his teeth. He said that now he was receiving strange instructions via radio transmissions to the tooth. I thought they were kidding me until the man came out of his room in a rage. He shouted that he had received orders to stop the poker game and throw the players out of the apartment. One of the guys who lived there shouted to him to shut up and go back to his room. At that point, the crazy guy jumped across the poker table and bit the man on the arm. We pulled them apart and held the offender down until we could get one of the few military policemen assigned to the unit to help us. The next day we shipped him to Istanbul in hand cuffs. I never heard of him again.

The QRC-45 Incident:

Our operations area at the top of Boztepe was surrounded by a fence and we had a guard shack at the entry gate. The fence was about five feet high but was not topped with barbed wire which was the normal style fence around USAFSS installations. As the ranking man on duty one warm, summer afternoon, I received a call from the guard at the gate that a man, who appeared to be a Turkish National, had jumped over the fence at the rear of the restricted area. I rushed outside and saw a Turkish man starting to dig a hole at the base of our QRC-45 antenna. The QRC-45, a C-Band Wullenweber antenna, was used by our non-Morse electronic interception section to home in on the location of monitored emissions and was classified technology at the time. I considered this violation of our secure area a significant threat.

I instructed the military policeman in the guard shack to lock the gate and accompany me to the base of the antenna. Together, we confronted the intruder. Recognizing me as the ranking person, he stopped digging and looked directly at me with a questioning look on his face. I told him in English to climb back over the fence. With his broken English and my slight understanding of Turkish, he communicated to me that he had been told by his employer to come to this point and dig a hole. I really didn't think he was a terrorist or a saboteur, but I felt required to evict him from the compound regardless of his excuse for being there. I told the military policeman to pull his .45 caliber automatic from its holster, jack a cartridge into the chamber and point it at the man to show him I was serious. This prompted a small grin on the intruder's face that I tried to interpret. I didn't know if it was a nervous grin or an arrogant grin, but it seemed to say, "You won't shoot me. I am a Turk in Turkey and you are only a guest in my country." We stood there eying each other for a few more seconds until I turned to the guard holding the gun; while pointing at the Turkish man, I told him to be ready to shoot if I so ordered.

I turned back to the intruder and could see that a transformation of his grin had occurred. He no longer looked confident and started to back toward the fence. My first instinct was that he understood English perfectly and had heard my instruction to the military policeman. When my eyes darted from the intruder to the military policeman, as the Turk climbed over the fence to vacate the secure area, I discovered the source of my success. The policeman's hand holding the weapon was shaking; he was sweating profusely and had a terrified look on his face in anticipation of having to kill someone. Apparently, the intruder quickly concluded that an accidental escalation of the situation could be imminent and he might be killed.

When I reported the incident to the unit Commander, he made it clear that we had dodged a bullet. He went on and on about what an international incident it would have been had we shot the intruder, and I guess it would have been really bad. The civilian contractors at TUSLOG were chastised for their poor supervision of Turkish nationals near the guarded compound and I think the incident was buried. My career, and most likely, a stint in a Turkish prison had been laid on the line that afternoon. I don't want to contemplate what my life might have been like if things had gone differently.

Arrested in Trabzon:

There was an outdoor movie theater in town that showed American movies dubbed into Turkish. It was funny to see stars like Randolph Scott and John Wayne speaking Turkish, but even that got old. We had many poker games and dice games, but mostly I entertained myself with reading and working. One evening after a poker game that lasted several hours, one of the players, Harvey, a fellow Staff Sergeant and a contemporary, decided he wanted to find some female company. He must have been drinking after-shave as well as the few beers we had or he had an overwhelming surge of testosterone because he decided he wanted to go to the "compound." The compound was a Turkish government controlled brothel in a less than desirable part of town. "Doc" and the Commander had declared the compound off limits and I think just about everyone obeyed that order; I know I did. Try as I might, I could not convince the young man that it was a bad idea. I couldn't physically restrain him, nor could I allow him to go out into that part of town alone, so I went along with him, all the while trying to change his mind.

When we reached the compound, I figured my problem was solved because the doors and windows were closed and there were no lights to be seen. Just as I was telling Harvey we should turn around and go back, he started to beat on the door to get someone's attention. We got attention all right, but it came from a six foot, four inch city police officer. He came around the corner straight up to Harvey and knocked him flat on his back with a right cross to the jaw. I was about fifteen feet away from where Harvey had been beating on the door and tried to intercede by shouting to the police officer that I could speak Turkish. He walked over to me and without a word, used his well practiced right cross to hit me square on the left side of my face. My head snapped back and hit the wall behind me before I crumpled to the ground. When I came to my senses, the officer was pulling me to my feet and my hands were constrained by a little gadget that slips over both thumbs and is screwed down to prevent release. Harvey was already up on his feet and constrained in the same manner. Still without any words, the policeman shoved us through alleyways until we came to a small police substation.

At the station, the officer and another policeman removed our money, cigarettes, wallets and belts, and required us to sign a ledger to record our arrest. Harvey signed in first. I don't know whether it was because the drinking had made him giddy or because he was very bright, but it came to him to sign the register as T. L. Ranger. When I saw that, I followed suit and registered as Richard Tracy. After we were placed into a cell, the two policemen had a long conversation and made several telephone calls. Finally, one of them handed the receiver to me through the bars; I placed it to my ear and said, "Hello. Who is this?" The voice at the other end told me he was a translator hired by the Air Force to deal with Turkish officials concerning American activities. I told him that there may be a problem because the police officer had beaten us up for no reason. He then asked if they beat us on the street or in the police station. When I told him it was on the street, he said we were lucky because that wasn't allowed and asked to speak with one of the officers. I guess it would have been okay to knock us around once we were in the station house but I was never able to confirm that.

After a lengthy conversation between the police officer and the translator, both of the policemen smiled as one of them unlocked the cell and indicated we could leave. They returned everything except our Turkish money and our American cigarettes. We did not protest and considered ourselves very lucky; all of us had been told horror stories about life in Turkish prisons. I never told anyone of the incident but somehow, part of the story must have spread. About a month later, at "Commander's Call," a monthly address to the troops by the Commander, Captain Carlson asked if anyone knew of a Dick Tracy or a T. L. Ranger in the organization. His question was unanswered except for a few barely audible snickers. I feel certain Captain Carlson knew the identity of the culprits, but in keeping with his style of command, he didn't push the issue any further. He had a special way about him that earned our respect.

There came a time when Captain Carlson, Jim Easley and I traveled to Karamursel to attend a mission planning conference. After our arrival at Istanbul International Airport, the Captain told me to call the Hilton Hotel and get rooms for us. In my naiveté, I identified myself as Sergeant Joyce from Trabzon and asked to reserve three rooms for the night. The clerk informed me that they were all booked for the evening. When I asked Captain Carlson what his second choice was, he told me I had messed up by letting them know I was a member of the U. S. Military, and that he would get the rooms. He called the Hilton Hotel and responded to the clerk's greeting by saying, "This is Carl J. Carlson from Apache County, Arizona. I am here at your airport with an associate and my male secretary. We need three rooms for the night. Please make the arrangements with my secretary." He handed the telephone to me and I disguised my voice as I made the reservations for the newly discovered vacancies. Captain Carlson had taken a page from Harvey's book and misrepresented himself. I tried to imitate his style for the rest of my military career.

Stoning Incidents:

Other than with shopkeepers, there were few social interactions between the local populace and the Americans stationed in Trabzon. We lived in two different worlds and did not understand very much of each other's cultures. This was driven home to me one afternoon as I walked down the alley toward my apartment building. There, I saw a young girl of about thirteen years of age cowering behind a power pole as local women and children threw stones at her. She either deliberately went out into public without her face and head being covered or didn't realize she had reached that state in development that required a veil and headscarf. Little girls played in the streets uncovered all of the time, but at a certain point in their development, custom demanded they be covered; this poor girl had violated the custom. I could not stop myself from protecting the frightened girl. Instinctively, I placed myself between the girl and the stone throwers and shouted in English that they should stop what they were doing. When that didn't stop them, I reached down and picked up some stones as if I intended to throw them at the abusers. That stopped them for a moment and the girl took the opportunity to run the sixty feet to the entrance to her home and escape any additional injury. I feel certain she remembers that day when an unknown foreigner risked injury and possibly an international incident to save her from further abuse or perhaps death. I remain proud of my actions that day, even though they were instinctive rather than deliberate.

I witnessed another stoning event some months later, only I was the one being stoned. In violation of the Commander's advice never to roam the town alone, I was on my way to visit some friends who lived near the dock area. As I crossed one of the many small neighborhood squares, I noticed a man standing on a wooden box speaking to a small crowd of men. I thought it was quaint, rather like the revolutionary days in America when politicians preached their opinions on street corners. My minimal command of the Turkish language did not allow me to understand anything the man was saying, but I knew enough to give the group a wide birth. After making my way around them and turning into the street I was seeking, I heard the speaker's voice rise up to a shout. I had my back to them as I walked away so I was surprised when small stones started hitting me and the ground around me. Again, instinct took over and I took off running down the alley toward my friend's place. After about a hundred feet, as I turned to enter his courtyard, I hazarded a look back. Only about seven or eight men had separated from the group in a half hearted attempt to follow me as they continued to throw stones. As I entered the doorway, they stopped and went back to listen to the speaker. Whether he was preaching against infidels or foreigners (I was both), I don't know, but he sure took advantage of an opportunity when I wandered into that square. After a few hours at my friend's place, we carefully checked the area of the square before I made my way back to my apartment. It seems a little frightening as I write about it now, but when you are twenty-four years old, you think you will live forever and little in the world intimidates you.

Aircraft Shoot Downs:

On June 27, 1958, a United States Air Force transport aircraft, a four engine C-118, tail number 13822, strayed across the border between Turkey and Soviet territory and was shot down by Soviet fighters. Considering the type of aircraft, and its crew, six officers and three enlisted men, it is reasonable to believe that it was not a reconnaissance mission; intelligence collection missions carried many more enlisted men than officers. At that time in the Cold War, the Soviets didn't care what the mission might have been; they jumped on every opportunity to shoot down our aircraft.[5] Now, fifty years later, it is generally accepted that the C-118 was operated by either the CIA or the State Department and was on a routine mission between the island nation of Cyprus and Tehran, Iran to transport classified equipment and documents. While trying to avoid thunderstorms in the mountainous area of southeast Turkey, the pilot became confused and crossed over the border into Soviet territory. The local Soviet air defense organization scrambled MIG fighters with orders to destroy the intruder. The initial cannon fire from one of the Soviet fighters caused a fire in the C-118 and the pilot ordered the crew to bailout. Five of them did but four were unable to reach escape hatches because of the fire and remained on board as the aircraft crash-landed at a partially constructed airfield in Azerbaijan. Immediately after the crash landing, as the four crewmembers ran from the aircraft, a huge explosion destroyed the burning wreckage. I suspect the explosion was part of a procedure in place to destroy classified information in the event of a force down in enemy territory, but I have no firm evidence to support my opinion. The incident occurred only a few hundred miles southeast of our location at Trabzon, but because we were so focused on or primary mission, we did not intercept any associated

---

5   A list of reconnaissance aircraft destroyed by Communists during my career can be found in Appendix A.

radio transmissions during the activity. Other Security Service units did copy radio transmissions and provided the intelligence to the highest levels of our government.

Security Service operated airborne voice and Morse intercept missions in the area along the Turkish border with the Soviet Union. The aircraft, normally a four engine C-130A Hercules configured as a COMINT (Communications Intelligence) reconnaissance platform, flew racetrack type flight plans between Trabzon in northeast Turkey and Lake Van in the southeast corner of the country. One sunny afternoon in late August of 1958, the interpreter assigned to a nearby Turkish military unit came to our operations area and asked to speak with the person in charge. That person happened to be me at the time, so I went outside of our secure area to speak with him. He pointed to the contrail of one of our reconnaissance aircraft that had been flying between Lake Van and Trabzon for several hours and asked me if I knew whose airplane it was. The collection missions were very highly classified and there was no way I could tell him the truth, so I told him I didn't know. He told me that his commander didn't know either so he was going to try to shoot it from the sky. I was personally aware that the local Turkish outfit didn't have the guns to reach an aircraft flying at 25,000 feet; I also felt secure that his headquarters knew why the aircraft was there and would not approve of any anti-aircraft action. Nonetheless, I reported the situation to the Commander and the Operations Officer and notified our chain of command up to the National Security Agency of our predicament. I didn't hear any gunfire that afternoon, so I assume people at a much higher pay grade than mine interceded and calmed down some Turkish nerves.

Sadly, we were to lose one of those reconnaissance aircraft only a few months later. On September 2, 1958, Soviet MIG 17 fighters shot down one of our aircraft when it strayed across their border. The C-130A, tail number 60528, crewed by four officers and thirteen enlisted men left Incirlik Air Base near Adana, Turkey and flew toward Trabzon to begin a planned mission between Trabzon and Lake Van. Instead of turning south at Trabzon, the aircraft flew straight past us toward the city of Batumi, just across the border in Soviet Georgia, as if the navigator confused the radio beacon from Batumi with the radio beacon emanating from Trabzon. Just before reaching the border with

Soviet Georgia, the aircraft turned south on a path that took it across the Soviet Armenian border on a vector toward the city of Yerevan, Armenia. The route flown paralleled the intended route between Trabzon and Lake Van. These facts, analyzed after the incident, led some to believe that the Soviet intelligence services arranged for the radio beacons at Batumi and Yerevan to mimic the beacons from Trabzon and Lake Van to lure the pilot over the border. To my knowledge, this reason for the border penetration has never been substantiated.

Busy working on our own mission, we were unaware of the plight of 60528. After it crossed the border, the Soviet Air Defense Command scrambled four MIG-17s and gave the order to "destroy the intruder." The eleven Security Service crewmembers that perished included nine linguists skilled in three different languages and two equipment maintenance personnel. After this incident, Morse intercept operators were included on flights to monitor the enemy air defense communications. *The Price of Vigilance: Attacks on American Surveillance Flights*, by Larry Tart and Robert Keefe, includes gun camera photographs from the MIG-17s taken as they destroyed 60528 and a transcript of the conversations between the fighter pilots and their ground controller. We at Trabzon heard about the destruction of 60528 a few hours later through normal advisories from headquarters. During the cold war, our reconnaissance activity was highly classified, so USAFSS-related aircraft losses due to enemy action were formally reported as transport or weather data collecting aircraft that had strayed over borders.

The Germans:

During my tour of duty at Trabzon, a lifelong friendship began when I met a German couple who lived in that city. Did you ever meet someone and instantly know that you would become friends? That is the way it was with the Zahns and me. It is now fifty years later and my wife Sylvia and I are still close friends with Peter and Uschi. Over the years, we have exchanged correspondence, telephone calls and visits, lived in the same city, celebrated births, suffered through family deaths and grown old together.

The Siemens Corporation of Germany assigned twenty-four year old Peter Zahn to supervise the installation of the electrical portion of a grain elevator under construction on the sea front. Peter, specially trained to operate in underdeveloped areas of the world, was primarily an electrical engineer. He was able to pick up foreign languages, fashion tools as needed, work with area tradesmen and deal with local political situations when necessary. He was, and is, a very special person. His twenty-one year old wife, Uschi, joined him shortly after he established residence in Trabzon. Uschi, the lone western woman in the city, and Peter had to survive the same conditions that faced us but with even less support from their employer than we received from the U. S. Government. We had the advantage because of the commissary runs to Ankara, where we obtained our canned goods and the kerosene needed for heating and cooking.

Not long after I arrived in Trabzon, George Mudrak, one of the men who lived in the apartment below my humble abode, asked me if I had met "the Germans" yet. When I said I hadn't, he arranged for us to meet on a Sunday afternoon; I was impressed by their friendliness. Both Peter and Uschi spoke very passable English, had perfect manners and pleasing personalities. Uschi, although rather thin from living on what was available on the local economy, was stunningly beautiful. Every normal man in our unit who met her lost a little bit of his heart to her, but always treated her with the utmost respect. To Peter and Uschi, the men in my unit represented everything that is good about America and Americans. Over their protestations, we gave them canned goods and American processed coffee when we could. The Germans were the antithesis of the Turks who always knew when a truck had made the round trip to Ankara and would seek out Americans to offer black market prices for our goods.

Uschi and Peter loved swimming and we were living on the coast of the Black Sea so the temptation to swim there was overwhelming for them. They asked for our assistance because Uschi risked being stoned if seen on the beach in a bathing suit. On several occasions, fifteen or twenty of us would use one of our large trucks to transport everyone to the beach. During those outings, we staked out a portion of beach as if it were our own for a few hours. The occasional Turkish women on the beach remained completely dressed with veils in place but would remove their shoes and walk in a few inches of water. Turkish men, on the other hand, romped in the waves completely naked to show their disdain for Uschi's perceived brashness. It did not take much effort on our part to ignore the "asheks," the Turkish word for jackasses, and we went about our own business. Peter and Uschi expressed extreme appreciation for our efforts on these days; the lonely American young men were happy to spend some time on the beach with a beautiful young German woman. It was a great deal for all of us.

One evening in Trabzon, when they were visiting with a few of us, Uschi got the wild idea to have her photograph taken in an Air Force uniform. We were both five feet eight inches tall, so she chose mine. Peter took the photograph but I never saw it until a few years ago when they sent a copy of it to us. The light was poor and the photograph is not what it could have been, but I think it is well worth including in this work. The following photograph is of Uschi Zahn wearing my uniform some time in 1958.

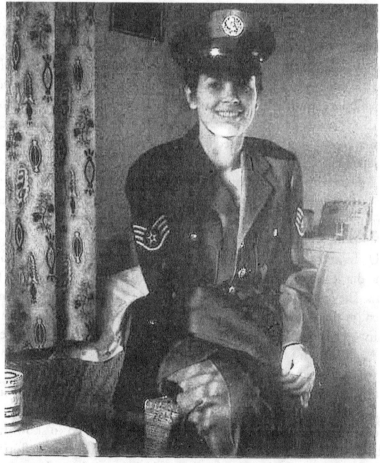

The beautiful Uschi Zahn. (Courtesy: Peter and Uschi Zahn)

Chapter 6 - Assignment Bremerhaven

When my year in Trabzon was completed, I was happy to get away from the five times a day call to prayers from the local minarets, the dusty roads, the terrible food and the arrogant Turkish population that envied anyone who had more than they had. I had earned a return to the Continental United States (CONUS), but I chose to take a one-year extension of overseas duty at Bremerhaven, Germany. My old friend, Herb Dennison, was stationed there with his wife, Pat, and their young son, Robert. Besides, I always wanted to visit Germany, so it was like killing two birds with one stone. Peter had also received his next assignment from Siemens; he was transferred to a remote town in Iran to work on a new project.

I discovered that Germany experiences a lot of dark, dank weather, and with the location of Bremerhaven on the coast, the weather was even less appealing than in other parts of the country. I was a young man and managed to find things to do during my off duty time, regardless of the weather, and even squeezed in a trip to Switzerland and two trips to Paris during that year. I enjoyed many evenings with Pat and Herb and enjoyed the camaraderie that existed among the men on shift work. My new unit used a three-day shift schedule in lieu of six-day shifts, so the sleep adjustments came around more often. Someone must have felt the change was beneficial to the men, but I didn't.

I was assigned to Able Flight as an Assistant Surveillance and Warning Center Supervisor. The first thing I noticed was that it was no longer a Trick; it was a "Flight." In the military, there are always new leaders and each one wants to stamp his signature on an organization. Someone up the chain of command decided that it would sound more "Air Force" if Tricks were called Flights, and Headquarters told units all over the world to make the change. At about the same time, someone in Washington, D. C. decided to change the phonetic alphabet that had been in use as long as anyone could remember. Able, Baker, Charlie and Dog became Alpha, Bravo, Charlie and Delta. This did not sit well with the old timers. Trying to make Able, Baker and Dog Trick change when Charlie didn't just wasn't right. Although Security Service tacitly accepted the new phonetic alphabet, the four Tricks in our units retained their names based on the old alphabet but did finally accept the change from Trick to Flight.

At the Bremerhaven assignment, I experienced my first dealings with a Flight Commander. More wisdom from above dictated that military officers should command the Flights rather than senior NCOs, as had been the practice. Not many, but some of these officers, were effective leaders. The ones that failed were those young Lieutenants with poor leadership skills that were thrown into the breech to deal with Senior NCOs who felt threatened by their loss of command. When a young officer tried to take control without showing respect to the more experienced Senior NCO, rancor and ineffectual mission control abounded. I worked directly for Technical Sergeant Thurman Thomas, the S&WC Supervisor, and he worked directly for the Flight Commander. The Senior NCO who managed the Morse intercept operations also worked for the Flight Commander. The fact that I can't remember the Flight Commander's name is proof enough that he stayed out of my business.

Each of the four Flights at a standard Security Service unit is assigned an S&WC Supervisor and an assistant. The S&WC Supervisors are the four most important people in the entire unit. Yes, a unit cannot operate without a Commander and his chain of command; and it needs administrative, maintenance, and support personnel of many types; but the S&WC Supervisor makes the decisions that are the most important. Not only is the S&WC Supervisor the operational decision maker, he must make many decisions in a matter of seconds and is expected to make the correct decision at all times. Often, the lives of other personnel depend on these decisions. The insertion of a Flight Commander into the mix was probably intended to move the decision making function from an enlisted man to a Commissioned Officer. During my time in Security Service, that never happened. The Flight Commanders did not possess the experience or expertise to make the decisions and the addition of another level of decision making only delayed the filing of important reports. We followed the standard procedure of having an Analyst look over the shoulder of the Intercept

Operator to relay aircraft identification and location information to the S&WC where it was plotted on maps and analyzed. The analyst then presented the information to the S&WC Supervisor who decided what to report to Headquarters and other intelligence agencies around the world. The S&WC Supervisor was a prestigious position in the unit, yet it was strenuously avoided by almost all senior analysts. Shift work was an annoyance and the responsibility an S&WC supervisor shouldered for his reputation and that of the organization was awesome. As I progressed in my career, I was one of those few who actually reveled in the position.

I was able to handle the stresses of the job save one. Every report produced by an S&WC Supervisor was analyzed, reviewed and picked apart by analysts working the eight to five o'clock day shift. Rarely had those Monday morning quarterbacks critiquing the work of the men on the line ever been on the line themselves. I only respected the opinions of Analysts who at one time had served as an S&WC Supervisor. They were the only ones who knew the demands of the job, and because they understood them, they very rarely accepted a position in the report review section. Thurman Thomas did a fine job in teaching me what he wanted in an Assistant and prepared me to be an S&WC Supervisor in the future. He and his lovely wife, Pat, accepted me as a friend and colleague. We correspond and remain friends to this day.

There was always activity that required reports. It was during the cold war and the Soviets were constantly flexing their military muscles. We regularly sent reconnaissance aircraft near their borders to provoke tracking activity by their air defense units. The one variation from the normal activity of a Security Service unit that I personally experienced was the high altitude photoreconnaissance flight program of the now world famous U-2. Every so often, Gary Powers would fly the U-2 between Peshawar, Pakistan and Bodo, Norway. Although we were all cleared for Top Secret Cryptographic Special Intelligence, the U-2 flights fell into an even higher category called "compartmentalized activity" which required additional, special accessibility. When an over flight was scheduled, the first page of the notification message instructed the communications operator to call the Flight Commander, the S&WC Supervisor and Assistant to the communications center to read the contents. After reading and memorizing the route and scheduled time of activity, we burned all copies of the message in the communications center. We then returned to our designated areas and waited for the Soviets to respond to the U-2 over flight.

When an over flight occurred, the Soviets regularly designated the target as "unidentified" and our analysts plotted the activity on the map board. Because of the high altitude, operators and analysts would scratch their heads and conclude the activity must represent practice operations. When the Soviet fighter aircraft invariably broke off their attacks short of the U-2's 70,000 foot altitude, the uninformed analysts concluded that the imaginary target was above the capability of that particular type of interceptor and the Soviets were just testing the decision making abilities of their Air Defense Commanders. As the information on the flight of the U-2 became available, Thurman Thomas or I would hand write reports of the activity as if it were routine and casually wander into the Communications Center; there the reports were transmitted at very high precedence to a list of top level addressees. Those of us cleared for the U-2 flight information never discussed it among ourselves or with anyone else.

I was stationed in San Antonio when the U-2 piloted by Gary Powers was shot down and remember analysts in the secure area where I worked wondering how a "routine weather aircraft," as our government called it, could get so far off course. I smiled inside because I knew who had been shot down over the center of the Soviet Union and couldn't tell anyone. When the government finally admitted the existence of the program and that Powers was actually shot down, I knew they weren't telling the whole story. Based on personal knowledge, I can tell you that the fighters and missiles used to attack the U-2 were incapable of shooting down the aircraft at its assigned altitude. In actuality, the U-2 flamed out from a mechanical failure and descended to an altitude low enough to be hit by a surface to air missile. During that activity, the Soviets also accidentally shot down one of their own aircraft with a surface to air missile.

The work was interesting, challenging and rewarding but the manner by which the men who worked in the Surveillance and Warning Center were tested never failed to annoy me. They called the tests, "smokescreen activities." The people on the day shift who evaluated our actual work would prepare imaginary intercepted radio traffic and show up in the middle of the night to test us. They didn't tell us the information was imaginary but the Communication Center Operator was told not to transmit any reports because a "smokescreen" was in progress. We never knew whether information was valid or imaginary. I suppose the theory was a good one, but to this day, I resent the unnecessary stress and strain put upon us; the job was stressful enough without smokescreen testing. It all seemed a little ridiculous to me; the worst thing they could do was to reassign me to a soft, eight to five job if I failed a smokescreen test and I knew that wasn't going to happen.

While stationed at Bremerhaven, the ill feelings between the citizens of our countries resulting from World War II were brought home to me in a poignant way. While stationed in Trabzon, I began a pen pal correspondence with Uschi Zahn's younger sister, Karin, who lived in Berlin. All German children were required to take English in school and this gave her an opportunity to correspond with a "real" American. We continued our correspondence after I moved to Bremerhaven. Karin told me in a letter that she would be spending a few days in Bremerhaven visiting relatives in July of 1959. We arranged for a time and an address in Bremerhaven where I could meet her and her mother, Frau Wieland, a proper and gracious lady with whom I had also corresponded over the past year. I borrowed a car from a friend and drove to the appointed place. Before I could reach the door to the house, Karin and her mother met me on the sidewalk where we introduced ourselves. Then, Frau Wieland, in an embarrassed manner, said, "David, I must apologize for not meeting you in my sister's house. She and her husband still have ill feelings about the war and would rather not have an American in their home. This is a big embarrassment to me and I beg for your understanding." I convinced her that I completely understood the situation and that it had no bearing on our friendship. As Karin was only sixteen at the time and I was much older, Frau Wieland, with typical German frankness, asked that I treat her like the young lady she was and added that Peter and Uschi had assured her that I was a gentleman. Karin and I spent some time that afternoon sightseeing in the Bremerhaven area and had an early dinner at an outdoor restaurant near the city park. I treated her like a lady and we have continued to correspond over the past fifty years. When Frau Wieland recently passed away, I felt as if I had lost a friend. The last time we enjoyed each other's company was many years after our first meeting when Sylvia and I were visiting the Zahns in Berlin in 1991. She insisted on treating the Zahns, Karin and us to dinner at a very nice restaurant in Berlin. I noticed the upscale service the moment we entered the facility and my first impression was confirmed when the menus were presented to us. The menus provided to the ladies were the same as those given to the men with one significant exception; the ladies' menus did not include prices. I knew I was in a high class establishment and that Frau Wieland was very appreciative of our long period of family friendship.

Chapter 7 - Assignment San Antonio, Texas

The year in Bremerhaven flew by, and in December of 1959, I boarded an aircraft and returned to the United States. After spending a few days in New York to visit my parents, I drove to San Antonio, Texas in a used car I purchased while on leave. I signed in at the Orderly Room at about 6:00 P.M. on Christmas Eve. Every organization in the Air Force has an Orderly Room. It is the administrative center of each unit and normally the location of the First Sergeant and his staff. During non duty hours, evenings, nights and weekends, an NCO called the Charge of Quarters, or more commonly, the CQ, mans the Orderly Room. I knew the NCO who was the Charge of Quarters that evening. He laughed uproariously when he saw me. "JD," he said, "you are the only guy I know who would sign in from leave on Christmas Eve." We both laughed about that, and I explained that I didn't have any particular place to go for Christmas and didn't want to waste my leave time. He told me that Jim Easley, my Operations Officer in Trabzon, was stationed in the outfit and had invited some of the guys to his apartment for Christmas dinner the next day. He convinced me that one more wouldn't matter and gave me the address.

Jim Easley greeted me with gusto when I showed up at his place the next day. We told stories about our time in Trabzon and had lots of laughs. Officers, he was a Captain by then, are not allowed to fraternize with enlisted men, but we in Security Service never did maintain military tradition and rules to a very high degree. None of us would ever jeopardize Jim's position with his peers, so while on duty, we maintained decorum but we enjoyed friendship with him and some other officers while off duty. That day he maintained the tradition of Trabzon veterans not being able to cook very well. All the fixings were there: hot rolls, sweet potatoes, mashed white potatoes, green beans, cranberry sauce and pumpkin pie. The trouble was with the turkey. Jim had forgotten to defrost the bird, so that morning he cranked up the oven as high as he dared and popped in our frozen entree. When we couldn't wait any longer, we removed the turkey and started carving. I can confirm that you cannot cook a twenty pound frozen turkey in four hours no matter how high you set the oven temperature. We were able to find cooked meat to a depth of about three quarters of an inch all around the bird, which was enough for all of us to have a taste. I have no idea what Jim did with the carcass.

I checked in with personnel on the next working day and was assigned to a section at headquarters that did in depth analysis of intercepted communications and published historical reports. There wasn't much excitement doing that work but it was nice to be in the United States for a while. While in that unit, I did have a strange experience in the spring of 1960.

One of the enlisted members of my organization was killed in an automobile accident and I was selected as the NCO to escort his remains to his home town of Fairbanks, Alaska. I received detailed instructions on the specific, formal procedures which render honor and respect to a fallen member of the military establishment, and started out on the long journey. The first step was to travel to the area of the accident and assume formal possession of the body. I supervised the transportation of the casket to San Antonio where we boarded a train for Los Angeles. From Los Angeles, we took another train to Seattle, the location of McChord Air Force Base, where an Air Force aircraft would take us to Fairbanks. Everything went smoothly until I arrived at the Seattle, Washington train station. It was about midnight and there was no one there to meet me. According to my orders, the base Mortuary Officer, Mrs. Murdock, was responsible to arrange our transportation to the base mortuary. I called the base Charge of Quarters and explained my problem. He was not able to authorize transportation but he was able to provide Mrs. Murdock's home telephone number.

The position of Mortuary Officer is one of those seldom required duties assigned to someone whose main responsibilities lay elsewhere, but none-the-less, it is an important one. When I called Mrs. Murdock, she was not happy to be awakened at midnight by a lowly Staff Sergeant. When I explained that I was calling from a pay telephone at the train station standing next to a large wheeled cart carrying the casket of a comrade and needed transportation to the base, she told me she would arrange for us to be picked up sometime after eight o'clock in the morning and hung up the telephone. My instructions were specific in that I could not leave the body unless I turned it over to a railroad freight car employee or another military member until I reached Fairbanks. I was not about to sleep on the ground at the Seattle train station.

I called the base Charge of Quarters again and asked for the home telephone number of the Base Commander. After suggesting that I rethink my plan because of the late hour and the fact that Staff Sergeants don't normally call the Base Commander, especially at his quarters, the CQ gave me the number and wished me luck. Although I woke him well after midnight, the Base Commander was amazingly polite and solicitous when I described my dilemma. He told me that he had Mrs. Murdock's home telephone number and that an ambulance would arrive at the train station within an hour. The ambulance arrived and we were taken to the base. The rest of the trip to Fairbanks, the funeral, and my return to San Antonio were uneventful. Forty-eight years later, I am still angered by the arrogant response I received from a civilian employee of the Air Force that showed such disrespect to a deceased Airman because she did not want to be inconvenienced.

By the spring of 1960, I was pushing twenty-six years of age and wasn't interested in the partying I did as a younger man, so I often spent time in my room reading. Barracks life had improved over the years; although we still had communal showers, urinals and commodes, now we had two man rooms with a sink and a mirrored medicine cabinet for shaving. Early one evening, one of the men who lived in the barracks walked by my open door and I noticed that he was carrying a school book. I asked him where he was going and he explained that he was taking a class at the local junior college. Then he said something that really got my attention. He said, "You know, JD, you're a pretty smart guy. You ought to take some night courses. Who knows where it will lead." I can't even remember his name, but he started me on a path that would lead to huge changes in my life. I took his advice and enrolled in San Antonio Junior College where I met my lifelong marriage partner.

While attending one of my first classes, Literature 601A, one of my classmates, another Security Service NCO, asked me if I were interested in meeting a nice young lady. He told me his lady friend,

Linda Stephens, had a friend attending the same school who might agree to a blind date. I was unattached to anyone and agreed; Linda arranged the blind date and the rest is history.

I am nothing if not a stickler for promptness. I do not like to be late and I resent it when others keep me waiting; I take tardiness on the part of others as an indication they think their time is more important than mine. Following my pattern, I parked around the corner from Sylvia's home in my brand new 1960 Dodge Dart, waiting for the exact time to ring her doorbell. At six o'clock sharp, I rang the bell and she opened the door with a smile. As I introduced myself, her very pleasant smile revealed the silver braces on her upper teeth. Unwittingly, she had chosen dangling silver earrings that evening, which meant silver from ear to ear when she smiled. I am, and always have been, as perfect a gentleman as I can be, so I acted as though I didn't even notice the blitz of silver that met my eyes. Besides, she had beautiful red hair and I was always a sucker for a redhead. Sylvia invited me in to meet her parents and to be inspected by her sisters before we went out that evening. I was not immediately smitten, but she may have been. Even after forty-seven years of marriage, Sylvia still tells people that when she opened the door and saw me, she thought, "I'm taking this one!" I guess I must have made a good impression.

It didn't take long to know Sylvia, and after a few dates, I didn't even notice the braces and began to ask myself if I might modify my plan to avoid marriage until I turned thirty. By the time she turned nineteen in September of 1960, and I had turned twenty-six in July, I had become convinced I couldn't possibly ever meet another girl as nice and sweet as she was. Is that love? Maybe it is the best kind of love, because it was based more on my respect for her and serious contemplation than on infatuation. We soon decided to marry and spend the rest of our lives together. That was the easy part; there were many, serious obstacles to be overcome with regard to her parents. To name a few: the more than seven year difference in our ages; I was a Democrat and they were Republicans; I was a Yankee and they were Texans; I had a tattoo and they thought only gangsters had tattoos. In addition to these problems, I was a Catholic and they were Methodists; she had been discouraged from dating servicemen and I was one; her father had two college degrees, was working on a third, and I had none.

Add my Yankee accent, which made it a little difficult for them to understand me, and my constant anxiety in waiting for them to finish sentences with their charming, slow Texas drawl, and you can imagine the challenges we faced.

There was a minor obstacle between Sylvia and me that took a while to overcome. I had been dating a young lady named Shirley before I met Sylvia. With the two names being so close, I would say Shirley from time to time when I meant to say Sylvia. To this day, whenever I start a sentence with the word, "Surely," she will quip, "Quit calling me Shirley."

In time, we wore down the opposition of Sylvia's parents and received their approval. Sylvia's family was long established in the neighborhood and had many relatives in the San Antonio area. In accordance with their customs, there were many bridal showers, teas and gatherings preceding the wedding. Sylvia's mother, Margaret, made her beautiful wedding dress. All of this activity was an introduction into the genteel South to me and I greatly enjoyed being accepted into the family. The problem of religion was discussed and Sylvia and I attended several meetings with her Pastor to discuss the ramifications of a mixed marriage. Whereas the Methodist minister was reasonable, the Catholic priest I contacted was not. He laid down rules with regard to my responsibility to raise any children as Catholics. I had seen many marriages fail for various reasons and assumed adding rules about raising children to all the other possible problems would not be a good idea. I told the priest I could not agree with the Church on this matter and that he should send my name to Rome for excommunication. He told me it doesn't work that way and that excommunication was an inferred action as well as an implied event. That is, if I believed I had committed an excommunicable act and it was one that the church considered excommunicable, I was excommunicated. The Catholic Church is big on rituals and rules. I left the meeting with a great feeling of relief. I was finally free from the Catholic Church and its hundreds of ways to encourage supplicants to feel guilt. I have always been kind of a black and white person; I make decisions and move on to the future. That was a very good decision.

Finally, at 7:00 PM on August 31, 1961, we were married in a ceremony at an overflowing Methodist church. My old friend Herb

Dennison was best man and five other friends from my outfit served as groomsmen. Because the reception held on the church lawn was alcohol free, I enlisted the help of yet another friend to ensure the groomsmen abstained from imbibing and otherwise behaved themselves during the evening. I heard more than one person inquire as to who the stranger in tuxedo hovering in the background was. It was my old friend, Mike Everson, the Aleut Indian from Alaska who, with his dark skin, seemed all the more mysterious among the otherwise completely Caucasian crowd. All the guys showed up on time and remained sober, and the wedding ceremony and reception went off without a hitch. We left San Antonio later that evening for our week long honeymoon in New Mexico and Arizona and began a union that endures to this day.

In the photograph above, purchased from a professional photographer, we are flanked by Sylvia's sister, Marilyn Kay San Marco, and my close friend, Herb Dennison, who was the best man.

Of course, we were as poor as the proverbial church mice. Military service did not pay well but Sylvia did a wonderful job of contributing to our finances. During our courtship, she finished her two year course in Secretarial Studies and applied for a civilian position in the USAFSS. Because our work was mostly overseas, the USAFSS hired many civilians in various positions to maintain stability in clerical staff and management. These civilians were all cleared by the FBI for access to our work areas. Sylvia excelled in her field. She had an excellent command of the English language, was trained in business formats, took notes in shorthand and could type at an astounding speed of one hundred and twenty words a minute. She was hired and assigned to a non-classified area while her background was checked and her clearance processed. Within months, her base salary was more than mine. I received additional funds for rations and was provided government quarters for married NCOs. The quarters were not great but they were clean, came with furniture and were adjacent to the base, which made them secure and convenient.

There were a few bumps in the road during this assignment to the Headquarters unit; I had a few problems with the UCMJ – The Uniform Code of Military Justice. While I was courting Sylvia, my life was very busy and it seems I was always hurrying from one place to another. On a Saturday evening when I was scheduled to be the Charge of Quarters, I was running behind schedule had hadn't had time for supper. I drove to the building that housed the Orderly Room, parked in front of the building in a no parking zone and ran upstairs to ask the day time Charge of Quarters to cover for me while I went across the street to get a hamburger for supper. He agreed, but when I returned to my car, there was a parking ticket on my windshield. I saw the military policeman driving away and caught up to him. I explained what had happened but the jerk wouldn't give me a break. Eventually, I was told to report to the Commander's office for the administration of an Article 15 under the UCMJ. An Article 15 equates to a misdemeanor in civilian law and the Commander is the judge and jury. He can administer punishment up to a reduction in rank, confinement to quarters for two weeks and a fine. I checked with the Provost Marshal for advice and learned some useful information. He told me that if the Commander was going to reduce my rank, the paper work would be on standard sized, eight by eleven inch stationery, but if the punishment was to be less, it would be on legal size paper. He also told me that the

Article 15 paper work would be on top of the Commander's desk and that I had the option of turning down the Article 15 and requesting a Summary Court Marshal.

I reported to the Commander as scheduled and at first glance observed that the paperwork was on legal size paper. When asked if I would accept the Article 15 instead of a Summary Court Marshal, I hesitated because the legal sized paper could have been a sham and the more serious punishment papers could have been underneath. I looked him in the eyes and did not discern deception, so I accepted the Article 15. My punishment was a tongue lashing and fourteen days restriction to the base. By a strange coincidence, Sylvia's parents and the rest of the family except her were scheduled for a ten day vacation away from San Antonio at the time. I often wondered how her father managed to have me confined to the base for that period.

PART III - MARRIED IN THE MILITARY

Chapter 1 - Period of Adjustment

After we were married, I had another brush with the UCMJ. Although Sylvia always knew me as David, all of my military friends called me JD, which I preferred instead of Jeremiah or Jerry. While paying for groceries at the commissary at Lackland Air Force Base, she signed the check, Mrs. J. D. Joyce instead of Mrs. Jeremiah D. Joyce as her signature appeared on the bank's signature card. The check bounced back from the bank with a notation of "improper signature." To bounce a check at a military facility is much worse than a parking ticket; I anticipated a lot of grief. I knew the procedure when I was called to the Commander's office for a second Article 15. Fortunately, we had a new, more understanding Commander. When I accepted the Article 15, I received a lecture about my inability to control the actions of my wife and was told that he would instruct military facilities in the San Antonio area not to accept a check from us for six months. I don't think the military is as strict today as it was then. Some things about the "good old days" were not really good.

Before too long, Sylvia became pregnant and on August 7, 1962 our son was born. We named him David Clayton after my father-in-law and me, but we always called him Clay. He was born in the base hospital on Lackland Air Force Base on a Tuesday afternoon. The Air Force discharged well babies as soon as possible, so I wasn't shocked to receive a telephone call from Sylvia at 8:00 A.M. on the following Thursday as I was about to tee off on the first hole at the base golf course. She told me she was being discharged and I was to come and take her home. I think my mother-in-law, Margaret, was a bit taken back with such an early release. Civilian hospitals hadn't yet accepted the well baby concept and kept new mothers and babies hospitalized for a week. Sylvia and Clay were home in less than forty-eight hours after his birth. Clay was one of those perfect babies; he was seldom fussy and was a healthy infant. It was lucky that his birth was uncomplicated; when he was six weeks old, we traveled overseas to our next assignment.

The first year of our marriage, Sylvia and I attended the Methodist Church. Since leaving the Catholic Church I was able to view the religious communities from a distance and developed less and less faith in organized religion. The 1961 Presidential campaign was underway and I was a strong supporter of John F. Kennedy. Although I am an Independent Conservative now, at that time in my life I was a registered Democrat. I am the perfect example of the well known pronouncement, often erroneously attributed to Winston Churchill but probably penned by Benjamin Disraeli, that, "If you are not Liberal when you are young, you do not have a heart; but if you are not Conservative when you are old, you do not have a brain." While attending a Methodist service on a Sunday morning, I heard the preacher imply that if Kennedy were to win the election, the Pope would be running Washington. It wasn't his ignorance that annoyed me; it was that his position in the church allowed him to make such a statement without being challenged. I wanted to stand up and take issue with his statement but did not want to embarrass my wife and her family. It was at that point that I decided I would never again allow myself to be preached to by anyone without an opportunity to counter preach. All this made me think more about organized religions and Christianity in particular.

My analysis of the teachings of the churches provided a simplified explanation of Christianity as practiced in this country. The Catholic Church teaches that everyone is "saved" when they are baptized but must live according to the dogma of the church in order to spend eternity with Jesus in Heaven once this life on earth is over. The Protestants generally teach that one must formally "accept" Jesus Christ as their "Savior" in order to spend eternity with Jesus in Heaven when this life on earth is over. I thought about Father Fry, who was a mean person and more than likely a pedophile, and the preacher who warned that the Pope would rule Washington if Kennedy were elected. I concluded I was as intelligent as both of them and more qualified to teach morality to any children I might have. I decided to completely leave Christianity and live a moral life without Jesus. I told Sylvia she should do as she pleased, but I had made up my mind. The genesis of my decision was the punishment meted out by the nuns. The culmination came as I squirmed in the pew without the opportunity to speak back to a preacher mesmerizing a congregation with ill advised political rhetoric. We have lived honest and honorable lives and raised two honest and honorable children outside the confines of Christianity. I will go to my grave without fear of the hereafter and supremely confident that my children were better citizens than any number of children reared as Christians.

Chapter 2 - Assignment Berlin

In early 1962, my name was close to the top of the list for an overseas assignment. Normally, that would not have been a problem; I would receive orders to a USAFSS unit, pack our personal belongings and fly off to my new assignment with my family wherever it happened to be. Things changed that year. There were very high tensions around the world between the United States and the Communist countries. The President decided that it was no longer safe to allow families to accompany military members overseas. This was a terrible blow to us. There was one exception to the President's decree. To prove to the world that we would not be cowed by the aggressive activity of the Soviet Union taking place in Berlin, he allowed families to accompany military members assigned to that city which was located one hundred and ten miles behind the Iron Curtain. There was a very serious caveat; anyone who volunteered for an assignment to that area was automatically denied. A member of the Air Force assigned there had recently defected to East Germany; the government felt that denying the assignment to volunteers might prevent a second defection. I knew there was an opening for a person of my rank and career field at our unit in Berlin but couldn't volunteer because that would exclude me from the assignment; it was a Catch-22[6].

Fate was to intervene. At the time my name came to the top of the list for an overseas assignment, Sylvia was secretary to the colonel in charge of personnel for the entire 10,000 man command. Someone in the office sought her out and told her I had been assigned to our organization located at Hof, Germany. She knew that she could not accompany me to that base and her disappointment was evident to her supervisor, Colonel Sarret. When he became aware of the situation, he instructed a subordinate to see if there was an assignment available

---

6   A theory found in Joseph Heller's novel, *Catch-22*, which suggests that when you think you have an answer to a dilemma, the government has a counter argument that trumps yours.

124

where she could accompany me. The only one available in the entire world was the one in Berlin. My assignment to Hof was switched to Berlin and our angst was alleviated.

In mid September, with Clay barely six week old, we climbed into our two door Mercury S-22 Sport Coupe and headed to New York to introduce my new family to my parents. Sylvia was breast feeding Clay, somewhat uncommon for American women in the early sixties, which made traveling with an infant much easier than expected. The trip was fun and the visit with my parents went well. They fell in love with Sylvia and were very happy to finally see me as a father at the advanced age of twenty-eight. After the visit to New York, we drove down the east coast to Charleston Air Force Base in South Carolina to catch a military aircraft for the flight to Germany. We turned in our car to be sent by boat to Bremerhaven and boarded a four engine, propeller driven, Super Constellation Military Air Transport Command aircraft. Sylvia, who at twenty-one had never been east of the Mississippi River, was on her way with a six week old infant to a point half way around the world from the only home she had ever known. It must have been quite traumatic for her. The weather was bad over the Atlantic and when we landed at the Azores for fuel, the layover was extended to repair some of the passenger seats that had broken loose during the rough first leg of the flight. I found it interesting see how respectful the male military members on the aircraft and in the terminal were of Sylvia's privacy when she nursed Clay. Eventually, the aircraft was repaired and we flew to Frankfurt, Germany. It was a good thing we were young and strong; lugging hand baggage and carrying a baby through and between terminals was quite a challenge.

After spending the night in a hotel in Frankfurt, on October 19, 1962, we boarded a special military train to finish our trip to Berlin. We had to surrender our identification cards, passports and special travel documents printed in English, French and Russian to the train commander to be inspected by Russian guards when the train reached the East German border. Our documents were returned to us early in the morning when the train reached the American Sector of Berlin. Because of the world wide coverage of the erection of the Berlin Wall, many Americans became aware of the situation in Berlin, but I don't think many of them could grasp the concept that we were living in a small island city deep inside a communist country. If the Russians wanted Berlin, they didn't have to attack the U. S. Army units stationed there; all they had to do was to change the signs on the fence and wall that surrounded us and inform the world that we were captured.

Because of the nature of my work and my knowledge of classified information, my family and I would never be allowed to fly into nor out of Berlin because of the risk of falling into enemy hands should the aircraft be forced to land in East Germany. Whenever we traveled to or from Berlin, we had to use special travel orders and transit East Germany in the sealed, U. S. Army train. If we took a vacation outside of Berlin, we had to hire someone not involved in intelligence work to drive our vehicle through East Germany to Helmstedt, West Germany, just over the border, where we could detrain and freely travel. The reverse of this procedure was required upon our return to Berlin.

Whenever a member of the Air Force is accompanied by family members on an overseas assignment, a sponsor of equal rank from his new unit is assigned to ease the arrival and familiarize him with the local area. Our sponsor had located a hotel room for us near Templehof Air Field which was the location of my new unit. Our room was on the third floor of a seven story building. An elevator was out of the question as the upper four floors remained in the same bombed out condition they were in at the end of the war in 1945. That was the beginning of our culture shock. Things were a little tough for us for a few days. The Cuban missile crisis began five days prior to our arrival in Berlin. People in the United States were hoarding food and water in anticipation of war and the people in my new unit were on duty every waking hour. I was left alone to find a place for my family to live. The hotel room, with the community bathroom facilities down the hall and a land lady who said Sylvia was not allowed to dry diapers on the heating radiator (yeah, sure), was getting old fast. Note the battle damage on the façade of the hotel.

Our first abode in Berlin - October 1962 (Photo by Author)

Fortunately, Peter and Uschi, who had completed their assignment to Iran and another one in Italy, were currently assigned to Berlin. On the first Saturday we were in town, I arranged to meet them at Uschi's mother's apartment, as it was closer to where we were living. Frau Wieland was overjoyed to be able to host us and greeted us as old friends. We arrived ahead of Peter and Uschi which made Frau Wieland's greeting all the more special for her. Sylvia was nursing Clay when Peter and Uschi arrived and Uschi immediately fell in love with her. While virtually all German women breast fed their children in 1962, they assumed very few American women did. A few minutes later, Peter fell in love with Sylvia and the love the Zahns have for her continues. Their son, Dirk, was born six months earlier than Clay, so the two women also had new motherhood in common.

At most overseas military installations there are family quarters available for use by accompanied personnel. There are never enough quarters to accommodate everyone; so many families live with the local citizenry. In military jargon, this is called "living on the economy." It was necessary for us to live on the economy until my name reached the top of the waiting list. Peter helped us find a place to rent – there would be a nine month wait before government quarters would be available for us. Our rented apartment was so close to the border between the American Sector of Berlin and East Germany, we routinely heard the guards open fire whenever a rabbit, or a person, set off alarms at the border. Our location was precarious enough that Sylvia and Uschi had a plan to meet at a specified point should hostilities occur. Uschi even insisted that Sylvia buy German style clothing and use a German made stroller for Clay so she would blend in with the local population rather than become a target as an American. I never worried as much as the ladies did. Their planning made them feel better so I encouraged them.

Finding safe, comfortable quarters on the local economy for accompanied personnel was a sore spot for Americans. Berlin was divided into four sectors at the end of World War II; America, England, France and Russia each occupied areas of about the same size. The Russians ruled their sector with an iron fist. The French were a little more understanding of the Berliners except when it came to housing their military personnel. They simply took the best quarters for their use and told the Berliners to move out. The Americans and the English treated the Berliners with respect and did not confiscate dwellings for their personnel nor did they put restrictions on land lords who chose to rent property to us. Americans paid exorbitant rent for places that barely met standards. I guess the governments were trying to make the civilian Germans love us.

In the apartment we rented, the furnace was in the cellar on our side of the building, so although the land lord controlled the thermostat, if he wanted to be warm we would be no less warm or even warmer than he was. Peter had gleefully pointed out the location of the heating system as a selling point when we inspected the apartment. It was good advice; that winter we went six weeks with the temperature never getting above freezing and many days it was below zero. We had a great deal of snow that year which actually can cause depression once the beauty of the initial snowfall dissipates. The weeks before our vehicle arrived from the United States were difficult because we lived away from other Americans and had to use trolleys and buses to get to and from work or shopping areas. Sylvia was a real trooper during the nine months we lived in that apartment. She had to deal with culture shock, a new baby, gunfire at night, strange furniture, separation from

English speaking neighbors, and no telephone or transportation while I was at work. We had a living room-dining room combination, two bedrooms, a kitchen and a half bath. The bathroom, with a commode and a sink, was located in a poorly heated entry area but the bath tub was located in the kitchen. That was a little strange but it was always warm at bath time. Sylvia had to wash cloth diapers by hand; disposable diapers were available but were far too expensive. It was a full time job just to survive. We went to the coin operated laundry facility located near the Post Exchange (PX) and did our shopping at the U. S. Army commissary. After a few months, we found a portable diaper washer in the PX and invested a good part of our spare funds to make the purchase. It was a barrel shaped container that held about four gallons of water. An electrically powered agitator hung down from the lid which was secured with clasps to ensure a water tight seal. It was worth every penny and made things a little easier for Sylvia. There were occasional unit social functions, but we were pretty much on our own when we lived on 25 Marien Strasse. Our friendship with the Zahns was particularly beneficial during that period.

Because we had a vehicle and the Zahns did not, we visited them more often than they visited us. We were with them on the evening of November 22, 1963 when President Kennedy was assassinated. Dirk and Clay were playing on the floor and AFRS, the American Forces Radio Station, was playing dinner music in the background. I had spilled a drop of coffee on the table cloth but Uschi was in the kitchen and didn't notice, so I moved a salt shaker over the stain to hide it from her. Peter laughed and explained to me that in a German home everything had a place and those things had to always be in their place. He warned me that Uschi would notice the shaker was out of place. Sure enough, when she returned to the table, she automatically moved the salt shaker and found the spot. We were all laughing as Peter opened the bottle of Bordeaux Blanc we had brought with us when the music was interrupted with the news that the President had been shot. Because the announcer reported it was a head wound, we concluded that it must have been fatal. Peter's telephone began to ring with calls from colleagues and soon the radio station announced the death of the President. After Peter received another call, he asked me accompany him outside of the apartment building. He wanted to show me the burning candles in the windows of apartments in every direction we looked. He wanted me to understand that Berliners held America and the President in high esteem. They all remembered the efforts of America during the Berlin blockade in 1948 and 1949, appreciated President Kennedy's 'Ich bin ein Berliner' speech during his visit in early 1963, and knew that America was the reason they hadn't been absorbed into East Germany. Berliners still have a close affinity with America.

Coping With a New Job:

My new organization, the 6912th RSM, gave me time to get my family settled and that was appreciated. My enthusiasm for the unit was soon to be dampened. The squadron was overwhelmingly dominated by linguists, commonly referred to as 203s (Air Force Specialty Code 203XX). There were many Russian and German language intercept positions operating twenty-four hours a day. There was one Morse intercept position and only one Intelligence Analyst assigned to each Flight. I was the fifth analyst and was assigned to the operations branch which worked the eight to five shift on weekdays. The analysts on the Flights administratively reported to their Mission Supervisors, but technically, they worked for me. It was an awkward situation - I had responsibility but little authority. Originally, the 6912th was a detachment of the 6910th RSM in Darmstadt but had grown into a separate organization. As it developed, the preponderance of linguists in the unit at all levels resulted in the usurpation of functions normally performed by Intelligence Analysts. The one analyst on a Flight was relegated to simply plotting the location of aircraft from behind a Plexiglas wall based on Morse code intercepts by the one Radio Operator on the Flight. Linguists performed both the initial analysis of the intercepted information and the intelligence reporting. This situation prevented the young analysts assigned to the Flights from developing their skills. For me, who had held important positions in my last operational units at Trabzon and Bremerhaven, this was a bitter pill.

The situation was exacerbated by the notorious superior attitude held by linguists in general. Not all linguists suffered from this personality trait. Usually, the older, more mature personnel realized their relative positions in the Intelligence Community, but many, too many, never matured. The problem started when young men were selected out of basic training to attend language school in anticipation of assignment to the USAFSS. They were constantly told they had special talents and were sent to nine-month long assignments at civilian colleges to attend classes in foreign languages. Once assigned to operational units, their superior attitude did not sit well with other operational and support personnel. In addition to wearing a false mantle of superiority, our linguists had to defend themselves against another criticism.

Although there was no basis for the opinion, it was perceived by service members skilled in other disciplines that linguists had a higher than average number of gay personnel; a situation that, when discovered, required immediate suspension of a security clearance. In the macho world of the military, homosexuality was carefully hidden. Although Morse Operators or Intelligence Analysts were occasionally discovered to be gay, there seemed to be more pointed criticism when a gay linguist was identified. This problem caused non-linguists to look with some degree of disdain upon those in the 203 career field. In those days, holding a security clearance was a tenuous thing. I remember one young man who lost his clearance because he chose to participate in the sport of sky diving. Officials in the USAFSS felt anyone who would jump out of a sound airplane lacked the good sense to protect secrets. In another instance, when a member of my organization received a serious head injury in a motorcycle accident, his clearance was revoked because, when asked if he planned to continue riding a motorcycle when he recovered, he replied in the affirmative. The strangest case of clearance revocation I can recall occurred during the miniskirt days of the sixties at Headquarters in San Antonio. There was a very attractive young woman who chose to push the miniskirt craze to the limit. The men flocked to the coffee shop if they thought she might be there, but the higher level officers felt she was a major distraction. She was asked to wear less revealing clothing but chose not to honor the request. Because of her refusal to comply with the request, her clearance was revoked; and since a clearance was required for her job, her employment was terminated.

My duty in the 6912th was an uncomfortable assignment to say the least. I taught the 202s assigned to the Flights how to do things to improve their value to the mission but I was prevented from using my skills in analysis and intelligence reporting. I was assigned every odd ball project that came along. I prepared intelligence briefings, performed field analysis of the Morse intercept material and supervised the installation and operator training for a ground-to-air warning system identified as the URC-53.

The URC-53 was a precursor to our current digital communications systems. It was the size of a very large desk, and through a complicated system of electronic parts, it allowed us to warn reconnaissance aircraft that they were straying too close to a border or that enemy aircraft posed a threat. A printout of a short message was sent to the reconnaissance supervisor in the rear of the aircraft and a three light warning bar was illuminated in front of the pilot to advise him of a dangerous situation. There were many bugs in the new system and implementation was frustrating at best. Eventually, the system was successful and was installed at units around the world.

While I was stationed in Berlin, we only had two aircraft shot down. One strayed out of an air corridor and the other one strayed across the East - West German border. There were three, twenty mile wide air corridors linking Western Europe with Berlin; the Southern, the Central and the Northern routes. The sole purpose of the Morse intercept position in our unit was to copy Soviet Air Defense (PVO Strany) communications that constantly reported the location of aircraft in the corridors. When an aircraft strayed across a corridor boundary, it was reported as an intruder and Russian fighters were scrambled. These boundary violations were reported to others in the Intelligence Community by the release of a message called the Border/Corridor Violation Report (BOCOVIR). Many of these reports were issued because PVO Strany reacted to the slightest intrusion. Normally, the violating aircraft returned to the proper flight path and the fighters returned to base.

During the day shift on January 28, 1964, an aircraft strayed out of the Central Corridor and did not get back onto the proper path. It was not one of our reconnaissance aircraft, so we could not issue a URC-53 warning. A BOCOVIR was issued and our German and Russian Linguists were advised to search for tactical air operations.

From the Morse intercept, we could tell that the Soviets had scrambled fighters and the target had been attacked. At the same time, a Russian Linguist recorded the activity between the ground station and the lead fighter pilot. The communications were what would be expected in a shoot down. The pilot reported acquisition of the target and the controller gave the order to attack. What struck me as being cold was the conversation prior to the actual firing on the aircraft.

The straying aircraft was a United States Air Force T-39 Sabreliner with three Air Force officers on board. The T-39 silhouette is very similar in shape but not size to the Caravelle, a sixty passenger aircraft manufactured in France. The lead fighter pilot reported to the ground controller that it was a Caravelle. From his position above the T-39, it would appear to be a Caravelle because he had nothing to relate to the size of the target. When the controller gave the order to shoot, the fighter pilot hesitated and again reported that it was a Caravelle, as if to question the advisability of destroying a passenger aircraft. Again, the controller told him to shoot and the Russian fighter pilot destroyed the Sabreliner. Three Air Force officers died in the incident. It bothered me that the ground controller thought he was issuing an order that could kill as many as sixty people in a civilian aircraft that had strayed off course. It was a cold order in a cold war.

Because the activity was completely controlled by the Flight on duty, I was not intricately involved in the reporting but was close enough to learn some disturbing bits of information. As it was explained to me, the excitement of the moment caused a serious error. The tape of the intercepted conversation between the ground controller and the Russian pilot was accidently erased. That was a disastrous mistake. A mistake of that magnitude could have a serious, detrimental effect on the military careers of many people. I honestly cannot say whether or not the incident was covered up by the unit, but I have always been suspicious of what transpired after the error. There was a clamp down on conversation about the shoot down, even within the secure area. As difficult as it is for me to believe, there is a possibility that the fact a tape ever existed was denied and all of the reporting was based on the intercepted Morse communications. If, in fact, a cover up occurred, it was a dangerous decision. We know now that the discovery of a cover up is normally much more serious than the original error. I would like to think I am completely wrong in my memory of this particular situation, but the facts, as I understand them, continue to bother me.

The second shoot down during my tour of duty in Berlin was of an Air Force RB-66 reconnaissance aircraft that strayed across the border between East and West Germany on March 10, 1964 in the general vicinity of the East German city of Magdeburg. Soviet fighters were scrambled and the aircraft was attacked. It crashed landed near the city of Gardelegen. All three Air Force officers on board were injured but survived. They were turned over to American authorities several days later. I was not on duty on the day of the shoot down so I cannot recall any more details.

On the lighter side of aircraft activity, we witnessed a successful defection from the other side while I was stationed in Berlin. On a sunny afternoon in July of 1963, a pilot assigned to the Polish National Air Force made his escape from behind the iron curtain and into free Berlin with his wife and two young children. I don't know how he defeated security at the airfield in Poland, but he did. He placed his wife and one child in the student seat of a Polish made TS-8 Bies training aircraft and put the second child in the instructor section with himself. Once off the ground he easily avoided radar detection by flying at treetop level until they reached Berlin. Several men from our unit were playing a soft ball game at a field next to our portion of Templehof Airport and immediately realized what was happening when the aircraft flew over the field displaying Polish markings. The players abandoned the game and ran to the landing strip to watch the action. As he had no radio contact with the Templehof tower, the Polish pilot used an ingenious way to land his aircraft. He waited until he saw a civilian airliner enter a landing pattern and tucked his aircraft in just behind the tail to follow it down to the runway. The procedure worked fine and after landing he taxied his aircraft over to hangar area, climbed out with his family, ascended the steps into the Air Force snack bar and requested political asylum. I was able to snap a photograph of the TS-8 Bies soon after it was rolled into the hangar and placed under guard. The pilot and his family were granted asylum and within a few days, the aircraft was returned to the Polish National Air Force.

*The Polish TS-8 Bies training aircraft at Templehof Airport,
Berlin in July 1963. (Photo by Author)*

The Family Grows:

The three years in Berlin were enjoyable only because of our growing friendship with the Zahns, vacations to West Germany and Italy and the birth of our daughter, Kelly Maurine. Sylvia became pregnant in May of 1963 and Kelly was born on February 17, 1964. By the time of her birth we had moved into U. S. government owned and managed quarters. The apartment, a third floor walk up, was very comfortable for us and the proximity to English speaking neighbors made things a lot easier for Sylvia. My job at the 6912th was still a bit of a drag, but we found ways to make life enjoyable. Clay was a good toddler and brought us great joy. Once we found that Sylvia was pregnant, I told her that I really wanted to ensure that Clay was completely out of diapers by the time our second child was born. I had never changed a diaper and didn't want to ever learn how. I think that dealing with cloth diapers on both Sylvia's and Clay's part had something to do with her success. By the time he was eighteen months old he was out of diapers and Kelly was about to be born.

At about ten o'clock in the evening of February 16, 1964, Sylvia told me it was time to take her to the hospital. I arranged for the lady across the hall to sit with Clay for the time it would take to reach the hospital and return. Once at the hospital, I turned Sylvia over to the first person I saw dressed in white and told her I had another little one at home. She assured me she could handle the situation and would call me when the baby was born. I returned to our apartment, and relieved the neighbor from the baby sitting job and went to bed. Early the next morning, before Clay awoke, the telephone rang. The nurse calling told me that I had a beautiful daughter and both mother and baby were fine. When I exclaimed, "I can't believe it! You have got to be kidding," she replied by telling me that she had been up all night working the late shift and had no reason to call me and make a joke. I tried to explain that we had wanted a little girl so much, that the reality was hard to believe. I suspect she had heard all of that before.

The rest of my day was a little difficult. The Army hospital hadn't changed their procedures in a hundred years. They insisted that any time a child was born, the mother and child had to remain hospitalized for seven days because that's what it says in the Regulations. I had to explain to Clay that his mother was going to be gone for a while. At breakfast, he looked at me and asked where his mother was. He was an early talker and we had no trouble communicating. As I listened to his question, the thought struck me that if I didn't correctly deal with this, he would be pestering me about his mother for a week. I told him that his mother was gone and that from now on it would be just the two of us. He looked me in the eyes and asked, "All gone?" I told him he had it right and I didn't want him asking about her all of the time. When Sylvia came home a week later he was really happy and I avoided a week of pestering, so I think I did the right thing. Clay and I ended up with a healthy and happy father-son relationship, although once I told him this story when he was an adult, he gave me a lot of grief for being so hard hearted.

I sent a telegram to Sylvia's parents with the news and then called Peter and Uschi. They were thoroughly excited and arranged to meet me at the hospital to see the new arrival. When Uschi saw Kelly, with dark hair like Uschi's and her almond shaped dark eyes, she loudly exclaimed in German, "Oh my God! She could be my daughter." As I write this, Kelly, now the mother of three children of her own, is forty-four years of age and the Zahns still think of her as a daughter. I survived the week caring for Clay on my own and when Sylvia came home we started yet another new life; one with a toddler and an infant.

Kelly, like Clay was a happy child. She was bright, and from the beginning was a quick learner. Sylvia was unable to produce enough milk to breast feed Kelly; probably because she had a toddler to chase after while caring for an infant. Child Psychologists tell us that a breast fed child will often be more sensitive than a bottle fed child. I don't know about that, but as adults, Clay mimicked his mother's tolerant nature and Kelly imitates my impatient, demanding personality. Others say Kelly is too intense because she was toilet trained by the time she was sixteen months old. I simply satisfy myself by believing they were just naturally different people; but in general, Clay was his mother's son and Kelly is her father's daughter.

Kelly is special in another way. Because she was born in an area legally identified as "American occupied Berlin," the local German government presented her with a German birth certificate and offered her duel German and American citizenship. We were advised that, although she is legally identified as a naturalized American citizen, she could never be President of the United States because she is foreign born. It is now my understanding that the advice was incorrect. A 2008 contender for election to the Presidency, Senator John McCain, was born to a military member in the Panama Canal Zone and his right to serve in that capacity was not been challenged.

Chapter 3 - Assignment San Antonio – Again

Not long after Kelly's birth, I received a promotion to Technical Sergeant. Promotions were hard to come by in the years between the Korean War and the beginning of the Vietnam War. I had been a Staff Sergeant for over eight years and was unhappy about it, but two other men promoted at the same time I was, each had twelve years in grade, so I felt lucky. By October of 1965, it was time to return to the CONUS. We shipped the car early so it would be at the port when we arrived, packed up our belongings and headed to our next assignment in San Antonio, Texas. It was difficult to leave our friends, the Zahns, but there were grandparents waiting in San Antonio to see Clay and Kelly.

A hundred pounds of baggage and two little children kept Sylvia and me busy throughout the trip home. After deplaning at LaGuardia Airport in New York City, we were ushered to the customs inspection area where the lines were long. Sylvia and I had fashioned little backpacks for the children to make them think they were helping us with the luggage, and being good GI dependents, they stood in line with us without straying. I remember dragging our bags forward with each movement of the line, being tired, worrying about the strain on Sylvia and the children and sweating in the overheated building when a customs agent approached me. He said, "Welcome home, Sergeant. You and your family need to follow me." I gave Sylvia a "What now?" look as we followed the agent to a side door out of the cavernous room. He opened the door for us and said, "I think we can trust you; you don't have to go through customs." It was forty-three years ago and I fondly remember that act of kindness. It buoyed our spirits and renewed our energy. We found a place to stay for the night and recovered our car from yet another customs area the next morning. After a short visit with my parents at the family home twenty five miles north of New York City, we piled into our little Mercury S-22 for the drive to San Antonio, Texas. I had removed the rear seat from the car and shipped it to San Antonio with our household goods. Then I installed a custom fitting piece of three quarter inch plywood behind the front bucket seats and placed blankets over the wood. My modifications made a great place for the children to play and sleep during the 2,000 mile trip. This, of course, was before seat belts were common or required.

Sylvia's parents were ecstatic about seeing three year old Clay who left them when he was only six weeks old, and eighteen month old Kelly, who they had never seen. Life was good for everyone. We purchased an eleven hundred square foot home that had three bedrooms, two bathrooms and a one car garage, in a housing development not far from USAFSS Headquarters at Kelly Air Force Base. In retrospect, it wasn't much of a house and the builder was throwing them up over night, but we made it a home and were happy there. The house cost $13,000 and we put just about all of that on the mortgage. The interest rate was six percent and the period of the mortgage was thirty years. With an escrow payment for taxes and insurance, our monthly payment was $104. We closed the deal at the title company office one evening after work at about 6:00 P.M. I distinctly remember coming close to regurgitating when I signed the document stating I promised to pay the mortgage company $104.00 a month for the next thirty years. I felt as if I had signed away my life to live in the little house at 135 Paradise Valley. I soon got over my stress and we went to work to make the house a home. Over the next year there were curtains to be purchased and installed, a fence to be built, and concrete to be poured for a walkway and a patio in the back yard. We planted plugs of St. Augustine carpet grass which flourished in the hot, humid San Antonio weather; we soon had to purchase a lawn mower and the other tools needed to keep a manicured lawn. We placed some decorative plants on either side of the drive way and trimmed the one lone native tree in front of the house the contractors missed when they cleared the land for development. Sylvia had her little piece of Texas.

San Antonio was a large city even back in the sixties and there were quite a few miles between our home and that of Sylvia's parents. This was bad because visits involved a thirty minute drive through heavy traffic, but good, because there were no unannounced visits. The same applied to Sylvia's sister, Penny, who lived in the Northeast side of town. We settled down into a routine of domestic tranquility, but

Sylvia decided she should go back to work to enhance our financial position and applied for her old job at the USAFSS. They were happy to reinstate her clearance and she accepted a position. We dropped off the children at a day care facility on the way to work and picked them up after work on the way home. It sounds like a good situation but it wasn't. It filled us with guilt each day when we dropped off the children and, of course, they came down with all sorts of minor childhood ailments. Then Sylvia started to contract one minor illness after another. She didn't realize it, but the burden of guilt associated with sending the children to day care and the stress of trying to be a mother, a wife and an employee took a toll on her. At one appointment with a physician for a rash on her leg, she broke into tears. The doctor asked if she were a working mother and when she said she was, he reviewed her medical history. Then he told her she could solve all of her medical problems if she resigned from her job and returned to being a stay at home mother. I agreed with the physician and she resigned the next day. Sylvia got well, the children got well and I was happy not to drop them off at the day care center every day. My job, though not as interesting as dealing with real time activity overseas, was rewarding and I continued to gain expertise in my field.

One day in mid May of 1967, while I was at a meeting, Sylvia called the office to speak with me. My next in charge, Staff Sergeant Troy Williams, took the message but forgot to pass it on to me. That evening Sylvia told me she had called and left a message with Troy, and wondered why I hadn't called back. The next morning, I cautioned Troy to make sure he passed along any messages from Sylvia because my brother, Danny, was in Vietnam and the message could be about him. Troy apologized and assured me it wouldn't happen again. That afternoon, Sylvia called the office to tell me she had just received word from my sister that Danny had been killed in combat. When I told Troy he would have to take over for me for a few days while I attended Danny's funeral in New York, he thought I was kidding. He refused to accept that I had just mentioned that possibility in the morning and now, in the afternoon, I was telling him it had actually happened. It had happened, and I had to go to New York.

When I was in the fourth grade, the father of a classmate was shot to death by his lover, and when in the eighth grade, a classmate was raped and killed by a predator. I only remember having a keen interest in the details of the investigations of these cases. I had no emotional connection to the incidents. In high school, a classmate sitting five seats away from me in the auditorium suddenly moaned and died during a stage presentation and during my high school graduation ceremony, one of the speakers died of a heart attack on the stage. It was probably my natural, youthful feeling that I would live forever that blocked any sensitive feelings during these incidents. My life progressed, and other members of my family died; a grandmother and a grandfather, an aunt and an uncle, my wife's grandfather and grandmother, yet I did not really experience grief. Then, on Mother's Day in 1967, when Danny was killed in Vietnam, it simply struck me that the inevitable had occurred.

Danny was a career Marine on his third tour of duty in that conflict. He did not have to go to the war zone for a third time, but he volunteered to do so. Through my position in the USAFSS, I was able to check on the combat activities on the day of his death. His platoon had been engaged in a firefight with a North Vietnamese Army unit at a position twenty-two miles south of Da Nang. One hundred and thirty-six enemy soldiers died that night and Danny, who was the Platoon Gunnery Sergeant, was among the six U. S. Marines who lost their lives in the battle. Danny took several rounds in the chest and probably died quickly. The citation that accompanied the posthumously awarded Bronze Star Medal stated that as he stood up to encourage his troops to repel the attack, he was struck by enemy gunfire.

Danny was the sixth of the nine children and there were three years between us. Perhaps because of our age difference, we never developed a strong relationship. Fourteen days after his death his remains arrived in North Tarrytown and I received word of the schedule for the traditional Irish wake and funeral; I packed my Class A uniform and caught a flight to New York. I felt as if I were simply fulfilling a responsibility rather than suffering any grief.

The funeral home may have been the one my father and I visited when I was a boy. This time I knew the person in the casket. Danny lay there with all of his brothers and sisters in attendance. I still did not feel grief. My mother mentioned the large number of medals that adorned the dress blue Marine Corps uniform that encased Danny's body. I agreed it was impressive to make her feel better, but I was thinking how ridiculous it was to imagine that military medals had any significance once you are dead. My mother and father were in a daze but there was no way I could understand their grief. Actually, I remember thinking that for the family to participate in a three-day-long wake was almost barbaric.

As is the Irish custom, there was a large reception after the burial where food and whisky were abundant. At one point during this party, a feeling of grief overcame me. The combination of liquor and seeing Danny's two children who no longer had their father didn't help matters. The fact that I had orders to go to South Vietnam within four months and the possibility that my two children could easily lose their father probably had a lot to do with my emotions at the time.

With three brothers who had experienced military combat, I had heard countless stories about friends taking care of each other in battle. During the year I was to spend in South Vietnam, I was never interested in risking my life for anyone. My goals were to do my assigned duties in a professional manner and to return to my wife and children alive and with all of my body parts intact.

Danny's death placed me in a difficult position. Because my parents had now lost a son in the Vietnam War, I had the option to request a change in my orders to prevent me from going to a war zone. As a patriot and a professional military member, I felt it was my duty to go to Vietnam, even though I could legally avoid that dangerous duty and ensure Sylvia she would not lose me in combat. I held the anti-war protestors in extremely low esteem, not the ones who moved to Canada – it took a certain type of courage to forego citizenship in this great country; it was the cowards I disdained. I could not allow myself to be even remotely associated with the people who advocated surrender and cowardice, so I elected to do my duty.

Chapter 4 - Assignment Vietnam

Training:

My assignment to Vietnam involved being on flight status. That is, part of the time, I would be a crewmember on board an aircraft. Each crewmember must meet certain physical and psychological thresholds to qualify for flight duty. In addition, only personnel who volunteer for flight duty can serve in that capacity. This status as a volunteer becomes a major Catch-22 when a particular training requirement comes into play.

All Pilots and crewmembers in the United States Air Force must complete a twenty-one day course called World Wide Survival Training. That is a benign enough sounding label to lull one into thinking it is just another routine requirement; it was not.

I arrived at Fairchild Air Force Base in the State of Washington on a Sunday afternoon, signed in at the Orderly Room and was assigned to a room in one of the barracks. The Charge of Quarters Sergeant told me to report to the base theater at 1800 hours (6:00 P.M.) that evening in fatigues[7]. Starting a training course at six in the evening on a Sunday was my first clue that this was not going to be an ordinary school. The students, who had come from bases all over the country, were complete strangers. Most ranks were included; there were lower ranking Airmen, Sergeants, young Lieutenants and middle-aged Colonels. The soft murmuring of the group of about fifty ceased as the lead instructor strode to the center of the stage at precisely 1800 hours. He was a perfect physical specimen and his uniform was as crisp and sharp as any I had seen in my fourteen years of military service. With a booming voice, he said, "Good evening, Gentlemen. From this moment, until the course is completed, you have no military rank. Each of you volunteered to be here, so if you can't handle that, simply

7   The fatigue uniform is designed for manual labor or combat operations. The name has been changed to Battle Dress Uniform (BDU).

143

get up and leave. You will be removed from flight status and returned to your unit." No one stirred; Catch-22 was in effect. Once he concluded no one was going to leave, he said, "To successfully complete this course, you must obey all orders from me and my assistants." As he pronounced the word, "assistants," eight of his clones strode out onto the stage and stood behind him. None of the nine, sharply dressed men wore any insignia of rank.

The lead instructor then set down a few more rules for the next twenty-one days. He informed the group that all movement would be in double time until further notice. For the uninformed, double time is a jog at twice the speed of a fast walk. He went on to explain that by Tuesday morning our leg muscles would be screaming from the double time movements but by Thursday morning, our muscles would have adjusted and the pain would be gone. He was correct. I can remember the pain and I can remember waking up on the following Thursday morning without pain. That man knew his business. Before releasing us to our assigned instructors, he pointed out that fainting was a weakness that required automatic removal from flight status, and that a fake faint to avoid punishment or work assignment would be treated as an actual faint. He told us that the first two weeks would encompass general survival techniques and that the last week was to test individual survival skills in the wilderness and as a prisoner of war. Finally, he told us not to trust each other because one of us would function as a traitor to the group once we were placed in the mock prisoner of war camp. As a parting shot, he reiterated the Catch-22 when he reminded us that we were all volunteers and had the right to remove ourselves from the program and flight status at any time.

For two weeks we attended class room presentations, field lectures and participated in interactive situations. We built solar stills to produce water. Using towers instead of the real thing, we learned how to parachute from airplanes. We learned how to release a parachute harness while being blown across a field by huge fans. Getting free from the harness and out from underneath a parachute after being dropped into a pool of water was a memorable experience. For several days, we took classes in self-defense that included training in a discipline that was a cross between Judo and Karate. The course taught us how to disarm and kill an assailant while unarmed. On the final day of that training, the instructor said, "I've taught you all I can in the few days available. Now let me give you some advice. If you are down in enemy territory, and you come across an oriental looking person who jumps into a Judo or Karate stance, don't try what you learned here; shoot him if you have a gun and run if you don't, because you will lose a hand-to-hand fight with a trained martial arts adversary." Everyone laughed, but it wasn't very reassuring.

It was the escape and evasion training that posed the most difficult hurdle. They taught us how to catch, kill and cook small game, to build a fire and to find shelter. After fourteen straight days of double-timing all over the base, we thought we were tough. On the third Sunday, we doubled timed out to the remotest part of the base at about 2100 hours (9:00 P.M.). It was time to test our newly learned skills.

They lined us up, side by side, and instructed us to get down on our stomachs and crawl from where we were to a lighted area a mile distant. To make it more uncomfortable, the base fire trucks had been there an hour earlier to wet down the rocky, weed strewn area. Instructors watched carefully to insure no one varied from the instructions and triggered simulated land mine explosions to add to the authenticity of the situation.

At the end of the mile long crawl, men dressed in black uniforms speaking English with strong eastern European accents pounced upon us. Each of us had our head covered with a bag made of thick black cloth and were told not to move. Once they had captured everyone, we were led to a mock prisoner of war camp. Someone shoved me into a four by four foot cell. He told me not to remove my hood and to stand in the middle of the tiny room without touching the sides. The guard said there was an opening in the door, and if he came by and saw me in any other position, the punishment for such a minor infraction was twenty or thirty push-ups with closed fists on the concrete floor outside of the cell. He also told me there was an old coffee can in one corner to use for biological functions. In earlier classes we were taught to concentrate on complicated issues to keep from breaking under the strain of this type of confinement. I decided to play a round of golf at the Lackland Air Force Base golf course in my mind. I imagined playing each stroke on each hole and it kept my mind busy. I played that course repeatedly for eighteen hours before I was taken from the cell. During the eighteen hours, there were shouted conversations as the guards took some men from their cell or returned others. There were loud noises and men crying out in pain. The guards located the highest-ranking person among us and forced him to empty the biological products from the receptacle in each cell. It was very difficult to believe that our captors were really on our side.

Eventually, with hood in place, I was removed from my cell and placed into a wooden cage with collapsible sides. They forced me into a squatting position and squeezed the sides of the cage together until I could no longer move. Then they proceeded to beat the sides of the cage with bamboo sticks and asked me questions they knew I could not answer. At this point, I had been awake for about thirty-three hours, hadn't eaten anything in a longer period and was very tired. When the guards tired of beating the sides of the cage, one of them pulled me out and stood there as I struggled with stiff and sore muscles. When I regained the ability to stand on two feet, he hustled me off to my cell. "That wasn't too bad," I thought, as the cell door slammed behind me. My respite was short; they gave me enough time to think they were finished with me, then came and got me again.

This time, after they pushed me into an interrogation room, my hood was removed. A tall, muscular, blond man in a black uniform with no discernable rank or nationality, snarled at me, "Sit in that chair." He questioned me for about fifteen minutes. I stood firm on name, rank and serial number. Then he had me stand with my back toward the wall and my feet on footprints painted on the floor about thirty inches from the baseboard. A few inches behind the painted footprints, I saw a four foot long, two by four nailed to the floor. There was a four by eight foot, one half inch thick piece of plywood wedged behind the two-by-four with the top edge nailed to the wall near the ceiling.

The interrogator had me place my feet on the footprints and lean back until my head hit the plywood with my arms hanging straight down toward the floor. I was in a painful position, balanced on my heels and my head as he shouted questions at me. When I didn't answer his questions, he started kicking the plywood at the level of my head with the bottom of his booted foot and continued to shout at me. Every time he kicked the plywood, pain shot through my head, neck and back but I stood firm on name, rank and serial number. After some time, the interrogator removed a piece of red felt from his pocket and threw it down onto the desk; it was the signal that the roll playing scenario had been interrupted. Of course, only the instructors had the pieces of red felt. The instructor told me that in his opinion, if captured, I would not reveal secret information, but that I would not survive captivity either. His advice to me was to work on the problem. He then placed the red felt in his pocket, replaced my hood, and quickly returned to his sadistic guard impersonation as he forced me back into my cell.

Later that afternoon, our hoods were removed and all of the prisoners were relocated to a barbed wire enclosure dotted with what looked like bomb shelters. They had curved concrete covered roofs and dug out floors covered with trash and rocks. When I arrived, they already had the ranking officer in our group standing in a water-filled pit up to mid chest and I could see what appeared to be horse manure floating on the surface. They broke us into small groups, forced us into the shelters, and told us to remain silent. I was able to get some fitful, much-needed sleep on the uncomfortable floor. One of our members called us together as night fell, and told us there was a prison break planned and that there would be help from outside. We made tentative plans as to what we would do if escape became possible.

At about 2200 hours (10:00 P.M.), the guards herded all of us into the prison yard and placed us into a ragged military formation. In front of us was a prisoner, stripped down to his underwear, tied to a post. The head instructor informed us that he knew there was a prison break planned and that the prisoner tied to the stake had tactical information. It was chilly in the mountainous area of Washington in the evening and the guy was shivering. Occasionally, one of the guards would throw a bucket of cold water on him and try to make him talk. I didn't see him break. Eventually, the guards forced us back into the bunkers and everything got quiet again.

As the next day dawned, there was a commotion in the prison yard. The guards had left during the night and a band of men who identified themselves as partisans had taken control. They quickly led us out of the camp and through the forest to their base camp where we were given food and some survival material. Each of us received a pistol belt that held a first aid kit, a compass, a canteen of water and a survival kit with enough rations for one day. They provided each of us with a map and indicated where we could find friendly troops. We rested during most of the day. Late in the afternoon, they gave each of us a potato and an onion and told us we would leave the next morning.

Just before daybreak, gunfire erupted and partisans ran through our area screaming for us to get away because there was an enemy attack underway. In a completely disorganized rout, we all ran into the forest, which was thick with underbrush and had few trails. This is where the earlier training we received was to be tested. Although some were able to team up with others, the camp raiders completely separated me from all of the other prisoners. The people who planned this exercise were prepared to rescue any of us who became hopelessly lost, and even had slow flying observation aircraft operating in the area during the following day to engage in searches if needed. This assuaged most of my anxiety about being alone in the forest, but not all.

Once I found a place to bed down for the night, I was able to start a fire and cook my potato and onion. It was a strange meal and one I never thought I would prepare, much less appreciate; but appreciate it, I did. As exhausted as I was, it was easy for me to get a good night's sleep. The next morning I studied the map they had given me and remembered the lesson I received from a local mountain man earlier in the program. He told us to travel in a straight line at all times, regardless of the terrain. He said that trying to avoid steep or difficult terrain by looking for a way around it would only cause confusion and disorientation. I started out early in the morning with my compass in one hand and the map in the other. Around noon, I came across a stream and decided to fish for lunch. I pulled up a few reeds which provided edible roots and uncovered some worms for bait. The survival kit had some fishing line and hooks and that put me in business. In no time, I had caught two very small trout, which I gutted and stuck on sticks. I started a fire with matches from the survival kit and cooked my lunch. The fish tasted fine as did the bulbous roots from the reeds. I had eaten the pemmican bar from the kit earlier in the day and felt fortified for the next leg of my trip. The compass pointed to the thickly wooded hill in front of me and I followed my instructor's advice. It was a steep climb and there were times I had to turn sideways to slide between the trees just to make progress, but I made it to the top. The other side of the hill posed a different problem.

I learned the meaning of the word windfall that day. In front of me were many acres of dead and downed pine trees that had been knocked over by an enormously strong wind. The fall had occurred many months, if not years, before because the branches of the trees had rotted away. All I could see were thousands of large tree trunks with the remnants of their branches sticking out at every possible angle. I had to pass this barrier if I were to arrive at my designated point. Up and over I went, up and over and up and over for hours and hours. The branch stumps jabbed into my body every time I slipped. I bordered on despair when I reached the middle because I was completely exhausted. After an hour of rest, I started out again and finally emerged from the area around 1600 hours (4:00 P.M.). After another hour of rest, I resumed my trek. Within fifteen minutes, I heard the engine of a truck and knew I was near a road. I clamored over a small hill and slid down into a ditch along a surfaced road. As I climbed out of the ditch, an Air Force truck drove past me and disappeared around a bend. I took off in the direction of the truck and found about half of my group sitting at the edge of the road. The mountain man had taught me well. I was only three hundred yards from the point on the map.

When everyone was accounted for, they loaded us into the trucks and transported us back to the base. We were taken straight to the chow hall. It was customary for the survival school classes to be able to order whatever they wanted for the evening meal after completing the course. I don't remember what I ordered, but I know I didn't eat much. After six days of meager rations and climbing through the forest, I had lost my appetite.

I weighed 140 pounds when I started survival school; three weeks later, I weighed 126 pounds. I believe most, if not all, of the 14 pounds were lost in the last seven days of the course. When I returned home, my wife counted over one hundred bruises on my body from falling onto those limb stumps as I crossed the windfall of trees. The World Wide Survival Course taught at Fairchild Air Force Base was the most difficult course I took during my twenty years in the Air Force. It was forty years ago and I can still easily recall most of the smallest details.

One more fact, at our debriefing they told us that the informer who had been leaking information about our prison break was the young man I saw tied to the post and shivering in the prison yard that night.

Getting to Nha Trang:

On September 22, 1967, I left San Antonio, Texas for my tour of duty in Vietnam. Sylvia drove me to the airport after I said good-bye to Clay and Kelly. On the way, I gave her advice on what to do if the Viet Cong[8] got me. I told her that if I died over there, she should marry a nice man who would be a father to the children. Then I said that, if they captured me, she should probably wait, because I felt I could survive. Finally, I told her that if I were reported missing, she should wait five years and then find a good man to marry. She heard all of this, but as I recall the conversation now, I don't think she absorbed anything I said. I do remember her noticing that the Braniff Airlines aircraft I was to board was painted Kelly green and she took it as an omen of Irish good luck. I kissed her good-bye and walked down the gangway to the aircraft.

The Flight to SeaTac airport in Washington was uneventful. I collected my B-4[9] bag from the baggage area and walked into the main terminal to find the Air Force liaison office. Before I could find the office, I came upon a desk with a large sign that read, Cam Ranh Bay Check In. My orders indicated I was to proceed to SeaTac airport, then to Cam Ranh Bay, Vietnam, and then to my designated unit, so I knew I was in the right place. I gave the clerk a copy of my orders and he scheduled my departure to Vietnam for the following morning via Trans World Air Lines. Everything seemed pretty well organized.

The following morning I boarded an aircraft filled with men of all ranks from all of the several services and departed for the war zone. It was a somewhat surreal situation. We were all in Class A uniforms instead of combat fatigues and the aircraft was overflowing with beautiful flight attendants. This had a calming effect on me. After a stop in Japan to refuel, we flew on to Cam Ranh Bay. It was September 23, 1967. By this time, the airlines had figured out that if the aircraft came in over the South China Sea directly onto the runway there was

8   The National Front for the Liberation of South Vietnam translates to "Viet Nam Cong San," which was shortened by GIs to Viet Cong.

9   A folding, canvas bag used by military personnel to carry enough clothing and living necessities to last a week or more.

little or no chance of receiving enemy fire, so it was a relatively safe trip to Cam Ranh Bay. Departures were scheduled the same way.

We unloaded and walked into the military terminal. The place was a beehive of activity. Men were lined up at counters in both Class A and fatigue uniforms. Others napped on the floor in corners or on benches while awaiting flights. Announcements made over the public address system were frequent and barely understandable. I noticed a trooper in full battle dress sleeping on a bench with one arm wrapped around his rifle and a leash wrapped around the other. At the end of the leash, a tiny monkey was jumping back and forth. I knew I had arrived in a strange place.

I found the counter for incoming personal and handed a clerk my orders. He told me that they had frequent trips to Nha Trang, my final destination, and that I shouldn't have any problem getting there. I wondered if that was all the help I was going to receive when he said, "Hey, do you see that C-123 out there? It goes to Nha Trang every day. Get your baggage as soon as you can and see if they'll take you. Oh, by the way," he said, "you better get into some fatigues." The C-123 parked just outside of the doorway behind the counter had camouflage painting. I went out and found the flight mechanic who was doing a preflight inspection of the aircraft and asked if I could catch a ride to Nha Trang. He said that would be no problem if I could be ready in an hour. I retrieved my bag from the baggage claim area, changed into fatigues and camped out under the wing of the C-123.

The C-123 is a particularly loud and shaky aircraft, but when in a combat profile, with Jet Assisted Take Off (JATO), the sound is almost unbearable. The crewmembers all wear headsets (earphones) to remain in communication so the sound is dampened for them, but for the passengers, it is, cover your ears and don't even try to talk. It was a short hop to Nha Trang. There was no terminal and no one to greet or direct me to my unit. I walked across the apron in the direction of a sign that simply read, "Operations." Inside there was a counter, several desks and many people in flight uniforms who all seemed to know what they were doing. I was completely lost. When I found a guy at a desk that wasn't being pestered by someone else, I asked him for help. I showed him my orders and he said, "Oh yeah, you need the 361st. Go out that door and turn left, turn left again and go about a hundred yards and you'll find them." I'm hot, sweating, carrying everything I own, and still have a hundred yards to go. I thought, "I could have been killed along the way, and no one would have known or cared. This is a strange situation."

When I found the Quonset hut with a sign that identified it as the operations office for the 361st TEWS[10], I noticed that, in very small characters, the sign also read, Det. 1, 6994 RSM[11]; I had reached my destination. The pilots and flight mechanics of the 361st TEWS flew the aircraft, but we of the 6994th RSM told them where to fly and operated the mission equipment.

I went inside and met Master Sergeant Jim Ali, the NCOIC of operations. He was familiar with everyone in the unit so he knew I was a new guy. Jim removed his ever present cigar, smiled, and said, "Hey, it looks like we have a NUG." I had no idea what that meant, so I just gave him a copy of my orders and my personnel file and waited for him to say something else. He said, "Relax, Joyce, we'll get you settled in."

"What's a NUG," I asked. Jim laughed and told me that NUG is a term for new arrivals. It meant new, untried and gullible. I was exhausted from my long journey, in a strange, threatening place, and could not see any humor in the term. Jim went on to tell me that I'd be working for Master Sergeant Dick Cheney and that he would arrange for us to get together. He hollered to someone in the back of the hut to ask if he knew of any openings for a new guy to live. The unseen person shouted back that there was a place on Airport Road.

Jim explained that it was a small base and everyone over the rank of Staff Sergeant was required to find lodging off the base by renting from the local Vietnamese. I was a Technical Sergeant at the time, so that meant me. This made me a little apprehensive. Jim noticed the worried look and told me it was no big deal and that I would receive extra pay for the inconvenience. Over the years men had rented places near the base and the area was well guarded and reasonably safe. He had a truck driver take my baggage and me to a building on Airport Road, which was adjacent to the base runway, where there was an opening. I met some off duty crewmembers from my outfit there and they clued me in to the routine.

We all chipped in to pay the rent. The property owner took care of

10   Tactical Electronic Warfare Squadron.
11   Radio Squadron Mobile.

maintenance, water and electricity. The requirement for some guys to live off base caused an unwritten procedure to develop to get the men back and forth to the base proper. Anyone driving a military vehicle would stop and offer a ride to any American standing on the side of the road. In my year there, the only times I ever had a transportation problem was during periods of high enemy activity which resulted in very few vehicles moving around the area. The names of the American occupied enclaves I remember were Airport Road, the School Area (a building adjacent to an elementary school) and VC Village. VC Village was the farthest enclave away from the base and the guys there always felt they were more or less surrounded by the Viet Cong (VC). We used facilities at the base when we were flying, but when performing non-flying duties, we worked in Quonset huts at a small Army Security Agency/Special Forces unit away from the air base, the 313th Radio Research Battalion. We referred to the location as the 313th or Camp McDermott. Although I flew on twenty-two intelligence-collecting missions while in Vietnam, I spent most of my time at the 313th. We had well built bunkers, lots of barbed wire protection and machine gun towers, so I felt relatively safe there.

The ARDF Mission:

ARDF stands for Airborne Radio Direction Finding. On its face, it was a simple mission. Our EC-47s[12] were equipped with instruments that could home in on enemy Morse code transmissions and determine a very precise location. We would then encrypt and transmit the position to the nearest Artillery Control Center and they would decide how much, if any, artillery to fire at the target. On occasion, if we determined we had located a high value target, an air strike could be requested. Post mission analysis provided intelligence used for strategic bombing missions. I was both a Morse code intercept operator and an Intelligence Analyst, so I could function in either capacity while on missions. The aircraft, built in the thirties and early forties, had no padding inside. They were so loud, we could only communicate with each other through microphones and headsets. Seven hours of the noise, concentrating on the mission and bouncing around in the

---

12   A two engine transport aircraft configured to intercept communications and determine the location of transmitters used by enemy units.

unstable air at four thousand feet altitude was mentally and physically exhausting.

Crews normally flew missions every three days, which means in a one year tour of duty they flew over one hundred missions. The program was a good one and provided much needed support to the troops on the ground. Everyone I knew who participated in the ARDF program felt he had significantly contributed to the protection of our ground troops in Vietnam.

The Following description of the ARDF mission can be found on the website for the 6994ᵗʰ Radio Squadron Mobile and is reprinted with permission.

At the earliest stages of the U.S. buildup in Vietnam, a system was needed to locate Viet Cong and North Vietnamese radio transmitters. Conventional ground-based Radio Direction Finding (RDF) methods proved difficult in attempting to locate low-powered enemy transmitters. The solution was Airborne Radio Direction Finding (ARDF)

The aircraft selected by the Air Force for its ARDF effort was the venerable C-47. The C-47 was a derivative of the DC-3 commercial airliner developed by the Douglas Aircraft Company. First built in the 1930's, the C-47 (Gooney Bird) distinguished itself as a transport in World War II, the Berlin Airlift, and the Korean War.

Prior to being sent to Southeast Asia, the planes had to be equipped with a multitude of electronic components so as to fulfill their mission. Thus was born the EC-47.

In 1966 squadrons were formed at Tan Son Nhut Air Base, Nha Trang Air Base, and Pleiku Air Base to conduct EC-47 ARDF operations. The flight crews consisting of the pilots, co-pilots, navigators and flight mechanics were assigned to the 360th, 361st, and 362nd Tactical Electronic Warfare Squadrons, respectively. The mission specialists, consisting of Morse Radio Intercept Operators, linguists, communications analysts, and equipment repairmen were assigned to the 6994th Security Squadron and its detachments.

The ARDF area of operation was South Vietnam, Laos (one six miles from the coast of North Vietnam), and later Cambodia. The Air Force ARDF program quickly demonstrated the capability to provide rapid determination of enemy locations and movements. Data was immediately transmitted to the ground where it was used to direct troop movements, artillery fire, tactical air strikes, and B-52 missions.

Later in the war, Nha Trang and Pleiku operations moved to Phu Cat and Da Nang Air Bases, respectively. In 1969 and 1970, EC-47 operations began at Nakhon Phanom and Ubon Royal Thai Air Bases (RTAFB). The last EC-47 mission was flown from Ubon in June, 1974.

Accomplishments:

During its eight years of operations in Southeast Asia, the 6994th made major contributions to building the intelligence picture of the battlefield in Vietnam. Countless commanders relied on Signals Intelligence (SIGINT) and ARDF reports when developing their battle plans. It has been alleged that 95 percent of the B-52 strikes conducted in Vietnam were based partially or in full on information provided by the 6994th.

One report of the effectiveness of the EC-47 came during a conversation between General William W. Momyer, the Commander of the 7th Air Force and Colonel Robert G Williams, Commander of the 460th TRW in May of 1967. Colonel Williams quoted General Momyer as saying:

"I want all of the personnel in this mission to know that the primary and basic source of intelligence in this country comes from COMPAS DART [The ARDF mission]."

The 6994th Security Squadron was recognized for its cryptologic excellence in 1969, when it won the Travis Trophy from the National Security Agency (NSA). The Travis Trophy is presented annually to the Service Cryptologic unit judged to have made the most outstanding contribution to NSA's mission during the previous calendar year.

In a message to the Commander, USAF Security Service, the Director of NSA stated:

"Information has been brought to my attention relative to an exceptional SIGINT contribution which was made by personnel of the 330th RR Co, and the 6994th Security Squadron in South Vietnam. It is noted that through the combined efforts of personnel in these units, timely and very vital intelligence information was made available to tactical commanders which contributed directly to the engagement with elements of the PAVN 325C Division on 10 May 1968. Further and more important, U.S. forces incurred very light casualties because of their knowledge of the situation

as derived from SIGINT." It was noted that this engagement took place within 800 meters of an ARDF fix made on 6 May 1968.

The NSA director continued:

"The efforts of all those involved in the production of SIGINT information which results directly in the saving of U.S. lives is deserving of the highest praise and I take this opportunity to extend my sincere gratitude and recognition for a job well done to those men involved."

Below is a photograph of two of our EC-47s in flight. The black nose on these aircraft distinguishes them from the heavily armed AC-47s used for firing machine guns and cannons at targets on the ground.

This is a ferry flight - we normally flew solitary missions.
(Courtesy: Rick Yeh, Webmaster of the 6994 RSM website)

The C-47 is a much-loved military aircraft; it is rugged, durable and trustworthy. It even operates well with just one healthy engine. Originally designed as a commercial passenger aircraft, first flown in 1933, the DC-3 was renamed "The Sky Train" when manufactured for the U. S. Army Air Corps. Military personnel are notorious for using nicknames, and the C-47 was no exception. Its nickname, "Gooney Bird," has lasted so long there are few who even know the original, government-mandated name. Whether configured as a regular C-47, an EC-47 or an AC-47, it is always a Gooney Bird. The name comes from an albatross found in the North Pacific Ocean that appears ungainly on land and in the process of getting airborne, but is a great flyer. I never met even one Gooney Bird crewmember who did not like and respect the capabilities of that aircraft.

I don't want anyone to think that I was a hero in the Vietnam War – I wasn't. In general, I remember the heat, the constant noise of aircraft and generators, the continuous threat of attack, the C rations for food and the loss of dignity with regard to biological functions and personal hygiene. I will relate a few incidents to provide a general view of what my time there was like, but please keep in mind, my experience pales to insignificance when compared to the troops who lived and died in the jungle or in prisoner of war camps.

The First Day:

A rude awakening on my first night in Nha Trang made me think that I had made a mistake when I volunteered for Vietnam service. My bunk was in a large room in the building on Airport Road. I had two roommates; both were Navy Chief Petty Officers. At about midnight, I woke to the sound of mortar[13] shells exploding on the runway. I jumped up, put on my boots and started to lace them up when one of the Chiefs asked me where I was going. I told him I didn't know but I was going to have my boots on when I got there. He laughed and told me the Viet Cong never fired more than five or six rounds before they took off running; he was right. Only five rounds landed and it was quiet again. The chief could have warned me what was going to happen next but he was having fun with the NUG. I had just gotten back to sleep when I heard an explosion that was close enough to shake the building. "Damn! What the hell was that?" Again, the chief calmly told me to relax. He explained that whenever the VC fired a few mortars at the base, the South Vietnamese Air Force would send up a couple of A-6 aircraft[14] armed with five hundred pound bombs to try to get the mortar crew, but never did. What I had heard was a

13   A mortar shell is a small, explosive projectile fired from a tube a short distance from the intended target.
14   A small, propeller driven, World War II vintage, fighter/bomber.

five hundred pound bomb exploding several hundred yards away and the sound was frightful. I can't imagine what it sounded like where it landed. Right then, I wondered how I would be able to survive a whole year of this. I wasn't a soldier or a marine; I was an Intelligence Analyst in the Air Force who was supposed to contribute to the war effort by using my brain.

The Viet Cong concentrated their mortar attacks on the aircraft parking areas and the motor pool. They believed the destruction of equipment and supplies was more worthwhile than the destruction of lives. They got lucky one evening and hit one of our C-130 aircraft parked on the apron. The C-130 was one we called the "Blackbird." It was modified for the extraction of downed crewmembers from behind enemy lines and was painted completely black instead of the common camouflage treatment. Their dangerous missions were very complicated. They had to fly over enemy territory, locate the downed airman, and drop a special harness and inflatable balloon used in the rescue. The downed airman had to climb into the harness and then inflate and release the balloon, which was connected to the harness by a cable. When the balloon rose to about 1,500 feet, the C-130, equipped with a "V" shaped boom that extended from the nose of the aircraft, snagged the cable connected to the airman and lifted him from the ground. Another mechanism, controlled from the open door at the rear of the aircraft, engaged the cable, attached it to a winch and pulled the man into the cargo bay. One of the crewmen actually asked me if I wanted to be picked up in a training operation so I would be familiar with the procedures in the event I needed to be rescued; I declined.

The Blackbird was always filled with fuel as it sat on the apron waiting to be launched for a rescue mission. During the attack on November 25, 1967, a VC mortar team got lucky and a mortar round hit the aircraft in one of its fuel tanks. The fire was immediate and began to spread to other aircraft. When the round hit, a flight mechanic was performing some maintenance work on his aircraft, a C-123, parked next to the Blackbird. Flight mechanics are just that – mechanics. They are not pilots but they spend so much time in the cockpit, many of them learn how to operate an aircraft. The mechanic in the C-123 had every right to run for cover; however, he chose to save his aircraft. Risking his life, he started the engines and taxied the C-123 away from the burning C-130. I viewed the scene the next morning. There was nothing left of the Blackbird except the remains of the four engines. They were being scooped up by a front end loader to be trucked to the scrap yard. The charred area on the apron told me the C-123 was doomed if that flight mechanic hadn't taken the action he did.

Day to Day:

Once I settled in to a day-to-day routine, I began to believe I could survive my tour of duty. Another analyst, Technical Sergeant Harry Calendar, and I both worked for Dick Cheney. The three of us became good friends and shared some comical and scary times together. They were the ones who taught me the local jargon so I didn't sound like a NUG anymore. VC was short for Viet Cong, the bad guys in South Vietnam. We more often referred to the VC as Charlie, the phonetic alphabet word for the letter C. We called any Vietnamese who was not a Charlie, a Zip. Where that nickname came from is a complete mystery to me. Indian Country was any area where the VC operated or held sway with the populace. Vietnamese criminals and thieves were called Cowboys. Again, the derivation of that name is unknown to me. We derisively called American troops stationed in Saigon, "Saigon heroes" because it was a well-protected area. Of course, everything is relative; the troops in Pleiku and Hue Phu Bai may well have referred to us as Nha Trang heroes. I discovered the weight reducing Vietnam Diet. The consumption of C-rations is a sure way to lose weight. I weighed one hundred and fifty pounds when I arrived and about one hundred and forty when I returned.

The United States government's idea of food for men in combat is something that can't be forgotten by those who had the dubious pleasure of being the consumers. Each case of C-rations was supposed to hold a variety of twelve different menus. Someone else must have gotten the other eleven menus because the only entre I ever found was canned pork and beans. I did make full use of the one-inch high cans of peanut butter and jelly often found in the boxes of rations. My favorite meal was to open a can of bread and remove the contents, which had so much preservative it felt and looked oily, and use the can to mix the peanut butter and jelly. When completely mixed, I spooned some onto the bread and ate my delicious concoction. There were lots of canned peaches and pears too. In each packet there was also a little box of four, non-filtered cigarettes. I remember Camels, Lucky Strikes and Chesterfields, among others. The cigarettes were stale, but we smoked them if we had nothing else.

In each case of individual packets of C-Rations, commonly referred to as C-Rats, were several can openers called P-38s. The can opener, an ingenious device designed in 1942 for the U. S. Army and catalogued as "Opener, Can, Hand, Folding, Type 1," was used by GIs as a tool for all sorts of jobs. No one knows for sure how the name P-38 originated. Some say it comes from the fact that it takes thirty-eight twists of the hand to cut out the top of a C-Ration can. I never counted the twists so I can't be sure. Below is a photograph of the practical P-38 with instructions for use. The hole in the opener was used to thread it onto dog tag chains.

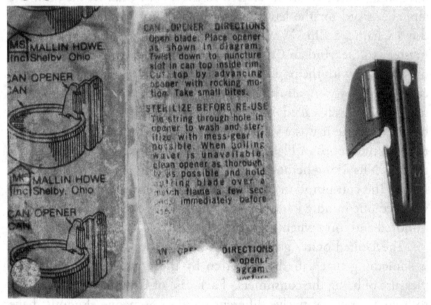

The famous P-38 (Photo by Author)

By the time the war ended in 1975, C-Ration cans and P-38s littered all of South Vietnam. Zippo cigarette lighters also littered the place. In those days, most of us smoked cigarettes and carried the basic Zippo cigarette lighter. The local Vietnamese were skilled at etching designs and words on the lighters, and most of us had that done. Mine, which I still have, simply has aviator wings etched on one side and

"Nha Trang, Vietnam, '67-'68" on the other. A favorite inscription of some of the troops who spent most of their time in the jungle mixing it up with the Viet Cong was, "Yea, though I walk through the valley in the shadow of death, I fear no evil, because I am the evilest one in the valley." Surely, Zippos so inscribed must have fallen from the pockets of many of the fifty-eight thousand who died in that country.

Shortly before I arrived in Vietnam, Dick Cheney and some friends were at a restaurant in Nha Trang that supposedly was a safe place to eat. Actually, there were no safe places in Vietnam. That evening, a VC operative detonated an IED[15] hooked to the outside of the flimsy wall of the restaurant. Dick, hit from behind, got some shrapnel in one ear but his best friend, Technical Sergeant Fred Sebers, received a wound to his head. Just a few days after Dick and I started working together, we received word that his friend had died from his wounds while being treated at Madigan Army Medical Center in Fort Lewis, Washington. Dick's story about that evening may have saved my life. About a month after I arrived in Vietnam, my Navy Chief roommates invited me to join them at a downtown restaurant for a meal. They assured me it was a safe place, but remembering Dick's experience, I declined. At about eight that evening, I heard a loud explosion; as I wondered about it, someone else in the house said, "Some poor guy just bought the farm." [16]

His statement was prophetic. A VC had ridden by the restaurant where my roommates were and hung a Claymore mine[17] on the wall which he remotely detonated a few seconds later. The shrapnel wounded one of my roommates in the hand, missed the other one completely, but hit the man sitting across from him square in the face. I remember my roommate saying, "Man, I could see his face disappear and I knew I should try to help him, but I was afraid there would another explosion, so I dove for cover instead. I still feel bad about that, but it was what I did." The VC would often set off an IED and then wait for rescue personnel to arrive before detonating a second bomb. The guy across from my roommate died that evening. Those Chiefs told me I was

15   Improvised Explosive Device.

16   World War II GI expression suggesting the insurance from a deceased soldier will pay off the mortgage on the family farm.

17   This is an American weapon that is shaped to direct shrapnel into personnel when fired.

lucky, because it could well have been me sitting across from them had I accepted their invitation.

Just after Christmas in 1967, we had to abandon the house on Airport road and find new quarters. I found a place that was next to an elementary school. Although the sound of the Vietnamese language is still annoying to me, the sound of the children singing at recess did give me a good feeling whenever I was around to hear them. The bad part about the new place was the cockroaches and other crawling things. We had our fair share of lizards climbing on the walls and ceilings that ate many of the offensive creatures but they couldn't eat all of them. I used a mosquito net when I was sleeping to keep them away from me. The problem was, roaches home in on carbon dioxide and moisture in exhaled breath and gather on the mosquito netting near the source. Many times, I would awake in the middle of the night to the sight of dozens of cockroaches just inches from my face. A simple slap of the netting would send them flying off to hunt elsewhere but it was disturbing. I didn't mind so much when I awoke lying on my back because they would be six to eight inches away; but if lying on my side, I could see them clinging to the netting only an inch from my face - a disgusting sight. Like everything else over there, I eventually got used to the roaches.

We analysts flew on missions from time to time but mostly we analyzed intercepted messages and tried to break codes. We were moderately successful and were able to identify and locate many enemy units through the use of the ARDF equipment. Below is a photograph of yours truly just before a mission. I'm the guy on the right wearing the hat. The other guy is Technical Sergeant Fitzpatrick (deceased); we all called him "Fitz." You can see that we are not wearing the one-piece flight suit normally seen on crewmembers. At that time, flight suits were made of a material that did not wick the sweat away from one's body and it was very hot and humid in Vietnam. Crewmembers had discovered that the jungle fatigues were much more comfortable and they became the normal uniform for most of us. The survival vest and parachute harness added to the discomfort caused by the climate. We did not wear our chest pack parachutes while in flight, but kept them nearby. We could snap the chest pack on to the front of the harness in a matter of seconds.

Fitz (left) was a really nice guy. (Courtesy: Richard P. Cheney).

Not long after this photograph was taken in late 1967, one of the Army cryptanalysts broke a North Vietnamese Army code and for a while, we were able to read many intercepted messages. One message in particular caused crewmembers to revert to wearing the uncomfortable flight suits. A very high echelon official in Hanoi sent a message to all units telling local commanders not to kill any captured American flyers. They were instructed to send them to the prisoner center in Hanoi. The message went on to explain that flight personnel could be distinguished from ground personnel by their one piece uniform which contained many zippered pockets. They were also instructed to feed captive crewmembers twice the amount of rice rationed to them, because Americans were normally larger than Vietnamese and required more food. Without divulging the source, this information was distributed and crewmembers quietly reverted to wearing the uncomfortable flight suits. The next photograph provides an example of the regular, old fashioned, one piece flight suit.

The one piece flight suit was not comfortable in Vietnam.
(Courtesy: Richard P. Cheney)

Cryptanalysts, by the nature of their business, tend to be different from the rest of us, and the one who broke the code that gave us the uniform information was no exception. We contacted his organization in Pleiku and asked for an explanation of his system to read the messages. After several attempts, the analyst sent a message to tell us he knew how to read the code but could not put it into words. My Operations Officer told me to catch a hop to Pleiku and learn firsthand how to read the code. I told him that if I did that, I would be returning with classified information over enemy territory, which was not authorized. The Captain told me to go anyway and said if I got shot down with the information in my possession, he would deny he ever authorized the trip. Things are done much differently in a combat zone than in other places. I caught a hop to Pleiku and spent a couple of hours with the cryptanalyst. He explained the system and I had no trouble putting it into words. When I was finished, I asked him why he couldn't have done that instead of causing me to come to a place that was more dangerous than Nha Trang. He told me he was really good with numbers and codes but had a hard time with writing about what he knew. I stuffed the notes into my pocket and caught a flight back to Nha Trang. We were able to read intercepted messages sent in that particular code for several months. One decoded message sticks in my mind. It was to a very low echelon commander and contained directions to a cache of buried weapons. The commander was told to pass under a specific bridge in his boat, land on the beach after completing the third left turn, find the bloated body on the beach, proceed one hundred meters to the North and dig until he located the "package." It was then I realized that the reason they were using such an unsophisticated code; it had to be understandable at the lowest level of command.

Jungle Survival School in the Philippines:

Those anonymous people working at the Personnel section of Headquarters, knowingly or unknowingly, did a favor for the men in my unit who were on flight status. Each crewmember flying combat missions in Southeast Asia had to attend the Air Force Jungle Survival School located on Clark Air Force Base in the Philippines. Fortunately, they shipped each of us to Vietnam without fulfilling the requirement. This situation necessitated a trip out of the war zone for a week of training. It was a welcomed break. I took my training during the first week of December 1967. Arriving at Clark Air Force Base was a wonderful feeling. Everything was clean and neat; there was no enemy activity; and I had a full day and night at a nice motel before my class convened. I found a telephone center and called Sylvia, which gave us great joy. I then called Harold Taylor, a long time friend of Sylvia's parents, who was the civilian safety and security advisor for the base. He invited me to have dinner with him and his wife, Conchita, once

I finished my training. My orders gave me two extra days after the jungle survival training ended so I was able to accept his offer.

The jungle survival was nothing like the worldwide survival taught at Fairchild Air Force Base. The attitude of the instructors was serious but very relaxed. They were diligent in their instructions because they knew what they were teaching would enable us to survive if we found ourselves on the ground in Vietnam. A few of the instructors were guest speakers who survived shoot downs in Vietnam, partly because of their jungle survival training.

They taught us how to find the many sources of safe drinking water in the jungle. We learned which snakes were poisonous; most are not. They told us how to choose green vegetation to eat. I still remember the rule. Everything that is poisonous is bitter and only ten percent of bitter vegetation is poisonous. If you eat a spoonful of bitter vegetation and do not regurgitate in twenty-four hours, it is probably safe to eat. We went out into the jungle at the far end of the base and learned how to make a shelter from banana trees and the remnants of a parachute. I had the first hand experience of learning that the jungle floor is teeming with crawling things and large rats.

While chopping down a banana tree with a machete, my blade bounced off a knot and sliced into the back of my left hand. Although the instructors had been adamant about reporting any injuries because jungles have uncountable numbers of infection producing bacteria, I simply wrapped the cut in a handkerchief and went on working. Later in the day one of the instructors saw the bloody handkerchief and raised cane about my failure to report the wound. He called in a helicopter to take me to the base hospital to have the cut cleaned and stitched. That was a new experience. The helicopter crew snatched me out of the jungle with a "horse collar" sling and took me to the hospital. The pilot landed at the hospital and arranged to pick me up at the same place at 6:00 A.M. the next morning for the return flight to the jungle training area.

I walked into the hospital to a depressing sight. On both sides of the hallway, gurneys with wounded troops from Vietnam stretched for several hundred feet. A medical airlift plane had recently arrived and the troops were waiting for processing and treatment. I did not hear a single complaint from these men who had every kind of wound imaginable. I felt a little embarrassed about my small, self-inflicted cut.

When I found an office with a medic inside, I stepped in and asked if he had time to look at a cut on my hand that happened in jungle survival school. He saw by the condition of my uniform that I had been living in the jungle for a few days and didn't question my story. He opened the homemade bandage and inspected the cut. This wasn't a doctor; he was an enlisted man with some medical training. He said he would have to scrub the area, apply medication and put in a few stitches and asked if I wanted my hand deadened for the procedure. I thought of those poor guys out there in the hallway, and then, my pitiful little wound; I told him to get on with the job without an anesthetic.

It did hurt when he scrubbed it and when he sewed the skin together but I controlled the pain with my mind. He bandaged my hand and I left the hospital through a side door without having to walk between the long lines of gurneys. Outside of the hospital, the first thing I noticed was the NCO Club, and it was a nice one. As I walked into the Club, the Sergeant-at-Arms directed me to the Stag Bar and warned me not to enter the main Club wearing my dirty fatigues. That was fine with me. The Stag Bar was a men only area where guys could wear fatigues or flight suits, drink, and use expletives without worrying about offending the fairer sex.

A delicious hamburger and a cold beer for supper sure beat the grass and leaves the guys in my class were eating that evening. After supper, I located the transit NCO quarters and got a good night's sleep on clean sheets. The next morning, the helicopter arrived at the pad on time and took me back to the jungle. It was daylight so he was able to land in a clearing and I returned to my group. It was the last day and night of the course and the subject was escape and evasion training. We were given the usual instructions, like stay below ridgelines, don't go into streambeds for water, don't use trails and, above all, maintain silence. Our pursuers were Negritos. Negrito is a Spanish word that means, "Little black person." They are small statured people native to Southeast Asia often mistakenly referred to as Pygmies. There are many tribes of Negritos in the Philippines, including the one that resided within the confines of Clark Air Force Base. The Air Force hired some of them as instructors in the jungle survival training. During the last phase of the training, their number greatly increased when they assumed the role of the enemy. Each crewmember in the course was given three hard plastic chits about three by five inches in size. Two chits were grey and one was red. At the end of the last day of training, the entire class ran into the jungle with instructions to evade the Negritos. If captured, the Negrito took one grey chit from the captive and released him. If captured again, the captor took the second grey chit and the game was over. The red chit was worth much more in payment to the Negritos. It was an emergency signal in the event a crewmember was injured and required assistance.

The Negritos could not capture us until after nightfall, but they had spies, invisible to us, posted all over the area to enable them to locate our hiding places without much effort. Most of the guys got captured twice; they never caught me. I made only a cursory attempt to hide during daylight; after nightfall, I gathered up my gear and left that spot. I made my way through the jungle toward the Negritos' base camp; it was easy to find because of the large campfire burning there. I worked my way into some thick vegetation away from the trails and quietly prepared for the night. Since this training was to help us in the event of a bailout over the jungle, part of our survival equipment was the silk from a parachute. I wrapped myself, including my head and face, and my gear over and over again, in the parachute. I had no problem breathing and the silk kept me warm. All night long, I could hear the Negritos coming and going as they captured crewmembers, discussed their plans and shared information. I was close enough to hear the crackling of the campfire. As experienced as they were at their job, they never once checked the area around their camp. I did not get much sleep that night; partly because of the commotion made by the Negritos, but mostly due to the rats on the jungle floor.

When there was no noise coming from the Negrito camp, I heard stirring in the litter on the jungle floor. The stirring stopped momentarily as the rat surveyed the opening in the vegetation created when I prepared my sleeping place. After a brief stop, the rat then bounded to the other side of the small clearing and went on its way. The rats continued to do this all night. They kept me awake because, as they scurried and jumped through the opening, some of them landed on me before bounding away. Without the protection of the parachute, I'm not sure I could have handled the situation.

The exercise ended at 6:00 A.M. the next morning when rescue helicopters flew into the area. The plan called for each crewmember to signal his location to a helicopter with a smoke flare. The helicopter would then hover over him and the trainee experienced the procedure of ground-to-air rescue with the horse collar and hoist. The Negritos were sitting around the remains of their campfire when I stood up, flare gun in one hand and swinging the chain with three chits with the other. They did not appreciate the big grin on my face at first, but after a few seconds, I noticed a few smiles. The rescue helicopter lowered the horse collar, which I promptly climbed into incorrectly. With hand signals, the hoist operator reminded me how to put it on correctly. I followed his instructions and he started the hoist. I waved to the Negritos as the mechanism pulled me upward and they waved back. As the operator pulled me into the helicopter, I thought, "This is fun but I sure hope I never have to do it for real."

At dinner with the Taylors in their home, I was introduced to another couple. I met the officer responsible for the security of Clark Air Force Base, an Air Force Major whose name now escapes me, and his wife. Both couples were very interested in my experiences in Vietnam and in the jungle survival training I had just received, and I was interested in the operation of such a huge base so there was no lack of conversation The Major told me he had established an excellent rapport with the leader of the Negrito tribe that resided on the base and that he employed members of the tribe as part of the base security force. Their employment was necessary because the Air Force Security Police were unable to control penetration of the base by a band of Philippine Communist guerillas who were stealing whatever they could find. It was a very large base with many remote jungle areas patrolled by military personnel in vehicles and on horseback, but the Communists continued to find entry points. As a last resort, the major contacted the leader of the Negrito tribe and offered to pay him if he could control the jungle-wise Communists. The Negrito leader agreed, and within a week returned to report that the problem had been solved. At the meeting he opened a cloth sack he proudly carried that contained the head of the Communist leader. The Major, a deeply religions Christian, was shocked and dismayed at the sight. He felt he was complicit in the killing and dismemberment of a fellow human being, albeit innocently. He told the tribal leader to refrain from killing intruders in the future and to simply capture them and turn them over to a military patrol. Somewhat hardened from my time in Vietnam, I thought the story was funny; but the Major, as he told the story, seemed still shaken by the experience. I wonder if he reported that incident up the chain of command.

I stayed on and chatted with the Taylors after the Major and his wife left. It was a nice change of pace for me to be in such cultured company and I enjoyed every minute. When the evening ended, Harold called for a taxi to return me to the transient NCO quarters. They promised to report to Sylvia's family that I had been a welcomed guest in their home and that I was doing fine. It was after dark when the taxi drove away from their house. I was surprised when we had to stop at a security checkpoint near the entrance to the compound that contained so many luxurious homes. The men staffing the checkpoint were well armed with automatic weapons and dressed in combat uniforms. The guards made it a point to be inconspicuous during the daylight hours, but were a commanding presence in the darkness. It struck me as sad that these homeowners had to resort to such stringent security measures when they were not living in a combat zone. A friend told me later that there were many places in the Philippines where it was dangerous to wander after nightfall.

The Secure Communications Project:

One of the problems with the ARDF program was communication between the aircraft and the Artillery Control Centers. Once we located the position of the target, it took time to encrypt the information, make contact with the Artillery Center, transmit the message, have it decrypted and send it to the operational artillery units. This processing time could give the target time to pack up and move if their commander suspected he had been located. It wouldn't take a very bright VC to figure out that an American aircraft, with strange looking antennae circling his position but not shooting at him must be triangulating with direction finding equipment. To solve this problem, our headquarters in San Antonio, Texas developed a secure FM voice communications system. The 6994th Security Squadron Commander at Tan Son Nhut Air Base at Saigon chose our Detachment as the first unit to install, test and implement the system. Our operations officer assigned me to function as the Vietnam area liaison for the pilot project.

We installed the equipment in our aircraft, the Army installed the ground equipment at their artillery centers and we tried to make the system work. There were many problems with the equipment and synchronizing the daily codes, but we kept trying. During one exchange of messages between me and my counterpart at the headquarters unit in Texas, I became annoyed with the tone of his writing. His final paragraph said something along the lines that if we are to be successful in our operations in Vietnam, we all have to work harder to make the new system work. As I replied to the first six paragraphs, which were all technical in nature, I became more and more annoyed about some faceless person, safely sitting in San Antonio, telling me to work harder when I'm in Vietnam getting shot at on a regular basis. I typed, "Re your paragraph seven – ridiculous." Before I sent the message to the communications center for transmission to San Antonio, I thought better of my statement and blacked it out from the original, but I failed to remove it from the carbon copies. The message was transmitted and I kept working on the project. As luck would have it, the first transmission was received in unreadable condition in San Antonio and they requested a retransmission. Because the original copy of all outgoing messages were sent to the Operations Officer, the operator in the communications center pulled the carbon copy of my message from the file for retransmission. The carbon copy did not have the "ridiculous" comment removed. This little communications quirk was to cause me some trouble.

A few days later, the Operations Officer, Captain Dickey, called me into his office and asked for an explanation for a nasty message he had received from San Antonio concerning my comment. A little research revealed how it happened and that was that as far as I was concerned. Some weeks later, Captain Dickey came into our Quonset hut and told me the Detachment Commander had called and ordered the both of us to report to the orderly room. I knew I wasn't due a promotion so I was really curious as to what the commander wanted. When I arrived, someone told me that the 6994th Commander from Saigon and the Pacific Security Region Commander from Hickam Air Force Base,

Hawaii, were in the Commander's office and wanted to interview me alone. At that point, I realized that everyone else, including Captain Dickey and the Detachment Commander, had faded away from the area. I was alone in the hut standing in front of the commander's door. A feeling of doom came over me. I thought something terrible must have happened to my family back in the states and I was here to receive the bad news. I knocked once and heard a gruff, "Enter."

I entered and saw two bird colonels[18], one seated at the Commander's desk and the other in a chair next to the desk. I guess I was supposed to know who was who, but I didn't. I walked up to the desk, stood at attention, saluted and said, "Sergeant Joyce reporting as ordered, Sir."

"At ease," snapped the colonel behind the desk. "At ease" does not mean, "take a seat and relax." To stand "at ease" is to stand at semi attention with feet spread apart and hands clasped behind one's back. He stared at me for several seconds before he said, "So, now I have a face to put on the famous 'ridiculous' remark." I've had it now, I thought. This guy is really angry. How did he know about that? My mind continued to race. When I made that comment, I didn't mean for it to be transmitted and if it were, I assumed it was going to a contemporary in rank. Now I was beginning to suspect that some Captain or Major or even a Lieutenant Colonel was the project manager at Headquarters, and he was not happy. The PSR Commander said, "Your smart aleck remark in the message you sent to San Antonio reached some very high levels. High enough that I got my butt chewed and that butt chewing is now flowing down hill. Can you explain yourself?"

I explained how the incident occurred; adding that I did, indeed, think it was ridiculous that some guy in the states was lecturing me when I'm risking my life every day. I had nothing more to add so I shut my mouth and stood there. I almost smirked when I thought, what are they going to do to me, send me home? The colonel sat there with his arms crossed and glared at me for several more seconds before he spoke. He said, "Joyce, I was sent here to administer counseling and punishment to you. You made plenty of people angry back at Headquarters. I'm not going to do anything because I agree with you, but you are going to tell everyone you know that I read you the riot act

---

18   The insignia for a full Colonel is an eagle. Referring to him as a bird colonel differentiates him from a Lieutenant Colonel whose insignia is a silver oak leaf.

and threatened to pull some stripes if anything like this happens again. Is that clear?"

"Yes Sir," I replied.

He went on, "I'm sure you noticed that there is no one in this hut but us. I arranged that so our conversation could not be overheard. If it ever gets out that I let you off the hook for this, I'll know it came from you, and then you'll see how angry I can become. Get out of here." I snapped to attention and saluted. He returned my salute; I did an about face and walked out of the office and the hut. All I ever said to anyone is that the PSR Commander really raked me over the coals for what I had done.

The project implementation continued and was successful, despite the aggravating remark from that jerk in San Antonio. We were soon able to communicate in a secure manner with the Artillery Centers within moments of obtaining the coordinates of a target. There is one lingering memory associated with the project that I just can't shake. While returning from a mission one evening after dark, I had the radio tuned to the FM frequency we used to call the Artillery Center in our operational area. The frequency was supposed to be dedicated for our use only, but I heard someone calling a ground station with clear, unencrypted voice transmissions. It was an Army helicopter pilot. He asked the man at the ground station how things were going. The operator on the ground replied that it was a bad day and he had six KIA[19] to be picked up and taken to a staging area. As I recall the helicopter Pilot's response, he said, "What? Are you crazy? You want me to land there in the dark just to pick up KIAs? You must be nuts. I'll come back at first light in the morning." Their unemotional, routine conversation when speaking of six men who had been killed in action gave me a sinking feeling. It sounded like the bodies were no more than pieces of wood lying on the ground. I pictured someone else speaking of my body the same way if I ended up dead. Death really had become common place.

A Flying Lesson:

One morning, while flying a mission, I looked forward toward the cockpit and noticed the co-pilot taking a nap. He was lying crosswise on the floor of the airplane behind the pilot and co-pilot's seats. In the co-pilot's seat was the flight mechanic, an enlisted man, and he

---

19   Killed In Action

was flying the aircraft. I had been told that pilots often let their flight mechanics fly the EC-47 after takeoff, but this was the first time I personally witnessed the activity. No one seemed to mind as long as the pilot did takeoffs and landings and supervised the flight mechanic. I was friendly with the flight mechanic on that mission, so after we landed, I asked him if he thought the pilot would let me fly someday. He assured me there would be no problem. Since I had input into who flew which mission, all I had to do was schedule myself to fly with that crew and he would convince the pilot to give me a lesson.

Some weeks later, while I on a mission with that crew, the pilot called me on the intercom and told me to come up front and take the co-pilot's seat if I wanted to fly the aircraft. Letting the flight mechanic fly the airplane was one thing - he had a lot of experience and would react well in an emergency; letting me fly was a different thing altogether. The rest of the crew probably didn't like the idea of a complete novice sitting in the co-pilot's seat while flying over enemy controlled territory. If the pilot were to be taken out by a lucky shot from the ground, I would have been next to useless in the cockpit. When people live with danger all day, every day, they tend to engage in dangerous and otherwise, ill-advised activities; this was one of them. As I climbed into the co-pilot's seat, it never entered my mind that I was increasing risk to the crew.

After putting on the headphones and tightening the seat belt, I put two hands on the yoke and looked to my left at the pilot. He asked me if I had ever flown an aircraft before. As he asked, I noticed he had pressed a button on his yoke, so I surmised it was the internal communications transmit button. I pressed a button on my yoke and said, "No Sir. I have never flown any kind of aircraft in my life." The pilot smiled as he responded that he didn't hear me because I had pressed the button that communicated with the ground controller. He told me to use the other button to communicate within the aircraft. Someone on the ground must have been laughing at the thought of a new guy receiving a flying lesson in a combat situation. We, or, at least, most of us, felt we were bulletproof.

The pilot then told me to keep my feet off the rudder controls but to hang on to the yoke because he was going to let go of his. The very first thing I did was try get the aircraft level with the clouds. That prompted the pilot to immediately tell me that I couldn't do that. He explained that the clouds aren't level with the earth and that every new guy tries the same maneuver. He pointed out the artificial horizon instrument on the panel in front of me and told me to keep the simulated aircraft level with the line bisecting the instrument and we would stay level with the ground. It wasn't difficult to stay level once I practiced for a few minutes. Next, he told me to turn to the left. As I turned the yoke to the left, the aircraft started to descend. He told me to pull back on the yoke, which I did, and the aircraft started to climb. Just when I thought I was doing fine, he pointed out that I had to keep watching the artificial horizon instrument while I was turning and pulling on the yoke. It was a "Eureka" moment. Flying was a lot more than just sitting there and steering the aircraft. The pilot explained again that all the new guys did the same thing when he told them to turn the aircraft and he knew of no better way to teach than to have the student actually make the mistake. He was right; I never forgot that lesson. He let me fly for about an hour and then suggested that I was ignoring my other duties and should return to my position in the rear of the aircraft. I thanked him and climbed out of the seat so the co-pilot could return, and the rest of the crew could quit sweating.

Riding Shotgun:

Vietnam duty was a twenty-four hour, seven day a week job. Every day was filled with duties and details. Before daylight one morning, I had the detail to ride shotgun to a pickup truck driver as he rounded up crewmembers for an early mission. As we turned on to the coast road, I noticed a large number of small Vietnamese fishing boats tied together floating on the bay just off the end of our runway. There were fifty or sixty of them from what I was able to tell in the darkness. As one of our EC-47s on a very early mission roared down the runway and then flew directly above us, I instinctively looked up. As I did, I saw tracer bullets heading toward the aircraft. I followed the line of tracers down to see the shooting was coming from a fishing boat in the center of the cluster. The driver saw the tracers, too, and slammed on the brakes. I jumped out of the truck and aimed my M-16 at the source of the fire, but in those few seconds, the aircraft was out of range and the shooting had ceased. I faced the decision of firing into a cluster of fishing boats at a target I could not see, or ignoring the incident. I knew that there must have been innocent Vietnamese civilians in the boats around the shooter's boat, just as I knew there were others who might have been complicit in the attack. I held my fire. If there is such a thing as psychological trauma, I suffered it that day; my indecision continues to plague me. The gunfire didn't hit our aircraft, yet I still struggle over the right and wrong of my inaction that morning.

Christmas Eve – 1967:

The day started out with a funny letter from my son. Clay was only five years old but was already able to print some words. I opened the envelope and found one piece of paper and a photograph. The letter said, "Dear Dad, I broke my arm. Love, Clay." The photograph showed him sitting in a chair, a big grin on his face, and a cast on his left arm. The letter from Sylvia that was also in my mail box explained that he had jumped out of his swing in the back yard and broke his forearm when he landed awkwardly. By the time I received the mail, all of his pain was gone and Clay looked so proud of his cast, I couldn't help but smile. The rest of the day didn't go so well.

Dick Cheney, Harry Calendar and I were working in one of our two Quonset huts at Camp McDermott around noontime when the crew from one of our early missions returned to debrief. The first thing one of the radio operators told us was that they had located a target not five miles away from where we were. We examined the data, and based on my analysis, concluded that a Viet Cong unit of about ninety men was approaching us, and in all likelihood, planned to attack. The next logical step was to inform the co-located Army unit.

The Special Forces unit commander, Major Fritts, asked me if I were certain the information was correct. I reminded him that intelligence gathering by its nature is not a solid science, but I was reasonably sure. He sent a couple of hundred troops to the area to engage the VC. At four o'clock that afternoon, I came in for a lot of good-natured ribbing from the Army. It seems I had erred in my analysis; the VC unit I had identified was, in reality, a four-man VC intelligence-gathering unit. I took the ribbing gracefully, but in the back of my mind was the thought of what could have happened had my misidentification gone in the opposite direction. If I had identified the VC as a small unit when it was actually a battalion, and the Army had sent out a Patrol instead of a Company, they would have been facing overwhelming odds. That thought shook me to my core. I am sure all of those guys have forgotten about the incident, but forty years later, as I write about it, I can still feel the weight of the decisions I had to make.

After the last mission had returned and the crew was debriefed, Dick, Harry and I went to the Army NCO Club to have a beer or two. It wasn't really an NCO club. It was a one-room shack with some stools, a bar and two tables. Behind the bar were some coolers where they kept the beer. Customers took their beer and were trusted to leave the proper amount of script[20]. As we sat there telling lies about other assignments, because I had heard enough about the afternoon's activity, we heard the telltale thump of incoming mortar fire. Maybe the VC were retaliating our killing the intelligence operatives in the afternoon, or maybe they just wanted to make their presence known on Christmas Eve; whatever the reason, they were sending presents over the wire to us. I don't remember if any words were spoken but we all headed for the door at the same time to run to the sandbag covered bunker that was right outside of the building. Dick and I made it out fine, but Harry got tangled in the wooden steps and yelped as he tumbled down. "Are you hit?" Dick shouted. Harry grumbled that he wasn't hit, but that he had twisted his ankle. We helped him to the bunker and looked at his ankle. It was seriously skinned and bleeding. Harry jokingly suggested he put in for a Purple Heart the next day. We began drafting the mock citation to go along with the medal. When we got to the part that we had consumed some beer and Harry stumbled down steps of the NCO Club, we started laughing because we knew that application wasn't going to be submitted. The mortar attack only lasted a few minutes and did little damage. We climbed out of the bunker and waited for the night shift to arrive. When they did, we caught a ride back to our quarters. On some Christmas Eves, my mind wanders back to that one in 1967.

Back on the home front that Christmas, there were some changes. Sylvia's parents had visited her and the children often since I left in September but she was still very lonely. She was also worried about her mother and father making so many trips through the San Antonio traffic to visit her. She expressed those feelings to her parents while they were together for

---

20   We used military issued money called script instead of American bank notes.

Christmas Eve. Her mother and father suggested she put our furniture in storage, rent out the house on Paradise Valley and move in with them until I returned. Sylvia agreed and moved in with them within a few weeks. She turned the house over to a rental agent who had no trouble keeping it leased. Those seven months living with their grandparents established a special bond between Kelly and Clay and Sylvia's parents.

Jackie's Bar:

As suggested earlier, when one lives in a war zone every day, there is a tendency to forget about routine dangers. Dick and I had fallen into that state and took chances we might better have avoided. This story is presented as Dick tells it to friends; I am not as clear on the details as he is. There was a rundown building not far from the edge of the base that housed a place known as Jackie's Bar. How the Vietnamese lady who ran the place got the name Jackie is lost to history. There were a few tables, some chairs and a reel-to-reel tape recorder that played American music. There was warm local beer (reported to be laced with formaldehyde for an extra punch) that tasted terrible, but it was a change in routine, so once in a while we would visit the place. It was off limits after dark but the military police were forgiving to some degree when it came to raiding the place.

One evening, Dick, the Operations Officer and I were drinking beer in Jackie's long after dark fell. Through a window, I noticed a military police jeep approaching the building. It was obvious to me that they were going to check for Americans who might be in the place during off limits hours. As I went through the window, I shouted "MPs" to the others but they couldn't get out in time. Dick and the Captain were stuck inside and had to come up with a story. The Captain realized he could be in big trouble for being in an off limits place and fraternizing with NCOs. When confronted by the MPs, he started to stammer, so Dick jumped in with his usual political acumen and came up with a reason for their presence. He told the military police that there was a rumor in our outfit that some of the troops had been visiting Jackie's after the allowed hours, and that he and the Captain were sitting there waiting to catch them as they entered. The police sergeant rolled his eyes as if to say, "Yeah, sure, I believe that." As he returned their identification cards, he told them it wasn't their job to check on Jackie's and suggested they get in the Captain's jeep that was parked alongside the building and go back to the base. As they walked toward the door, the MP Sergeant said, "By the way, don't forget to pick up your Buddy who went out of the window when we pulled up." It seemed we had dodged yet another bullet and Dick had bailed out the Captain. While discussing the incident later in the evening, Captain Dickey confirmed that they really did teach him the earlier mentioned lesson that, "All enlisted men are stupid, but some are crafty and bear watching" when he was in Officers Training School.

The Tet Offensive:

Millions of words have been written and spoken about the 1968 Tet[21] offensive in South Vietnam; I, like everyone else in Vietnam, was affected by the experience. Overall, I have to say that during the offensive I was often confused as to what was happening anywhere beyond a few hundred yards from my location and spent a great deal of time simply trying to stay alive.

The war in South Vietnam was ebbing and flowing with heavy casualties on both sides. Our bombing campaign on North Vietnam had crippled their economy, so political forces in the North decided to implement an offensive suggested by the Viet Cong leadership early in 1967. The politically powerful leaders in the North were convinced that, with the implementation of the offensive, there would be a popular uprising of most of the citizens in South Vietnam and the Americans would be defeated. The plan called for a simultaneous attack on 36 provincial capitals and over 100 other towns during the early morning hours of January 31, 1968. They chose this date because they knew people would be celebrating their New Year Holiday and would have compromised defenses.

The plan called for a probing action on January 30 to assess our reaction to simultaneous attacks. I was at Camp McDermott early that evening, debriefing returning crews when the teletype machine connected to our organization in Saigon began to clatter. I got up and read the message. The operator had simply typed, "Incoming mortars, going to bunker." While I was reading his message, I received a similar message on the other teletype machine from our organization in Pleiku. How strange is that? I thought,

21   Tet is the name of the Vietnamese New Year holiday.

just as a mortar shell exploded not far from my hut. I didn't bother to tell the guys in Saigon and Pleiku that I was getting hit too; I just headed to a bunker. After the attack, I chatted with the faceless guys at the other end of the teletype machines about the coincidence. The best we could figure was that the VC were sending us a message that they were capable of coordinated attacks. Those three little attacks were nothing compared to what was going to happen the next day.

After being in Vietnam for several months, I had come to learn that when the local people disappeared from the streets and yards, or if a power outage occurred, there was a good chance that an attack of some sort was imminent. Neither of these things was happening when I returned to my quarters on the evening of January 30th. To the contrary, the streets were full of people preparing for the holiday. Old timers had told me that there would be a great celebration at midnight, so I stayed awake to witness the festivities.

At midnight, tremendous amounts of celebratory fireworks ignited and people all over the city fired their weapons into the air. The Viet Cong also started firing their weapons, but not into the air. They initiated a mortar and small arms attack on the city. With all of the noise created by the celebrating citizens, it took a while for anyone to realize an assault was underway. My first realization came when I saw American helicopter gunships firing at targets on the ground not far from where I was standing. Nha Trang was the first city attacked. At about two o'clock in the morning, attacks began all over the county. The Viet Cong never assaulted my compound with ground troops, and by dawn, the helicopters had driven them away from my location. I was out of communication with my unit and had no idea of what had happened. I could hear sporadic small arms fire and minor explosions, but there was not a soul on the streets. I ventured out in hopes of catching a ride to the base or Camp McDermott. A few steps from my building, I saw a South Vietnamese guard hunkered down behind a mini bunker. In front of him I saw what appeared to be two piles of dirty rags; the two piles were actually the bodies of two Viet Cong soldiers; the guard had killed them some time during the night as they tried to enter my compound. I knew if I asked him the typical new guy's question, "Are they VC?" the answer would be, "They're dead, aren't they? They must be VC." That's how it was; if it was a Vietnamese and it was dead, it had to have been a VC.

I stepped out from behind the bunker when I saw a blue, Air Force pickup truck racing up the dirt street. The pickup slid to a stop and as I jumped into the bed, another American, who I had not been aware was near me, jumped out from behind a low wall and climbed into the truck. As we raced toward the base, I kept wondering how I could have missed the guy hiding behind the wall. If he had been a Viet Cong, I would have been an easy target.

We made it to the base without incident and I caught another ride to Camp McDermott. Once there, I learned that similar attacks had occurred across the entire country. Our aircraft launched and flew out to find targets. With messages coming and going, crews to be debriefed and the analysis of raw intelligence, the day flew by in a blur. Late in the afternoon, we were informed by our Army hosts that they anticipated an attack on Camp McDermott some time during the evening or early morning. Captain Dickey asked for volunteers to be on hand to destroy classified information in the event the camp was overrun. At Dick Cheney's insistence, the captain eliminated all married men from the group solicited for volunteers except Dick, Harry Calendar and me. The three of us had worked closely together for many months and the captain knew we were dependable and efficient. Dick, Harry and I, along with seven single guys, volunteered and the rest of the unit departed for the air base which was very well guarded. After the last crew was debriefed, we organized all of the material and equipment that might require destruction. During that process, Captain Dickey came into our hut and asked for volunteers again to make a trip to the air base to pick up some steel helmets and ammunition. Dick Cheney and I volunteered. I never knew why Dick stepped up, but I volunteered because I wanted to be sure that I had a steel helmet and my share of ammunition.

We put on flak jackets and drove off in a jeep. Dick drove and I rode shotgun. It was dark and the ominous sounds of small arms fire and explosions in the distance made it a scary trip. The worst thing that happened was when we were stopped by the notoriously trigger happy South Vietnamese Military Police at a checkpoint. They thought we were crazy to be on the road but waved us through after recognizing us as Americans. We made it to the base and back to Camp McDermott with the helmets and ammunition clips without incident. We weren't even stopped by the South Vietnamese on the return trip; they had abandoned the check point for safer pastures. Captain Dickey told us we were great guys to volunteer for that mission. Dick and I didn't think it was a big deal. I got what I wanted - a helmet and pockets full of loaded M-16 magazines.

When the attack came, it was minor in scope. It started with incoming mortar shells. We all ran out of the vulnerable Quonset hut and headed for the bunkers. For some reason, everyone else ran to the left and I ran to the right. I found myself alone in a bunker with an M-16 and no other help. The bunker was made of half moon shaped pieces of heavy gauge steel covered with sand bags. When a round hit the bunker roof at the other end from where I was sitting, the sound was deafening. When I could hear again, I heard someone from a machine gun tower shout, "I think they're in the wire," followed by hundreds of rounds machine gun fire.[22] All I could do was to sit with my M-16 aimed at the bunker opening and hope they didn't get through the wire; they didn't. When it got quiet again, we left the bunkers and exchanged stories. Dick Cheney tells a story about tripping over Captain Dickey who was dodging real or imaginary fire as they raced for the bunker. We turned off the lights and settled down with a floor for a bed to wait for dawn. That was one hairy night.

The next day was a regular workday. Although we were silly from lack of sleep and dealing with the situation, we launched and recovered ARDF missions. The 5th Special Forces troops along with a Republic of Korea (ROK) infantry unit stationed nearby had pretty much saved the bacon of a bunch of Air Force troops not necessarily highly skilled in combat operations. It got quiet again and I made my way to my quarters. Soon after I arrived there, fire fights and helicopter attacks resumed. The activity wasn't too close; probably a mile away. We were armed, but not for serious combat. I only had my .38 caliber side arm and a .25 caliber automatic pocket weapon. Several of us were sitting on a walkway with a low wall protecting us when I had a wild idea. I asked if anyone had used the shower today. No one had. I was

---

22   In Vietnam, the Viet Cong and North Vietnam Army used Bangalore torpedoes to break through our concentrations of barbed wire. They are long pipes filled with explosives that can be shoved through the wire and detonated. This weapon was designed by an English officer in 1912 while stationed in Bangalore, India.

dirty, sweaty and just a little scared, yet I had an urge to take a shower. The opportunity to take a shower in Nha Trang was a rare thing. We didn't have hot water, but we had a tank of water on the roof that could be drained through a shower head after it had been warmed by the day-long sunshine. The first person to show up in the afternoon enjoyed something less than a cold shower, but not anything near a warm shower. This was my chance. I told the others not to run off while I was in the shower without telling me. The shower only took a few minutes. As I was returning, Dick aimed his camera at me so he could prove I was crazy enough to take a shower during a combat situation. The strange photograph is below.

The C-Ration diet kept me slim. (Courtesy: Richard P. Cheney)

Not long after my shower, a firefight broke out in the street just a few yards from us. We ran down the steps and to the courtyard gate to see if we could help. What we found was a perfect example of the "fog of war." Tracers were coming from both ends of the street, but it was dark and we could not determine who was doing the shooting. We had no idea which side was which. It could have been Viet Cong and Americans shooting at each other; Viet Cong shooting at Viet Cong, or Americans shooting at Americans. There was no way to determine which way to shoot, so we didn't. After a while, the shooting stopped and we returned to our perch on the second floor walkway to watch the helicopter gunships attack enemy ground units. That evening I observed an incident of bravery that remains clear in my memory.

There was sporadic ground fire by the Viet Cong trying to bring down our helicopters and the chopper pilots were having difficulty in suppressing the unit manning the weapons. The pilots came up with a plan to get the job done that was ingenious, but dangerous. Helicopter gunships normally operated with all lights extinguished while involved in a nighttime fire fight which gave them an advantage. That night, two pilots figured out that if one of them turned on running lights and headed toward the area of the ground fire, the enemy troops would open fire and expose themselves to the second gunship, flying behind the first with no lights. The ploy worked to perfection. The first gunship flew toward the ground with machine guns blazing and the Viet Cong answered with everything they had. As the first chopper peeled off to the left, the second gunship unloaded everything he had at the location of the Viet Cong shooters made obvious by the tracer bullets coming up from the ground, and eliminated the threat. The pilot of the lead gunship laid his life on the line to fool the Viet Cong into making themselves an easy target. I don't think I could have done that during my craziest moment while in Viet Nam.

The Tet offensive lasted from a few days to several months, depending on how quickly the enemy could be defeated in the many areas of activity. Over all, the estimated fatalities associated with the offensive were 3,400 – 6,000 American and 30,000 – 80,000 Viet Cong and North Vietnamese Army troops. A large number of civilians also died. The number of wounded on both sides was astronomical.

The aggravating attacks in the Nha Trang area lasted for a few weeks. During that time, some of us flew local area missions in aircraft of questionable airworthiness to locate mortar teams that were pestering both the Air Base and Camp McDermott. We were constantly feeding the Army information on Viet Cong infantry movements that enabled them to retake the city of Nha Trang. One memory that sticks in my mind is activity by the ROK (Republic Of Korea) troops. They had a "take no prisoners" policy and wanted the Viet Cong to know that. Whenever possible, they would dangle the bodies of Viet Cong troopers from power poles or anything else high enough to display their handiwork. The Koreans told us that these symbols of their ferocity caused the Viet Cong to bypass their locations for fear of similar treatment. I'm not sure I fully understand or appreciate this activity, but that is the way it was.

The U. S. Army appreciated our assistance during the Tet offensive. They singled out a few of us for award of the Army Commendation Medal. Dick Cheney, Harry Calendar and I were among the lucky few. When the paperwork reached the bureaucrats at our headquarters in San Antonio, they decided the U. S. Army could not award a medal to a member of the Air Force. They returned the paperwork to the U. S. Army Commander in the Nha Trang area (II Corps), a Brigadier General. That general promptly sent the paper work and the denial from USAFSS Personnel to the commanding general of the USAFSS with a request for approval. Our Commanding General overruled the Personnel department and awarded the medals to us. Although the Air Force also awarded the Air Medal and the Bronze Star to me, the Army Commendation Medal is extra special because it is so rare to find it on the chest of a member of the Air Force.

While working with the Special Forces unit, I met a man with a rare specialty. He was a highly trained sniper in a special category. He was an assassin and his targets were marked for termination by the CIA. He was a quiet, unassuming individual whose job was to execute specific individuals. He showed me a uniquely designed medallion he carried in his pocket and told me that it was something everyone selected for his job carried. I didn't know whether to believe him or not. There was no reason not to believe him, but I wasn't one hundred percent sure he wasn't just pulling my leg. I was to see an identical medallion many years later that convinced me he told the truth.

The skirmishes continued in the Nha Trang area for several weeks. Those of us living in enclaves organized a guard duty roster to ensure protection during the nighttime hours. I had an experience during that period that had a profound effect on me. It was around two o'clock in the morning on a very dark night in February of 1968 and I was on guard duty. Instead of sitting and watching, which could lead to dozing off, I chose to keep walking around the buildings occupied by Air Force personnel. As I slowly walked down a dirt path, a shot rang out behind me. Instinctively, I dove for cover in the foliage that lined the path. On the way down to the ground, in my mind, I said, "If anyone is controlling this world, I need help right now." Being an Agnostic, that was as close as I could get to a prayer. When I hit the ground and rolled under the bushes, that voice in my head said, "You can't count on anyone but yourself; quit praying for help." As I lay there, perfectly still, I pondered my dilemma. If I moved to try to get the sniper in my sights, he might be able to find my location and shoot again, but I couldn't lie there all night. Finally, I conjured up the courage to twist toward the direction of the shot and saw nothing but blackness. In all probability, the sniper thought he had hit me and took off in the opposite direction as soon as he fired the shot. This little incident of momentary prayer has given me pause to think about the cliché that there are no atheists in foxholes. For me, the conclusion is that abject fear will cause an otherwise non-prayerful person to reach out for any possible help when there isn't even a straw in the wind to grasp.

After the Tet offensive ended and the communists retreated to lick their wounds, activity reverted to normal. There was the occasional mortar attack on the Air Base and Camp McDermott, and booby traps would explode, but we settled into a routine. Just as we began to become complacent, the Viet Cong shot down one of our aircraft.

The Shoot Down of Brew 41:

Before I arrived in Vietnam, my unit lost an aircraft. Tide 86 was the tactical call sign of an EC-47 brought down by enemy ground fire on March 9, 1967 with the loss of the entire crew. Seven good men died that day. We were to lose another Security Service aircraft during my tour of duty.

I was on the ground at about eleven in the morning on March 11, 1968 when I received a teletype message from our unit at Pleiku. The operator told me that one of our missions, call sign Brew 41, had requested we at Nha Trang be notified that they were down at Dak To. I notified Captain Dickey and he began working on contacting the crew. There could be no reason to land at Dak To, a small Army base, other than mechanical problems. As we analysts scratched our heads trying to figure out how the EC-47 could have landed on a fifty foot wide, fifteen hundred foot long PSP[23] runway, Captain Dickey returned and informed us that Brew 41 had crash-landed after taking enemy fire. The entire crew survived with only minor bruises.

In addition to airframe and engine damage, the hydraulic systems on Brew 41 were inoperative after being hit by ground fire. The pilot, an old Lieutenant Colonel named Dobyns was able to keep the aircraft in the air just long enough to reach the Ben Het Special Forces camp at Dak To where he accomplished a crash landing. There was no fire and the crew was out of the aircraft within thirty seconds of its coming to a halt. Once it was determined it was safe to reenter the aircraft, the pilot and the two radio operators removed our classified documents and cryptographic equipment. They then proceeded to Pleiku where one of our other aircraft landed to pick up the crew and return them Nha Trang late in the afternoon.

A group of us greeted the crew on the tarmac with a few GI cans filled with iced down beer and one bottle of Champagne to celebrate their survival. One of the radio operators walked up to me and handed me the five-by-five inch, metal-clad cryptographic mechanism used to activate the secure air to ground communications system. It had dents but still appeared to be functional. Before I could ask anything, he said that he had tried to destroy it with the fire ax carried for that purpose before they crashed, but it was impossible. We both laughed because it was obvious the plan to destroy the item looked good on paper but didn't work when implemented.

I asked the radio operator about the shoot down. He told me everything was routine until he heard a loud clank and the aircraft shuttered. The other radio operator told the Aircraft Commander that he could see damage on the number one (left) engine. The Aircraft Commander requested a damage assessment from the crew and then called out a mayday situation on his air-to-ground radio. Dobyns was able to keep control of the aircraft for a while until the number two

---

23   Pierced Steel Planking used to construct short, temporary runways.

engine started to race out of control. In addition, the rounds from the 37 MM anti-aircraft gun had compromised the hydraulic system making the flaps inoperable, and caused the landing gear to drop down putting excessive drag on the aircraft that was already difficult to fly. In response to the mayday call, air rescue dispatched two Jolly Green Giant helicopters to the area in case of a bail out. A Forward Air Controller (FAC) flying a small, single engine O-2 aircraft joined the group and gave Dobyns a damage report from his perspective. Two A-1E Air Force fighter aircraft, we called them Sandies[24], flew up alongside Brew 41 to offer support. The lead Sandy Pilot said they would stay with the EC-47 crew whether they crash landed or bailed out of the aircraft. Dobyns told his crew to dump anything they could from the rear of the plane; out went the side door, the direction finding equipment, the radios, the typewriter, the spare parachutes and harnesses, the box of M-16s, the life raft and the box of psychological warfare leaflets carried as a cover story in case of capture. Every removable object except parachutes went out the door. Dobyns had to shut down the number two engine and, although the number one engine that took the brunt of the hit kept running, they continued to lose altitude. The FAC recommended a bail out because there were some high hills between their location and friendly territory. Dobyns told the FAC that it was too late to bail out because they were only 500 feet above ground level. Over the intercom, Dobyns then told the crew they were now too low for a bailout and to buckle up and hang on. The radio operator told me he could look up and see the fruit on the trees as they flew between the last two hills before they lined up with the PSP runway. Dobyns was a superior pilot and he made a controlled crash landing that destroyed the aircraft but saved the lives of the crew.

Colonel Dobyns struck me as somewhat of a caricature of an old time Air Force pilot. He was five eight or five nine, thin as a rail and had a classic Irish face. He had a quick, easy smile and wore his flight hat just far enough to the side of his head to be a little out of compliance with Air Force Regulations. To his crew, he was the hero who saved them from bailing out over enemy territory and got their fatally damaged aircraft safely on the ground.

The Squadron Commander gave the crew of Brew 41 a few days off

---

24   Slow flying, single engine, World War II era fighters used for close air support of ground operations.

from flight duty to recover from the physical and psychological impact of the shoot down. I happened to be monitoring the radio when they departed on their next combat mission. The same radio operator, who had related the story of the shoot down to me, called on the radio after takeoff and advised they were returning to base with an engine fire. He went on to request that the stand-by radio operator meet them on the apron to replace him on the mission. I spoke with the radio operator later in the day. He told me that, after being shot down and then having an engine fire on his next mission, he felt his number was up and didn't want to fly anymore. He only had three weeks left before his tour ended, so I was able to assign him to duty not involving flying (DNIF) for the remainder of his tour without telling anyone why. I think he may have mentioned my favor to another crewmember because I received a similar request some months later. We had a guy in the organization who was serving his third tour of duty and had over four hundred combat missions on his record. He came to me about three weeks before his scheduled return to the States and asked if I could place him on DNIF. He looked me square in the eyes and said that, after all those missions, he had a feeling he had pushed his luck too far. It was no problem to grant his request, and I never told anyone about the arrangement.

Writing parts of this story, all these years later, I relived that awful feeling one feels in his stomach when in danger and your body releases adrenaline. I could not have survived my time in Vietnam if I had felt that way all of the time. We have something in our psyche that enables us to adjust to constant danger, preventing the excess release of adrenaline. This ability is little different from the defense mechanism that allowed me to ignore the plight of the waifs I saw on the streets. If I had let those scenes tear my heart out, I would never have made it home.

R & R in Hawaii:

In World War II, the government sent troops overseas to fight against Germany, Italy and Japan. The length of their tour of duty was "the duration of the war plus six months." During the Vietnam War, it was different. For Air Force personnel, the tour of duty was one year. Each member was also afforded a six day Rest and Relaxation (R

& R) trip to a variety of areas. The destinations I recall are Australia (Sydney), Malaysia (Kuala Lumpur), Thailand (Bangkok) and Hawaii. There may have been others, but I was only interested in Hawaii. By visiting Hawaii, I could arrange for my wife to fly there from the mainland and be with me for five or six days.

For entrepreneurs in Hawaii, the visits of troops from Vietnam to meet wives and families from the mainland were a huge source of income. They leased thousands of condominiums and upscale hotel rooms to sublease on a weekly basis to those visitors. The troops didn't care what price was demanded. To get away from the war zone for a week and see one's family was invaluable. I made my arrangements for a one-bedroom condominium on the twelfth floor of a high rise building on Oahu and sent the information to Sylvia so she could arrange her trip. I scheduled my R & R to Hawaii for the second week in May of 1968.

Sylvia and I had coordinated the trip to the last detail. She was to meet me at the military arrival center at nine o'clock in the morning on May 7th. Murphy's Law[25] went into effect and last minute changes were made. For reasons unknown to me, someone rescheduled my aircraft to leave Cam Ranh Bay twelve hours earlier than originally planned. I caught a hop to Cam Ranh Bay and was able to get there in time to board my aircraft, but I ran into a glitch. After I handed my identification card and shot rerecord to the Air Force clerk at the counter, he told me my shot record was out of date and I needed a cholera immunization. I pleaded with him to ignore it because I had to catch my scheduled flight to Hawaii to meet my wife. He told me that he couldn't let me on the aircraft with an outdated cholera shot, but then, with a wink, he said there was a doctor giving shots behind the column across from the counter. I went behind the column, recorded a cholera shot in my shot record and returned to the counter. The clerk checked my documents again and directed me to the waiting area for my flight. It was just one more thing done in Vietnam that was against regulations.

It is a long flight from South Vietnam to Hawaii, especially when a stop in Japan is made to top off fuel. The trip took about ten hours and I was exhausted when I arrived twelve hours earlier than the original

---

25   If anything can go wrong, it will go wrong.

schedule. We were herded out of the aircraft and onto buses that took us to the military reception area where I assumed Sylvia would be waiting for me. As my bus pulled in to the off loading zone, I stared out of the window scanning the faces of wives anxiously waiting for their husbands to exit the bus. Finally, a pretty, young woman with long red hair caught my eye. There she is, I thought, just as some guy who had already climbed off the bus ran up and hugged and kissed her. Whoops! That can't be Sylvia, I thought. Everyone on the bus had someone waiting except me. Then I realized there was no way Sylvia could have been contacted and told of the new schedule before beginning her trip to Hawaii. I processed through the reception center and, at about ten o'clock at night, caught a taxi to the condominium, happy that we would have the extra hours together. Those hours were to evaporate.

I arrived at the condominium building with happiness in my heart and a smile on my face. I knew Sylvia would be overjoyed with my early arrival. I bounded up the steps to the entrance only to find a locked metal gate that prevented my entry. A sign told me the gate would reopen at six in the morning. Well, that makes sense, I theorized; they are trying to protect their customers. I saw an all night coffee shop across the highway and made my way there to use the telephone. All I had to do was, contact the owner who had rented the condominium to me and ask for the telephone number of Sylvia's room. She would be able to come down and let me into the building. The line was busy.

After an hour of getting a busy signal every time I called, I contacted the operator and asked if she could help. She checked the line and told me there was nothing wrong. I told her of my strange situation and asked if she could break in on the user and get the information I needed. She told me that my situation was not unusual, and that in all likelihood, the owner of the condominium had the telephone off the receiver to prevent being awakened. That was quite a situation. I was in a coffee shop at midnight looking at the actual building and floor where the wife I hadn't seen in over eight months was, and I couldn't get into the building.

There wasn't much business at the coffee shop at that time of night, and by now, the lady behind the counter was well aware of my situation. We agreed it was comical but not funny. I could only drink so much coffee but I didn't want to leave the area. I convinced the lady to let me curl up in a booth at the rear of the shop and try to get some sleep. Under any other circumstances, she probably would have called the police if some stranger wanted to sleep in the coffee shop, but I had won her over with my strange plight.

The night finally passed and at six o'clock I was at the gate when the maintenance man opened it from the inside. I took the elevator to the 12th floor, found the proper room number and knocked. A cautious voice asked, "Who is it?" I told her it was her husband and she said something like, "It better be," and opened the door.

We had a wonderful second honeymoon. I had also arranged for a rental car, so we toured wherever and whenever we chose. We visited an old friend, Bill Chapman, and his family stationed on the Island. It was as if there were no war and life was one unending party. All too quickly, the five days were over and Sylvia drove me to the departure area for my return to Vietnam. I knew I would be home in a matter of three or four months, so our parting was not as devastating as expected. Before I boarded the aircraft, I picked up a paperback book to read on the long voyage back. It was George Orwell's novel, Nineteen Eighty Four. The combination of leaving my wife and civilization, returning to the war zone and reading that overwhelmingly depressing book put me into a funk that was to last for weeks. At Cam Ranh Bay, I remember talking with an Army sergeant on his way to Hawaii to meet his wife. He asked me how my trip was. I told him the pain of having to come back to Vietnam almost outweighed the joy of seeing my wife. It took many weeks for me to get back to normal – Vietnam normal.

R & R in Thailand:

Dick Cheney and I were lucky enough to have a second R & R trip. In early July, near the end of our tours of duty, there were some cancellations for an R & R trip to Bangkok and anyone who could get permission from their commander could utilize the openings. Dick and I had the Commander's permission and we jumped at the chance.

As was the case in Hawaii, the free spending inclination of troops on R & R did not escape the entrepreneurs in Bangkok. The visitors to Bangkok were a somewhat different group than those who chose Hawaii as an R & R destination. The visitors to Hawaii were normally men who went there to visit their wives and families; the visitors to Bangkok were more interested in partying. The governments of the United States and Thailand knew that and planned accordingly.

After deplaning, they bused us to a securely patrolled reception center. Every passenger received a thorough briefing on how to act while in Thailand. We were assigned hotel rooms and given an introduction to Thai customs, advice on unsafe areas and a lecture on dealing with Bangkok's ladies of the night. The lecturer told us that the official position of both governments was for us to avoid these women at all costs. He then went on to say that he knew some would ignore his advice and explained how things worked in the Bangkok red light districts.

He told us that each woman in the sex trade was required to have identification and a matching government issued, circular, wooden chit with an emblazoned number. The city health department checked these women for diseases once each week. He cautioned us again about avoiding the red light districts, but strongly advised absolute avoidance of any woman not in possession of the described identification items. At the end of the lecture we boarded civilian busses that took us to our hotels.

The first thing I noticed was the driver sitting on the right side of the bus. I had never thought about which side of the road they used in Thailand; they drive on the left. He drove like a Kamikaze Pilot as he made his way through Bangkok's busy streets and byways. I wondered if I would die in Thailand instead of Vietnam; it was an adventure just to get to our hotel. When we pulled into the hotel's bus unloading zone, we were met by a bevy of men and women thrusting free glasses of beer into the open windows of the bus. Thousands of GIs had visited Bangkok before I arrived and the locals knew that the free spending men on R & R would spend even more after they had consumed some of the local brew. I don't know who paid for the beer and the servers. Perhaps a consortium of hotel owners, the chamber of commerce, the purveyors of jewelry for which Bangkok is known and the local bar owners paid for the service. I accepted a glass of beer that was warm and just a little bitter. I knew right then that I wouldn't be consuming a lot of that.

I enjoyed four days out of Vietnam and acted like a tourist. I found a fancy barbershop and got a decent haircut. I luxuriated in having warm showers and clean sheets. Dick and I met for a few meals and American beer at an NCO Club we located in the city and we took a paid tour to visit the sites listed in the tour books. I can recall two things about that tour. The one hundred and forty foot long, gold leaf covered reclining Buda at a temple called Wat Pho, and the visit to a snake farm where we handled and learned about the huge snakes of the region. I took another day to purchase and mail some sapphire jewelry and bronze dinnerware to Sylvia. At each jewelry establishment, we were met by an attractive young lady proffering glasses of cold beer. I drank some of the beer but didn't succumb to the temptation to over indulge.

On the evening before our return flight to Vietnam, Dick and I enjoyed a fine dinner at the NCO club. As we walked across a parking lot on the way to our hotel, a peculiar incident occurred. Not four feet away from us, the left rear tire of a parked car exploded. Without a word or a glance at each other, we simultaneously dove for the ground looking for cover; we had been In Vietnam too long. When nothing else happened, we looked at each other and started laughing. As old as I am, that was the first, and only, tire blowout I have ever heard, and it happened when I was gun shy. We must have looked ridiculous laying there on the asphalt parking lot. The next day we took the short plane ride back to Vietnam. Dick had only a few weeks left on his tour and I had just a few months.

The Return Home:

The clerks in the personnel assignments section at headquarters did another favor for me. They overstaffed my unit in Nha Trang. Maybe they were hedging their bets on how many of us would be killed and we fooled them. At any rate, because of the overstaffing, I received orders to proceed to my next duty station, San Vito Air Station at Brindisi, Italy, effective on August 1, 1968. That amounted to seven weeks taken off my one-year tour. I had done my duty and survived; now, all I wanted was to put the whole mess behind me. I turned in all of my flying gear, jungle fatigues and jungle boots to the supply section. I couldn't understand why others wanted to keep the equipment as souvenirs of their service. I retained two khaki uniforms, one pair of low quarter shoes, two sets of underwear and socks, and a hat. All I carried with me when I left Nha Trang en route to Cam Ranh Bay was an AWOL bag[26] containing the extra clothing and my shaving kit.

As I stood in line at the passenger terminal in Cam Ranh Bay, Staff Sergeant John Zornes was in front of me. John had all of his personal gear, all of his flight gear, a Montagnard[27] crossbow and a bunch of other items he had picked up over the past year. I told John that he was way over the forty-pound weight allowance, but he wasn't worried. He told me he had always placed his fate in the hands of Jesus Christ and that he was sure Jesus would solve his problem. When the clerk weighed John's baggage, he told him he would have to leave part of it behind. John turned to me and pointed out that, since all I had was an AWOL bag, maybe he could have some of his stuff assigned to me. The clerk agreed with the suggestion, and I didn't care, so John got all of his baggage on the plane. I hastened to point out to John that from now on he would have to consider me as being Jesus Christ in the body of J. D. Joyce. John did not appreciate my blasphemous comment but I thought it was hilarious and displayed my feelings with an uproarious laugh.

When we boarded the TWA aircraft, it was truly like stepping from one world into one another. Everything on the aircraft was clean and neat, and the aisles were filled with stunningly beautiful stewardesses wearing miniskirts. I was astounded and literally speechless. If there was an equal opportunity law in the sixties, the airlines paid it no attention. To be a flight attendant, you had to be female, very attractive and young. Once a stewardess had a few years on her, or added a little weight, she was discharged. When one of these women leaned down toward me and asked if I needing anything, I caught a faint scent of perfume and knew I was really leaving Vietnam.

The joy and happiness of the trip home abated just a little when

---

26   A small bag one might use when planning to be Absent Without Official Leave (AWOL) instead of a duffel bag which is much larger and would draw attention.

27   The Montagnards were members of an indigenous tribe of non Vietnamese that formed a reliable fighting force in the battle against the Viet Cong. This ethnic group has suffered severe repression and brutal treatment since the Americans left Vietnam.

we stopped to refuel in Japan. We were able to leave the aircraft and wander around the terminal for an hour. I noticed another group of men wandering around the terminal; they were fresh faced, young U. S. Army troopers on their way to Vietnam. They laughed and kidded each other the way young men do when trying to cover their apprehension. I knew as I watched them that some would return home in body bags, and others would return with wounds of varying severity. I felt sorry for them and the scene depressed me.

After boarding the aircraft for the next leg of our flight, my depression dissipated and I settled in for the long voyage to Seattle. Flying from the Far East to the west coast of the United States through many time zones can cause tremendous jet lag, but I was so happy and relaxed I was able to sleep a great deal during the flight. When we landed at SeaTac International Airport, I was wide awake and ready to continue my journey to San Antonio. I went to the Braniff Airlines counter and booked a flight that departed within the next two hours. Then I went into the men's room, shaved the stubble off my face, cleaned up as best I could and changed into the clean underwear and uniform I carried in my AWOL bag. I put the dirty uniform and my shaving kit into the small bag and placed it into the waste container. When I left the men's room, all the physical traces of Vietnam were behind me. I called Sylvia and gave her my scheduled arrival time. I talked with Clay, who was excited, and with Kelly. She didn't remember me because she was only three and a half when I left, but she told me she would know me from pictures she had. She said she would know me because I had "a point on my head." I found out later she was referring to my prominent widow's peak.

As my aircraft neared the San Antonio area, I explained to one of the stewardesses that I was returning from Vietnam and wondered if she could arrange for me to deplane first. She received permission from the captain and those in the first class section who would normally be the first to deplane. When the door opened, there were many smiles from the stewardesses and first class passengers as I stepped into the tunnel that took me to the terminal. As I entered the terminal, Clay ran away from his mother toward me and I could see Kelly, shyly hiding behind Sylvia's skirt. Sylvia's parents were also there to greet me. I saw more smiles from the deplaning passengers as they passed the members of my family hugging me. It was great to be back in a civilized world with my family; it was as if the tour in Vietnam had never happened.

Six months after I left Vietnam, I received a cardboard tube in the mail that contained an additional, informal award from the Commander of the 5th Special Forces unit with whom I worked for six months of my time in Vietnam. The certificate, displayed below, made me an honorary member of the 403rd Special Operation Detachment of the 5th Special Forces (the Green Berets). It was very nice to learn that the ground troops appreciated my efforts while we served together.

I proudly display this on the wall in my office. (Photo by Author)

Chapter 5 - Assignment Italy

After being where the action was for so long, I couldn't bring myself to go back to the old grind at Headquarters in San Antonio or NSA at Fort Meade in Maryland. I asked for an assignment to Europe and was given a two and a half year tour of duty at San Vito Air Station at Brindisi, Italy. Brindisi is located on the heel of the Italian boot on the Adriatic Sea. The weather is almost always great and there are plenty of opportunities to soak up Italian culture. Italy is a wonderful, inviting place populated by people who believe that living comes before working and family comes before everyone else. Those are good rules, if you can follow them, and for the most part, Italians do. They have a *domani* (tomorrow) attitude. Although the trip from Texas to New York, then to Rome and then via domestic Italian aircraft to Brindisi was long and tiring with our hand baggage and two children in tow, we looked forward to an enjoyable assignment.

We had a very nice sponsoring family and the unit gave us plenty of time to find accommodations on the local economy. Similar to our situation in Berlin, we had to live on the economy until I qualified for government quarters. What wasn't similar to living on the economy in Germany was the inconsistency of available of electricity and water. At any given time, water, which was not potable, would be turned off for a few hours to an entire day. The electric service was the same. Those living on the economy learned never to have an abundance of food in the refrigerator for fear of spoilage if the electricity was off for several days. Because we couldn't drink the local water, we always had five and ten gallon plastic containers of water on hand which we filled at the Base. We learned to keep the bathtub filled and a mop bucket handy to flush the toilet.

We rented a second story walk up apartment in a six hundred year old building near the docks. There were no other Americans living in that area so we had to use our wits to survive. Having had the experience of a bathtub in the kitchen in Berlin, we were not surprised to find the same layout in such an old building. We purchased a propane fueled kitchen stove from an American who was leaving Italy and Sylvia set out to make the place a home for us. As was the case in Berlin, we did not have television or a telephone, and we had only one vehicle. Sylvia had sold our car in San Antonio and we purchased a brand new Fiat 124 station wagon for $1,500. The Fiat was a little larger than a Volkswagen but not by much. Sylvia communicated with the Italian neighbor ladies by using her English-Italian dictionary, but that became dicey part of the time because some of the ladies were illiterate. Somehow, she made herself understood and the Italian women welcomed her with open arms. They especially took a shine to Clay and drove him crazy by pinching his cheek and saying, *"Chabello"* which means, "cute little boy." On one occasion, when they saw Sylvia spank Clay on the rump for something or other, they took great pains to tell her that one should never spank a boy child. They told her it was alright to spank Kelly, but to keep from breaking a boy's spirit, Italians never spank their sons. That gave us an insight as to why so many Italian men act like spoiled little boys.

A Death in the Family:

I was assigned as the Surveillance and Warning Center Supervisor on Able Flight and plunged into learning the units under our surveillance. The previous Supervisor had already departed and the Assistant who was running the center was happy to be relieved of the responsibility. He had only a few months left on his tour and wanted to leave unscathed. I had only been there about six weeks when I received word that my father had died and my mother wanted me to return for the funeral. I really did not want to go back for the funeral but some hidden sense of duty told me to make the trip. I was given an emergency leave, which carries a high priority for boarding military aircraft, and headed home. My assistant reluctantly took the reins of the Center and Sylvia assured me she could handle being alone for a week or ten days. She gave me a shopping list for some curtain rods and other things she needed that we couldn't buy in Italy, and sent me off to the funeral in North Tarrytown.

As can be imagined, my mother, who had lost her husband of forty-five years, was in shock. A wake and funeral very similar to Danny's took place. Again, I felt it difficult to experience grief. By now, I had been married for seven years and my entire being revolved around the care and protection of my wife and children. I do recall being somewhat overcome as we returned from the cemetery, but I think it was the reminder of the finality of death and its eventual application to my family and me that caused those feelings. My mother told me she was certain my father had died from the blow of losing Danny. Danny was killed in May of 1967 and I left for Vietnam in September of that year. According to my mother, Danny's death consumed almost every waking moment of my father's life; and when he wasn't speaking of Danny, he was expressing his fears about losing me. She felt the only thing that kept him from dying sooner was his desire to see my safe homecoming. She said that once he knew I was out of Vietnam, he lost his desire to live and died of grief over Danny's death. At the time, I was able to accept her explanation as valid when some of my sisters expressed their belief that she was correct. As mentioned earlier, I recently found that he had again succumbed to his addition to Morphine and may have died from an accidental overdose. Whatever the cause, his request to the nuns that they pray for him to die in his sleep rather than thank him when he did favors for them seemed to have paid off. On his last evening, he told my mother that he hadn't felt that well in a long time; then he went to sleep and died. I didn't waste any time after the funeral and returned to Italy with the unwieldy package of curtain rods. Sylvia had a great story to tell when I got home.

The large propane tank, called a *bombola*, used to fuel our gas stove had emptied and she decided to replace it without help. She drove to the *bombola* exchange store and traded in the empty one for a replacement. Getting the empty tank down the long, steep flight of stairs was not a problem for her, but carrying the full tank up those stairs was another thing altogether. With minor help from six year old Clay, step by step, she reached the top and dragged the tank into the apartment. The muscles in her arms would be sore for weeks to come, but that was to be least of her adventure. She hadn't noticed the rubber washer at the connecting point when she disconnected the empty cylinder and didn't notice the new one supplied with the full cylinder. She simply connected the hose as tight as she could and hoped for the best. She thought she should test the connection before trying to light a burner so she lit a match and held it to the joint. What occurred was a flame of burning gas from the washer less connection. In a panic, she chased the children out of the kitchen, soaked a towel with water and placed it over the flame. After lifting the towel to see if the fire was out, she saw it wasn't and concluded she needed help. She went to the Italian neighbor lady and dragged her into the kitchen to point out the problem rather than try to explain. Before long, the apartment was filled with several neighboring families to include husbands, children, grandparents and anyone who might have been visiting. She described it as an overflow crowd with every one speaking at once and shouting words she did not understand; but she was consoled by hearing laughter which told her the crisis was over. One of the Italian men correctly connected the gas tank and they all left with a funny story to tell their friends in the morning.

Day to Day Living in Italy:

Living in Italy and working at the 6917th Security Group left me with many wonderful memories. Soon after my emergency leave, I attended a Commander's call where I was awarded the Bronze Star for my service in Vietnam and a few weeks later I was promoted to Master Sergeant. That made me an official "fast burner."[28] I only had fifteen years in the Air Force and it normally took twenty to make MSgt. I got along well with my flight Commander and had a great crew of analysts under my supervision. The assistant S&WC Supervisor departed for the CONUS and I was assigned Technical Sergeant Dean Welch as an assistant. We got along well and he would eventually develop into a highly respected S&WC Supervisor on his own. The Italians were friendly enough and the country offered many opportunities for exploration. While we were stationed there, we visited Naples, Pompeii, Rome and the Vatican, Florence (twice) and many small, out of the way villages with special meaning in Italian culture and history. Some of the trips were organized Able Flight social functions, some were associated with a visit by Sylvia's parents and still others were made with Peter and Uschi when they visited us.

During the summer of 1969, the pressure of the job was getting to

---

28   One who is promoted at a faster rate than the average member of a military organization.

be a bit much so we took a vacation to Austria and Southern Germany to help me unwind. I traded vehicles for two weeks with a friend who had a Volkswagen camper so we could stop at campsites along the way and save money. We went at a leisurely pace as we drove north through the Italian country side and learned more about Italy. After noticing that many homes in a particular area had concrete stairs to nowhere on top of their flat roofs, I had to inquire as to the root of the custom. What I discovered was a surprise.

In some of the less urban areas, an old law states a person can own land but not the air above the land. The land owner had the right to build a home on his land but could not prevent someone else from building a structure above it unless he could prove he intended to build there; thus evolved the stairways to nowhere. The staircases served to prevent others from building in the free air above the land owner's home.

One evening on the trip to Germany, we saw an example of what well behaved children we were rearing. We stopped at a campsite in the far northern part of Italy and set up our equipment. While exploring the campground, we noticed a nice sitting area outside of the office/market complex where patrons could sit and enjoy a bottle of wine. At about seven in the evening, we told Clay, who was nine, and Kelly, who was seven, to stay in the camper while we went to share a few glasses of wine. We admonished them not to leave the camper. We did not want them wandering around outside without close supervision. We were only gone about an hour, and when we returned to the camper, we were greeted with a unique demonstration of brotherly love and admirable behavior.

Kelly had developed an intense need to urinate but Clay refused to let her leave the camper because of our instructions. Between them, they came up with an answer to their dilemma. When we slid open the door on the side of the camper, there was Clay stretched out on the floor with his hand holding a paper cup as Kelly squatted over it to urinate. It was both a cute and satisfying scene that will be in my mind for as long as I live. He was a wonderful brother to her.

Sometimes it seems as if the tour in Italy was our best assignment. There were Flight parties for all sorts of reasons and parties for members of the S&WC for no reason what so ever. Whether by illegal eminent domain or perhaps some legal mechanism, the Americans at San Vito had staked out an area on the Adriatic shoreline and called it the "American Beach." For most of the year, we had beach weather. To leave work at 8:00 A.M. after a mid shift and head directly to the beach with my family was a common event. I could catch a few hours sleep on the beach and then take a nap after supper to get ready for the next midnight shift. Everyone in the unit sported a suntan - the "in" thing in the sixties. Following is a photograph of Kelly and Clay on the beach showing off their tan lines. By today's standards, we probably would be accused of child abuse for letting our children spend so much time in the sun.

The source of our pride and happiness. (Photo by Author)

That beautiful beach, with the azure water of the Adriatic lapping at the sands, also had an insidious effect on some lives. Wives of the young men stationed there wanted to look their best in a bikini; that meant that often there were many beautiful, oil soaked bodies, lying around in the sun working on tans, including Sylvia. The following photograph, found in the family archives, suggests that the boss' wife, a mother of two great children, was able to hold her own competing with those young ladies back in 1969. In the photograph she is getting ready to "catch some rays."

The other source of my happiness. (Photo by Author)

With a large contingent of single, testosterone loaded men assigned to the base, there were bound to be flirtations and illicit romances. Whenever an affair was reported to the unit Commander, the man involved had his clearance immediately revoked and everyone involved was shipped back to the United States with no explanation to the rest of us. We were simply told to make do without the missing person and not to ask questions.

There was one young man who will swear that Sylvia saved his life. We showed up at the beach one morning after a midnight shift to find the red, swim at your own risk, flag flying. The life guard told us it was because of the riptide and said she had no obligation to attempt a rescue of anyone who got into trouble in the water. Sylvia advised me not to enter the water, as I was only a mediocre swimmer; being a strong swimmer, she felt confident to enter with some of the young men. Sure enough, a young man named Murphy got into trouble and called for help. Sylvia and one of the men who was a really strong swimmer went to his rescue and brought him to shore. He was shivering from shock and fear as the life guard and I spoke with him. He swore that Sylvia helped to save his life that day and he had trouble finding the words to thank her for risking her life for his. Sylvia seemed to think that the incident wasn't all that serious and that the man helping her did most of the work.

We eventually found a nicer place to live in Brindisi. It was a modern apartment building that housed some other American families and that made things easier for Sylvia. While I was at work on a day shift, Sylvia answered the door bell to find a group of Italian women at her door jabbering a mile a minute. One of the women was waving around a windshield wiper and kept returning to the word *"bambino."* She gathered that the lady was referring to Clay and reverted to the protective mother mode as Clay approached the ruckus. Sylvia kept saying no to whatever the questions were and was reaching the end of her patience when an English speaking Italian man made his presence known and offered to translate. The woman was trying to say that some little boy had broken the windshield wiper off of her vehicle and someone had told her that Clay was a witness to the incident. All they wanted was for Clay to describe the perpetrator. Sylvia had perceived a threat to her son and had risen to the occasion. The incident reminded us of the briefing we had received about Italians when we first entered the country. We were told that when in a heated discussion, Italians tend to get right up in your face and raise their voices with no intention of doing you harm. Americans, on the other hand, dislike violation of their personal space and being shouted at, so relatively innocuous situations often unnecessarily escalate.

There were other problems getting along with the local populace. The Italian drivers are a special breed; lines painted on the highways and streets, put there to delineate traffic lanes, mean absolutely nothing to them. They follow what many worldwide travelers know as "French driving rules." The rules, supposedly instituted by French drivers, are simple. Drive on any portion of a roadway you wish, but do not hit another vehicle from the rear or on either side and avoid oncoming traffic. These rules work fairly well as long as everyone is aware of them and they are scrupulously obeyed. Drivers unaccustomed to "French rules," are at first terrified, become cautious, and then learn to participate in competitive driving. I am reminded of an incident late at night in Paris. I had hired a taxi to take me to my hotel and panicked when the driver flew through a red light on the Champs Elysees. I shouted to him that he had just run a red light and could have killed both of us. He smiled at me in the rear view mirror and said, "I have a brain. I could see there was no traffic. The red light has no brain; it doesn't know if there is traffic. I will not be controlled by a brainless red light." He had a point but it was a scary ride.

Add the Italians' love of speed and somewhat questionable level of maintenance of their vehicles to "French rules," and you have a mixture ripe for disaster. All new arrivals at San Vito Air Station were briefed on the traffic situation on Italian roads and were shown photographs of fatal accidents to drive home the point, but accidents occurred anyway. There were 1,600 military personnel assigned to the base. The 2,400 family members of those personnel brought the American population in the area to 4,000. In the two and a half years we were stationed at San Vito Air Station, there were sixteen American fatalities on the roadways. Those were the days before seat belts were mandatory, and in many cases not even available; that added to the carnage. When compared to the fatality rate in the United States for the same period, the statistics tell a grim story. With our death rate of sixteen over a thirty month period, the Americans stationed at San Vito Air Station experienced a rate of 1. 6 traffic deaths per thousand of our population per year. At the same time, in the United States the traffic death rate was .26 per thousand of population per year. Our personnel were roughly six times more likely to die in a traffic accident than citizens in the CONUS. We took this risk in stride as just one more thing to deal with while stationed overseas.

One evening, after catching a ride home because Sylvia needed our Fiat that day, I noticed an unusual silence on her part. After dinner and after the children went to bed, Sylvia turned down the radio and said she had something serious to discuss. When I asked what could be so serious, she replied that it was really bad. I jokingly asked if she had fallen in love with another man. She replied that it was worse than that. Adding to the joke, I asked if she had fallen in love with another man and had become pregnant by him. She replied that it was worse than that. Subconsciously somewhat relieved, I ask her what could be worse than that. She told me she had been driving in a rainstorm in Brindisi looking for the apartment of a girlfriend when she ran into a parked car and left the scene of the accident without calling the police. For a military man to learn that his wife left the scene of an automobile accident in a foreign country is almost as bad as finding that his wife is pregnant with another man's baby. When I asked why she didn't call the police, she told me she got out of the car to try to find the owner but an Italian man standing on his second floor balcony caught her attention and shouted, *"Via, via."* To Sylvia that meant get back into your car and go because no one saw the accident except him and he wasn't going to tell anyone.

That was the kind of incident that can ruin a military career. I immediately drove to the base and reported the accident to the military police sergeant on duty. He mulled it over for a few minutes and then told me he would make a notation that I had reported the accident but would take no action unless someone from town reported it to base officials. That way, I was covered for reporting the accident but if it were never reported by the civilian, nothing would ever come of the incident. Sylvia told me she couldn't discern any damage to the little Italian car but definitely remembered feeling the bump when the collision occurred. We dodged another bullet.

Sylvia found that in the southern part of Italy, Italian men have little respect for women. They love and appreciate the female form, but consider women as property. Any woman walking down a sidewalk alone was thought to be inviting attention. It was common for a man or a boy to reach out and pat her posterior as she passed or try to engage her in conversation. As an American, Sylvia was not aware of this behavior when we first arrived in Italy. She told me of being pestered in the park where she took the children for fresh air and sunshine and of being followed around a department store by adolescent boys when shopping alone in Brindisi. To stop at a stop sign or red light with the driver's side window down was an invitation to the nearest male to reach through the window and grab her inner thigh made visible by her miniskirt. She quickly learned how to wind up the car window in a hurry to catch an arm or wrist. I trace their behavior back to what the Italian women told Sylvia about never spanking a boy child; these males never grew up and felt entitled to do as they pleased. Eventually we qualified for government NCO quarters at the Air Station, which was a welcome change. It kept us off of the very dangerous road between the town of Brindisi and the base.

Arrested Again:

We were all cold sober when we arrived at the NCO club. There were about twelve of us so we pushed some tables together and ordered a round of drinks. Sylvia and the wife of a friend headed to the ladies room as the round was being served. The Sergeant at Arms approached our group with a scowl on his face. I had no idea that this man, for reasons still unknown, had a visceral dislike of me. He said to one of our group, "Welch, you know you have to wear a tie when you are in this club. You're out of here! "

I stood up and said, "Hold on a minute. There's a guy completely passed out lying across a table over there. Even though he's wearing a tie, he's the one who should be tossed out of the club." The Sergeant at Arms did not appreciate my interference and told me that I was also to leave the club. I told him that I hadn't violated any rules and that he would have to call the Security Police if he wanted to throw me out of the club. At about the time Sylvia was returning from the ladies room, the Sergeant at Arms was approaching the tables with two Security Policemen. He must have planned the incident because the policemen appeared within seconds. When Sylvia asked what was happening, someone told her that her husband was about to be arrested. This was quite a shock to her as only a few minutes had elapsed since we entered the club. One of the Security Policemen asked me if we could discuss the situation in the Lobby. I agreed and several of us moved to the area just inside the door to the club. At that point, the other policemen asked if we could discuss the problem in the parking lot. When I told him that I would not agree to that because it would be tantamount to having been ejected from the club for no reason, he replied, "I can drag you out of here if I have to."

Bruce Rice, an NCO who worked for me, stepped in between the policeman and me and said, "You're going to have to go through me first, buddy." As the policeman reached for his baton, I realized the situation was escalating to the point of a problem. I told Bruce to back off and told the policeman that if he wanted to talk to me in the parking lot, he would have to arrest me. He did and they took me to the Security Police building, booked me, and charged me with resisting arrest, encouraging a riot, and disgracing the uniform in front of foreign nationals (the band). Fully aware of whom I was, the Desk Sergeant released me on my own recognizance.

The next day, my neighbor (the NCOIC of Operations), Chief Master Sergeant Jack Morris, commented to me, "I noticed on the police blotter that you and Welch raised some hell at the club last night." I simply replied that the policemen had made a mistake. At the beginning of my next shift, the OIC of the Security Police cornered me and told me I would not be hearing from those two policemen as long as I was on the base and that the blotter had been rewritten.

Some months later, when seated next to the base commander at a formal function, I took the opportunity to mention that I felt I had done nothing wrong the night I was arrested. Colonel Rice replied, "If I thought you had been wrong, you'd have been in my office the next morning. The incident never occurred." I guess he was serious, because less than a year later, I found my name on the list for promotion to Senior Master Sergeant.

A Transfer to the Day Shift:

On a day shift late in the summer of 1970, I received a call to report to a Captain who worked in the Operations area. He told me he had a few things that needed attention by someone with writing skills and asked me to take a two week temporary assignment to rewrite some Standard Operating Procedures (SOPs). It doesn't take much of a writer to write an SOP but I guess not many people want to or can do that sort of work. I accepted the offer and turned over the S&WC to Dean for those two weeks. By the end of the second day, I had rewritten the first SOP and turned it in to the Captain. When he appeared shocked that I had given him what he thought was a first draft after only two days, I added to his surprise by telling him it was for his final review.

When he approached my desk the next morning, I figured I was headed back to shift work if he didn't have any more work for me. I wasn't going back to shift work anytime soon. The Captain told me he was happy with my work and had discussed it with Colonel Ramey, the Operations Officer and second in command of the base. Colonel Ramey wanted to speak with me about doing some work for him when I finished my detail with the Captain. It didn't take long to write the remaining SOPs and I was given an appointment to meet with the Operations Officer. Colonel Ramey first expressed his displeasure that the Base Plans Office somehow ended up within the Operations area and thus became his responsibility, and then told me of his problem. The USAFSS Inspector General's (IG) team had recently inspected San Vito Air Station and, among several deficiencies, found that the many base plans had been ignored for years and were woefully out of date. The colonel told me he was aware of my writing skill as well as my reputation for getting things accomplished. He asked me if I thought Dean Welch could take over as permanent S&WC Supervisor if I were to be assigned as the NCOIC of Base Plans. This was a big surprise to me. The idea of working an eight to five hour shift to finish out my last eight months at San Vito was very appealing. My only hesitation came when I wondered what the job would be like once I had rewritten all of the plans. Something reminded me of the principal that the requirements of all jobs will expand to meet the hours available to the employee; I didn't want that to happen. None the less, I told Colonel Ramey that Dean was ready to take over and that I would accept his offer. Colonel Ramey was a sly old officer. He told me I would report directly to him and that there would be times that what I said would be understood as to have come from him, so I should choose my words carefully. Then he said, "This is a high level position. I will leave it up to you to determine how many hours you need to work. Don't ever ask me for time off; you should know if you can be gone from the job. Just let me know that you won't be available if you are to be gone from your office."

It was yet another Catch-22. Yes, I was free to set my own hours, but I would end up working many more than forty hours a week. I was assigned one assistant and went to work. There were plans for natural disasters, bomb threats, attacks by local militias, destruction of classified material, base traffic, the maintenance of base facilities and responses to penetrations of the secure area to name the ones I can remember. There was a tremendous amount of rewriting, updating and exercising the plans to be done before the IG's follow-up inspection in December. I was able to accomplish all of that and even had an occasion to implement the disaster plan when the base was pummeled by a fierce wind storm in the late fall of 1970. Colonel Ramey and the Base Commander were impressed with the efficacious manner with which the natural disaster plan worked during the storm and the results of the eventual re-inspection. I am certain they were instrumental in my promotion to Senior Master Sergeant, one step below the highest level an enlisted man can reach, when I only had seventeen years of service. I continued on the track of success as a "fast burner."

During our time at San Vito Air Base, we received and accepted an offer to sell our house on Paradise Valley in San Antonio. Our renters were happy there and wanted to make it their permanent home. With no home to return to and being young and adventurous, we applied for another assignment in Europe and received orders for a three year tour of duty at Darmstadt, Germany. A few days after receiving the orders, the Air Force changed all tours of duty in Germany from three to four years. That was fine with us; I only had three and a half years left before I could retire from the Air Force and if I wasn't promoted to Chief Master Sergeant by then, I intended to leave the Air Force and try something else.

Chapter 6 - Assignment Germany

In February of 1972, we over packed the little Fiat 124 and headed to Germany. When we reached Northern Italy, I felt like Hannibal crossing the Alps - in the reverse direction. It was snowing and cold, and the trip over the slippery surface was harrowing as we climbed the long, winding road to reach the entrance to the St. Bernard Tunnel through the Alps at St. Rhemy. I worried about how bad the roads would be once we exited the six mile long tunnel on the Switzerland side at Bourg-St-Bernard and checked to ensure that my snow chains were easily accessible. It was a pleasant surprise to emerge from the tunnel into bright sunshine and clear roads. It was a good omen; our trip through Switzerland and into Germany was an enjoyable adventure. We were seasoned travelers and knew that a smile and an attempt at the local language was all that was needed to solicit information from the local populace. The Swiss are nice people and are accommodating to strangers. We had snow free roads all the way to Darmstadt, which was unusual for February. Once in Darmstadt, we found a hotel and I sought out the housing office to sign for the government quarters that had been reserved for us.

As the saying goes, we won the war but lost the peace. German nationals were hired to administer the base housing for military personnel. Along with that administration came union rules and a little bit of corruption. A German national from the housing office escorted us to our ground floor, three bedroom unit on a bleak, windy morning. The condition of the unit was deplorable. As we entered, the first thing we noticed was paint peeling from the ceilings in hundreds of places throughout the apartment. The wood floors were in terrible shape with many spaces between boards. The appliances were old but relatively clean and serviceable. When I noticed tears on Sylvia's face, I told her not to worry because the first thing I would do would be to scrape the ceilings. The housing office representative sternly said I would not be allowed to do that. When I asked why, he told me the unit was scheduled for repainting in a few months and that only union personnel were allowed to perform that type of work. I smiled and asked if he wanted to follow me to the PX where I would buy a paint scraper to do the job. He warned me again not to do any work. I took the clipboard out of his hand, signed for the apartment, handed it back to him and told him to leave. I started scraping the ceilings that afternoon. A few months later, the apartment was repainted and the floors were repaired and resurfaced; no one ever mentioned the freshly scraped ceilings.

After settling into our quarters, I started my new job at Operations. I was assigned as the S&WC Supervisor for Dog Flight. The previous supervisor had already departed for his next assignment and the Assistant Supervisor, Technical Sergeant Don Peavy, was temporarily supervising the Flight. Those are always touchy situations. The troops get used to taking instructions and orders from a familiar person and tend to be suspicious of the "new guy." In addition to that, the temporary supervisor becomes used to being the leader and can develop hurt feelings if the transition back to assistant is done without consideration. I introduced myself to Don and asked him for a briefing on the enemy units that would become my concern. I went on to say that I needed him to continue to control the Surveillance and Warning Center until I felt familiar enough with my new mission to be comfortable. I had stumbled upon the perfect approach. Within twelve working days I was ready and took command. I never noticed any resentment from anyone in the unit and Don Peavy and his wife, Jill, remain our friends some thirty-seven years later. Below is a photograph of Jill and Sylvia circa 1972.

Jill (left) and Sylvia – two beautiful ladies. (Photo by Author)

As a seasoned S&WC Supervisor, I kept things running smoothly. We had the usual amount of activity which involved close calls by some of our aircraft but no shoot downs to report. Early on a morning shift on May 11, 1972, I was required to release a CRITIC report which may or may not have qualified for such a high priority. In the intelligence community, a CRITIC report takes priority over every other message anywhere in the world and is routed to the very highest level of decision makers in the United States government. The information for this particular CRITIC came from an officer at the I. G. Farben building in Frankfurt, Germany which was the headquarters for the U. S. Army Corp in the region. Through secure teletype communications with our unit, he reported that a bomb had exploded at the entrance to the building at approximately 7:00 A.M. I immediately issued a CRITIC report which simply stated the time and location of the explosion, and then issued a CRITIC follow-up report with the scant details I had available. The Red Army Faction (also known as the Baader-Meinhof Gang), which had perpetrated terrorist attacks in Europe since 1968, exploded three pipe bombs within a few minutes of each other. The Officers' Mess, which was the target, was destroyed with the loss of one life, an Army Lieutenant Colonel who was a decorated Vietnam veteran.

I was neither lauded for my decision to issue that particular CRITIC, which was not based on our internal development of intelligence, nor was I criticized. It was just one of many split second decisions made by S&WC Supervisors in units around the world who put their careers on the line every day. I didn't realize it at the time, but I was becoming a dinosaur. It never entered my mind to ask or even contact the Flight Commander before I sent the CRITIC. As suggested earlier, the USAFSS was trying to switch the decision making function to the Flight Commander, but with their general lack of experience, it wasn't a good idea. My relationships with Flight Commanders were usually contentious; they probably resented my style.

During a midnight shift some months later, my Flight Commander told me that Headquarters in San Antonio had instituted a new proficiency program for S&WC Supervisors. We were to be required to pass written examinations at various intervals to prove our worthiness to remain in the position. I could not help but broadly smile, barely stifling a chuckle. My brain started to evaluate the other NCOs in the unit who would or could do my job; none came to mind. The silliness of the conversation was enhanced when he said I would be required to submit two hundred questions to be considered for inclusion in the proposed examinations. I told him if it were a direct order, I would go through the motions and supply the questions but they would not be very difficult ones because I didn't want any that might cause me to fail. He reconsidered his request and I never heard anything more on the subject, nor was I ever given a proficiency test to prove I was worthy to continue in my position. As mentioned earlier in this narrative, there was a never ending supply of NCOs who did not want the responsibilities of an S&WC Supervisor and there were very few who had the personality and skills required for the job.

Someone in Operations, either the NCOIC or the Operations Officer, didn't like me. I came to work on an evening shift late in 1972 to find that two new Master Sergeants had been assigned to me. I was a Senior Master Sergeant and by now, Don, based on his sterling record, had been promoted to Master Sergeant. We were both fast burners who worked perfectly together and now I had to deal with two surplus Master Sergeants that out ranked Don. There was no way I was going to let my team of analysts be degraded. I assigned each of the new Master Sergeants to subsections and told them to let the Staff Sergeants in charge of those sections call the shots. I let them know that if they didn't like the assignments they should take it up with the NCOIC of Operations. A decent Flight Commander would have gone to the Operations Officer and had that dead wood transferred off of the Flight, but that didn't happen.

Late in 1971, when I sewed on my Senior Master Sergeant stripes, we were offered an apartment in the area reserved for Senior NCOs. The upgrade was nice, so we decided to accept even though it meant another move and dealing with the housing office again. When government quarters are vacated, they are expected to be in perfect condition with regard to cleanliness. The housing office was happy to recommend a German cleaning crew to do the job for a price that would guarantee the unit would pass inspection. It was fairly obvious to me that someone in the housing office was getting a kickback from the cleaning crews. I declined the offer and told them we would do the cleaning ourselves and save the money. After moving to the new quarters, Sylvia and I prepared the old quarters for inspection. When the housing office inspector entered the apartment, he asked which cleaning crew had done the job. I told him we had cleaned the place ourselves. He told me it would not pass inspection. I told him to do his thing and tell me what might be wrong. In the kitchen, he removed a drawer and reached in to check the wood strip nailed to the wall in the back of the opening. When he found a speck of saw dust that had been there since the building had been constructed decades before, he showed it to me and said the kitchen failed inspection. He then took out a five mark coin and scratched the floor at the rear of a bedroom closet and told me there was dead wax on the floor that had to be removed. I realized none of this would have happened if I had paid a cleaning crew. I told him to submit his report to the housing office and I would get back to him.

I promptly went to the Army Lieutenant Colonel who was the titular head of the military housing section and told him I had a problem. After explaining the situation and my belief the housing office was getting kickbacks from the cleaning crews, he decided to inspect our place himself. We walked into the vacant, clean apartment and didn't get past the living room before he announced that the apartment passed inspection and I was not to worry about a thing.

Life wasn't all about work and dealing with the corrupt housing office; I had a family and friends, too. Jill Peavy, originally from England, and Sylvia hit it off perfectly. There were social functions of all sorts, visits from the Zahns, camping trips to sites around the country and meals at each other's apartments. The Peavys had two daughters of about the same ages as Clay and Kelly, so we had a many things in common.

We vacationed in Spain twice during these years and found the Spanish people to be friendly, polite and accommodating. On one occasion, when I needed a break from the job, Sylvia, the children and I, drove to the Barcelona area to camp out for a week. I remember crossing the border from France, where local governments had a blind eye to the primitive condition of their public facilities, and into Spain, which presented orderliness and cleanliness to visitors. We had a great time on that trip and recharged our batteries. The following year, we took a second trip to Spain with another couple, Jack and Dale Lilly. This time we drove further down the coast line to a resort area where we rented a villa for two weeks. It was another great trip with wonderful weather, great company and friendly local citizens. Life was good; we enjoyed our friendships, parties and vacations, but we also had the usual problems encountered by parents.

One afternoon in the spring of 1972, the son of one of my neighbors came to the door of our third floor apartment to tell me that Clay was at the bottom of the stairwell and could not walk. When I reached the entrance to the stairwell, Clay was lying on the floor and was covered with dust and twigs. When I asked what had happened, he told me he didn't know but that all of a sudden on his way home from school, he found he couldn't walk. I said, "Come on, Clay, if you got into a fight and lost, it's okay. You can't win them all." He insisted that there was no fight and that he had to crawl home because he couldn't walk. I still wasn't sure about what had happened because it didn't make any sense to me. I said, "Clay, if I pick you up and carry you up three flights of stairs and you can walk, I'm going to be really upset. Are you sure you can't walk?" He assured me he couldn't walk and I carried him up the stairs to our apartment. Sylvia took over and in no time we were on our way with Clay to the base medical facility. I carried him down the stairs and we all got into the car and drove to the dispensary. As I carried him up the steps to the door of the facility, I offered him another chance to admit he could walk, but he said he couldn't. We turned him over to a nurse who put him into a wheel chair and took him to an examination room.

Ten minutes later, the nurse returned to tell us we had to leave Clay with them for transportation to the Air Force hospital at Wiesbaden where he was scheduled for surgery the next morning to repair a protruding hernia. I felt a little bad about being so hard on him, but that was me. Clay got to tell his Dad, "I told you I couldn't walk!" We laughed about this episode in our lives for years to come. The surgery went fine, and like most children, Clay bounced back in a hurry and there were no lasting consequences.

Near the end of the school year in 1972, Clay came to me with a problem he was having at school. He told me that the teacher had organized the class along the lines of a government to teach a civics lesson and that he had a problem with the head of the student government. He explained that the student had assigned a heavy load of extra work to him for speaking out in class and he didn't think it was right. I didn't think it was right either, and told him to forget the extra work and that I would take it up with the principal. I promptly went to the school and told the principal that Clay's teacher was wrong to let a child's contemporary assign punishment and that she should be fired. The principal called for Clay's file and reviewed the contents before any further discussion. When he was finished, he asked if I were in the unit moving to Augsburg during the summer. When I confirmed that I was, he noted that Clay was an "A" student and said that Clay would receive an "A" for the final semester and that he would not be required to attend school any more that year. I agreed with his decision and told him again he needed to give the teacher some serious guidance. Clay of course was thrilled with the decision and was forever proud of his father for interceding.

The move of our unit to Augsburg in southern Germany that summer was a difficult undertaking. The mission had to be covered by other units while the physical move was made in as short a period as possible. Because of our key positions in the unit, the S&WC Supervisors were given high priority with regard to the logistics of the move, so it was not too difficult for us. In our new building at Augsburg, the S&WC was known as the "Fish Bowl." We worked in a large, high ceilinged room on a level lower than the where the day workers had their facilities. There were large glass windows on the upper portion of a wall at one end of the room that offered a complete view of our activities. The Operations Officer and any authorized visitors could watch through the windows as the analysts plotted the positions of aircraft on a large Plexiglas board. They could easily see the large communications area, the report writers and the S&WC Supervisor and his assistant. I never did get used being watched when on a day shift. Thankfully, there rarely were any observers during the evening and midnight shifts.

Augsburg offered us the opportunity to explore the Bavarian area of Germany, which was quite a change from northern Germany. There is a cultural distinction between the north and south of Germany much like the separation between the north and south of the United States with regard to regional accents. There was also a difference in religious preference. Citizens of southern Germany are almost all Catholic whereas the citizens of northern Germany tend to be Lutheran. Those in the south are more laid back than the uptight, strict, northern Germans. I had been studying German for some time and felt I had a fair command of the language until I got to Bavaria. They have a very strong south German accent that is difficult to understand. It was like someone from Massachusetts trying to understand someone from South Carolina; it took a lot of effort.

PART IV – CIVILIAN LIFE

Chapter 1 - The Australian Adventure

I had the highest possible evaluations of my performance at all levels for many years. Apparently, I must have angered some Lieutenant or Captain along the way that was now a Major on a promotion board because I had not been selected for Chief Master Sergeant as I neared my twenty year point, so I made plans to retire from the Air Force. I looked at it as their loss, not mine. I was also extremely unhappy with the political climate in the United States during 1972 and 1973 when Richard Nixon was President. I looked into emigrating with my family from America to Australia and found the idea appealing. Everything I read suggested it would be a favorable move. Sylvia and I discussed the pros and cons and decided to try a new country. We purchased a 1973, right hand drive Ford Capri to take with us to Australia and had it delivered to us in Augsburg. I submitted my papers to retire effective on the first day of 1974 and made plans for the move. The Australian government was happy to issue Visas to us as émigrés and we anticipated the start of another adventure. I had sixty days of leave on the books so I left the service at the port in New Jersey at the end of October 1973 with a formal retirement date of January 1, 1974.

We shipped our household goods and vehicle to Brisbane where I had arranged for a rental apartment to use upon our arrival. The only belongings we had with us when we arrived in the United States en route to Australia were the clothes we carried. We visited my mother and sisters in upstate New York and continued on to San Antonio to visit Sylvia's family. I had arranged to travel to Australia on my own to make the logistical arrangements and for Sylvia and the children to follow sometime later. I've made many mistakes in my life, and the decision to immigrate to Australia was one of them.

When I arrived in Australia, the first set back I encountered was the loss in value of American money. On February 13, 1973, President Nixon announced a ten percent devaluation of the American dollar. If that statement means little to you and sounds confusing, attempt to decipher the explanation he gave the following day:

"When people see the headline "devaluation," they have to realize we are not talking about the value of the dollar here.

The other point is the trade package. We are not talking about another round of lowering tariff barriers . . . although we have an outgoing policy. That is only one-half, I suppose, of the story. We are talking about the other side as well. We must go up as well as down. That is the only way to get a fair deal and a fair shake for American products abroad.

We have gone into too many negotiations abroad, in which all we have done is to negotiate down, whereas others have negotiated up. We are going to ask the Congress for the right for our negotiators to go up or down. Only by going up can we get them to go down with some of the restrictions they have."

I'm not sure I will ever understand that statement. What it meant to me in Australia was that the budgeting of what money we had saved and the value of my Air Force retirement pay had to be reconsidered. I was not astute enough to understand the implication of the devaluation when it was announced. I was also not aware that the Australian economy had entered a slight recession since we had made our decision to emigrate. It didn't take very long for me to determine that I had made a disastrous mistake, and that no matter how bad the politics were in my own country, it offered better economic stability than anywhere else in the world. When I now hear others complain about America, I can truly and honestly tell them that they should emigrate if they don't like things here.

I contacted Sylvia and told her to cancel her flight because I had changed my mind and would be returning to San Antonio. It was a devastating blow to my ego that would take some time to heal. We had lost just about everything we owned but we were young, I was forty and Sylvia was only thirty-three, and we were sure we could pick ourselves up and start again. Thanks to being ridiculously anal when it came to the inventory of our household goods, I had numbered and identified the contents of each box so I was able to tell an agent in Brisbane which boxes to send to auction along with the Capri. The proceeds from the auction paid most of the expense of shipping the remainder of our goods to us in Texas. We were able to reclaim most of our cherished items and photographs. We convinced ourselves to restrain from looking back and began to dig ourselves out of the hole we were in because of my poor judgment.

Chapter 2 - South Texas Living

With her excellent secretarial skills, Sylvia had no trouble finding work. With her income and my retirement pay, we were in a position to purchase a little home. We accepted the charity of some of her family when they offered pieces of used furniture and we used her mother's Sears charge card to purchase some other items. The first thing we paid off was the Sears card once we had sufficient income. Purchasing a vehicle was another matter. We found one within our budget we felt would be reliable and applied for a loan through the USAFSS Credit Union. When the car dealer called to tell me the loan was not approved, I was shocked and hurt. I called to find the reason and was told that I didn't have enough income to qualify. At the time we applied, Sylvia hadn't started her new job and our only income was my small Air Force retirement check. When I called the credit union and asked to speak with the CEO, I was told that people didn't just call and ask to speak to the CEO of such a large organization. I told the clerk that I was a charter member when the organization founded in 1956, and that I had a beef with the way I had been treated. I didn't mention that I knew the CEO when he was only a Master Sergeant. Sure enough, I was connected to Fred Barrett, the CEO. I told him who I was, what had happened, that I had never been late on a loan payment and, as a member for eighteen years, I ought to be trusted to meet my obligations. He said, "I'm glad you thought to call me, JD. I'll make sure the loan is approved as soon as I hang up the phone. Welcome home; I'm sure you will be just fine." I don't like asking for favors but we really needed transportation. Sylvia and I were used to having just one vehicle so we were able to get by with that old, ugly, Ford Torino until we were on our feet again.

In the early seventies, the American economy was experiencing a slight recession. The OPEC oil embargo that lasted from September of 1973 to March of 1974 added to the recession and made it extremely difficult for me to find employment. There was no demand for

223

experienced foreign intelligence analysts. I applied everywhere with no luck. In addition to the employment problem, there was the problem of schooling for the children. In anticipation of starting school in Australia, they spent very little time attending school during the 1973 fall semester. I enrolled them in the grade levels they would have been in had there been no interruption in their education. In both cases, the advisors told me it was not the proper thing to do and that they both should be set back a year. I told the counselors that they were very bright children and could make up any deficiencies. I asked for and received the books used during the fall session and went to work to help them catch up over the Christmas holidays. Clay and Kelly made us proud. By the end of the spring semester, Kelly was recognized as the outstanding fifth grade student in her elementary school and Clay had a B plus grade average in his middle school. The children had done their part in our recovery.

I continued to look for work with no luck until early summer when two opportunities arose. In my naiveté, I wasn't even aware of one of them. I had applied for employment at the local telephone company and taken their aptitude tests, and they subsequently called to schedule a physical examination for me at a local health center. I thought it was just another step in the application process but was told later that the company would not have incurred the cost of a physical examination had they not intended to offer a position to me upon passing the exam. As it happened, at the same time the Veterans Administration called me into their personnel office, and based on a civil service examination I had taken several months earlier, offered me a position as a Veterans Benefits Counselor. There were many problems for veterans attending school through the GI Bill and the Veterans Administration decided to station counselors at some of the colleges to assist them. At the interview, I was advised that since there were many applicants I would have to decide on the spot if I wanted the job and would also have to choose a location to serve. After so many months of looking for work with no success, I felt obligated to accept the position. Upon stating my acceptance, I was offered the opportunity to work at Victoria Junior College in Victoria, Texas, New Mexico State College in Las Cruces, New Mexico, or Stanford University in Palo Alto, California.

I am nothing if not a decision maker; in fact, Sylvia likes to say that I use the "ready, shoot, aim" approach when it comes to making up my mind, so I had little hesitation in making a selection. Palo Alto and Las Cruces each sounded more appealing than Victoria, but we had been overseas for about five and a half years and I was certain Sylvia would have killed me if I accepted a position far away from her parents. Victoria is a small town about one hundred and ten miles south east of San Antonio. It is so humid there, the local people go to San Antonio to "dry out," and San Antonio is brutally humid. Everything in Victoria is air conditioned all year round. If you wear glasses, whenever you leave an air conditioned building or vehicle, the lenses become covered with moisture from the humid air. Lawns do not have sprinkler systems and never have to be watered by hand because it is so humid; yet they have to be cut twice a week in the summer. The big, black mosquitoes are ferocious; homeowners require gloves and mosquito netting just to mow their lawns. I told myself that people do survive in Victoria because I saw them, so I ought to be tough enough to survive. Survival is one thing; enjoying survival is another. Although I try never to second guess decisions, there were many times in Victoria when I wondered what living in Las Cruces or Palo Alto would have been like.

The Veterans Administration sent me and a large number of other newly hired counselors to a training course in Carollton, Georgia, to prepare us for our new careers. While I attended the six week course, Sylvia resigned from her position, began packing and put our house on the market. On one weekend, I returned to San Antonio and we drove to Victoria to find a place to live. We decided on a new home that was within a few weeks of completion and made a deal for the purchase. The following week, Sylvia sold the house in San Antonio and arranged a closing date to accommodate our move to Victoria. This transfer, unlike so many others, went smoothly.

We moved into the new home and, with the exception of the terrible humidity and mosquitoes, our lives were good there. We met nice neighbors and began to fit in to the local society. Sylvia found work at a local accounting firm where her skills were greatly appreciated. Clay and Kelly started school in the fall and had no academic problems whatsoever. I worked three days a week at Victoria College, which was collocated with a branch of the University of Houston, and two days a week at Bee County Junior College at Beeville, a small town about fifty miles away. There was plenty of work and it was gratifying to be able to help veterans who would otherwise be seriously frustrated with trying to obtain an education. I like to think that my counseling helped some of them succeed in life.

Even small towns have their share of jerks. One day, when he was twelve years old, Clay came to me with a problem he was having with a couple of local boys. He liked to take a short cut across an open field to get to his middle school, which made him vulnerable to harassment from older boys. He told me that two of them stopped him and told him to turn over his lunch money or they would hit him with the bicycle chain brandished by one of them. He felt he had no choice so he gave up his money, but he wanted to know what to do about the situation. He told me he did not want the boys to force him to take the long way to school by staying on the sidewalks, but knew he couldn't fight the bigger boys. I thought about the problem for a bit and came to a solution.

I told Clay that bullies tend to avoid victims that fight back; instead they pick on those who are more vulnerable. I advised him to take his short cut whenever he wanted and the next time they approached him, to give them some advice. He was to tell them that it was obvious that he couldn't fight two guys but that his father wanted them to know that if they hurt him, he would kill one or both of them. I told Clay that when they scoffed at the threat, he should tell them how it would happen. He was to tell them that I had been forced to kill children in Vietnam (a lie) and that it wouldn't bother me a bit to kill some kid who was threatening my son. He was to describe how I would wait for the chance to catch them one by one and fake a violent fall as I smashed their heads into the nearest rock until they were dead to make their deaths look like accidents. The look on Clay's face was one of shock as I outlined the plan, and I am sure when he told the boys about my plan a few days later, his belief that I would kill one or both of them showed through in his presentation. He was never bothered again; and he viewed me in a different way for the rest of his life.

Kelly was having a problem, too; but it was insidious and would escape our attention for many years to come. She was either born with, or developed, an intense desire to be perfect in everything she attempted. Anything less than a 100% correct grade in her school work was unacceptable to her. Although we never consciously encouraged perfection, we always congratulated her for her success at school. I discussed this trait with her when she was an adult woman because it had caused problems between us during her school years. She told me she knew that when she did well in school, it pleased me; so she felt if she did even better, it would please me even more. Her explanation hurt me. I remembered the days I sent her to bed crying because I refused to let her study more than I thought she should. All through primary school, secondary school, college and into graduate school, she never failed to obtain straight "A" grades, and in almost every case, the grade was based on 100% accuracy on tests. This perfectionism and her very high IQ were to plague her later in life, but while we were in Victoria we could not see into the future.

After I started college at night school in San Antonio in 1960, I continued to take evening classes whenever they were available. While in Victoria, I took the remaining courses to qualify for an Associate Degree in Liberal Arts. I wanted to continue my education but there were no courses available there beyond my two year degree, so I took a break from school. Within about two years, the GI bill program that had been in such disarray was running smoothly and my presence in Victoria was no longer needed. Based on my success there, I was offered a promotion and a transfer to the main office in Houston. It is a tossup as to whether Houston or Victoria has the worst weather, so we didn't anticipate any improvement in that area. My in-laws were very happy to have us and their grandchildren so near, so we thought we would give Houston a chance. Deep down inside of me, I really did not want to live in Houston, but I did not express that to Sylvia. We arranged to meet a realtor in Houston on a Saturday morning and Sylvia, Kelly and I drove the 120 miles up the coast. Clay remained back in Victoria with some neighbors. The Veterans Administration's main office was on the south side of Houston, so we began our search for a home in Pearland, a suburb a few miles south of there. When we found a place we thought we would like in a nice neighborhood, I was shocked that the price was $20,000 higher than I expected. When I mentioned this to the realtor, she told me that yes, it was high, but one had to pay for "restrictions." I didn't know what she meant, so I pursued the issue and asked for an explanation of the "restrictions." "You know what I mean," she replied, "restrictions" as she touched my side with her elbow. Again, I told her I didn't understand. She said, "Look around you at the neighbors. They all look like you. That is because of restrictions." Then I realized she meant that the neighbors or neighborhood association had conspired to only sell to white people.

My first thought was, how would I explain to my children that I had paid $20,000 extra for a home to keep from living near non-white people when I had raised them to treat people of all races equally? It was all very depressing and we did not make an offer on the home. Sylvia and I discussed the situation on the way back to Victoria and she let me know that she really didn't want to live in the Houston area either. With our feelings out in the open, we agreed that we had always tried to live where we would be happy and we probably would not be happy in Houston. It struck us that when we were on our honeymoon in 1961, we thoroughly enjoyed our visit to Albuquerque, New Mexico. We remembered it as a pretty city with an excellent climate, and decided we should think about living there.

The following Monday, I called my boss in Houston and told him I needed a few days off. We left the children with their grandparents and drove the 800 miles to Albuquerque. We drove in and around the city, visited malls, the Old Town area and model homes. We read the classified ads in the local newspaper and concluded we should be able find jobs without too much trouble, and decided to make the move. When we returned to Victoria, I called my supervisor in Houston and told him that I intended to forego the promotion and resign. He was kind enough to agree to keep me on board until our house sold and wished me luck in Albuquerque.

Chapter 3 – A New Beginning in Albuquerque, New Mexico

Within a few months, we sold our home, packed our belongings in a U-haul truck, attached one of our vehicles to the rear, and started out on another adventure. I had made a quick flight out to Albuquerque to find and rent an apartment for the six months I estimated it would take for us to get established and buy a new home, so we had a place waiting for us when we arrived in August of 1976. Again, Sylvia had no trouble in finding employment but I did. Sylvia went to work for an engineering firm where she fit in perfectly. Whether it was the economy at that time or my lack of employable skills, I had difficulty finding work.

We lived in a second floor apartment at the corner of Pennsylvania Avenue and Montgomery Boulevard in the Northeast Heights of Albuquerque. Montgomery Boulevard was, and is, a very busy thoroughfare. One evening, not long after we arrived in Albuquerque, we heard the telltale sounds of a horrendous automobile accident. A quick look over the balcony told us there had to be serious injuries. As we called the police to report the accident, Clay, who was fourteen, ran down stairs to see if he could help anyone. When the ambulance arrived with only two paramedics, one of them asked Clay to give him a hand with one of the drivers. Clay helped remove the man from the heavily damaged pickup truck, but when the paramedic checked for vital signs, he told Clay to step back because the man was dead. By then, another ambulance had arrived and Clay, shaken by the experience, returned to the apartment. He had a difficult time describing his feelings about being near to, and touching, a deceased person. None of us could know at the time, but Clay was to be associated with death many times in the future.

In September we enrolled Kelly in a middle school that was within walking distance of our apartment. Sandia High School, where Clay was to be a freshman, was also within walking distance of our temporary home. When I offered to go with him to enroll, he told me if he were old enough to go to high school, he ought to be old enough to enroll without help. Some years later he told me of his experience that day.

After walking the few blocks along Pennsylvania Avenue to reach the school, he began to get uneasy. Clay had never been to a big city school and when he saw the large number of students of all sizes and types, he panicked, and walked right on by without entering the school grounds. After passing the confines of the school, he gathered up his courage, turned around and walked back toward the entrance; again terror gripped him and he went right on by the school. He didn't want to return home and admit his fear, so he turned and made his way into the school yard. It took all day but he successfully got registered for the proper classes and even signed up to play the snare drum in the marching band. On his way out of the school, a bully started to hassle him but it only lasted for a few seconds. An older, bigger student pushed the bully aside and said something along the lines of "quit picking on the freshmen." When Clay told me this story, he also told me that he vowed then and there to return to the school yard when he was a senior and look for bullies hassling freshmen to pay back for the help he received. With an attitude like that, it shouldn't have surprised me when he eventually decided to become a police officer.

While attending Sandia High that year, Clay observed two more deaths. One occurred when an automobile being pursued by a police cruiser pulled over to the side of the street across from the school yard and stopped. The sound of the siren and the flashing of lights caught the attention of the students and they watched to see what would happen. As the police officer approached the stopped vehicle, the driver's side door opened, a shot was fired and the driver fell out of the car. He had committed suicide in front of the large group of high school students. Clay had a tendency to exaggerate and even make up stories on the spur of the moment just for fun, so I hesitated to believe this one until I read about it in the newspaper the next day.

The next death he witnessed occurred at the same intersection as the first. Sylvia and I were returning from a shopping trip when we came upon a massive traffic jam at the corner of Pennsylvania and Montgomery that prevented us from reaching the parking area for our apartment complex. We parked our car on a side street to find Clay just returning from the scene of the accident; he was ashen faced and shaking. When we asked what happened, he told us he had just felt a boy die. Someone had sped through a red light and a high speed accident resulted. Clay was in the apartment and heard the crash. When he saw the carnage, he grabbed a blanket and ran down the stairs to the scene. The first thing he saw was a blood soaked, eighteen year young man lying on the road. He suffered extensive internal injuries and many lacerations when he was ejected from the vehicle through the windshield. Clay covered him with the blanket and looked around for anyone else he could help; then the boy grabbed his hand and asked him to stay there. The boy told Clay he was dying and grabbed tighter and tighter until he died. Clay told me he had to pry the boy's hand from his and had come very close to regurgitating on the spot. From the balcony, we were able to see the boy's covered body on the pavement; we had no reason to doubt the veracity of Clay's story that time.

Our financial situation began to get a little sticky around October because we had put down an initial payment on a new home under construction based on the assumption I could find work and we would be able to qualify for a mortgage. I finally landed a job as an inside salesman with the local Bekins Moving and Storage Company. One of my duties was to separate the daily mail. When I noticed a letter from my mortgage company a few days after I started work, I knew it was to check on my employment so I intercepted it and took it home with me that evening. I filled out the form that requested confirmation of my employment and an opinion as to my longevity potential in the position. An illegible, scribbled signature was all that was needed to establish that I was an excellent employee with great potential. I mailed it back to the mortgage company in the stamped, addressed envelope. With my new job, Sylvia's employment and my retirement income, we were approved for the loan. At about the time the loan was approved, I received an offer to go to work for the IRS. I was not a very good salesman; I didn't have the personality for the job, so I accepted the offer from the IRS.

The job at the IRS was as an entry level clerk typist, a GS-4 rating. It paid as much as the sales job but had better potential. I had been a GS-9 when I left the Veterans Administration and knew I could climb my way back up the ladder. I was the only male clerk typist in the organization, and thus, had to be better than all of the women to gain their respect. Gaining their respect was the easy part; gaining the respect of the men was another story. I received a lot of grief from ignorant, thoughtless men who couldn't understand how a man could take a job normally performed by a woman. I knew I was putting bread on the table and paying the mortgage, and was confident that eventually I would leave those same men in my dust.

We moved into our 2,100 square foot, three bedroom, two and a half bath home on Christmas Eve of 1976. In the spring, we installed a sprinkler system, planted shrubs and covered the front yard with gravel as is the Albuquerque style. Clay was in high school and had an old Volkswagen Bug for transportation and Kelly took the bus to her middle school. Life was good for us. I had been promoted to the position of "Taxpayer Representative," which meant I answered questions from taxpayers all day long. A three week long school in Los Angeles prepared me for that job and others to come. That spring, Sylvia left the engineering firm and went to work at Sandia National Laboratories on Kirtland Air Force Base where the pay scale was higher. At that time, before the introduction of desk top computers, secretaries had to have short hand and excellent typing skills. The staff in the personnel department at Sandia was happy to see her application.

By late in the spring of 1977, I had completed another IRS school and was working as a tax auditor at the Albuquerque office. The work was challenging and I looked upon my position as an enforcer of the law. I felt that every time a taxpayer was forced to pay their legally levied taxes, I was recovering money that had been stolen from me, an honest taxpayer. Many funny cases came across my desk. One of the most comical was the case of the young lady who had had breast augmentation surgery. She had taken deductions for the surgery, transportation and lodging expenses to have the procedure performed in Dallas, as well as new brassieres, dresses and blouses. She was accompanied to the audit by her police officer boyfriend in full uniform, a common form of intimidation. When I established that he was not her tax representative, I advised him that he could only observe and could not make any comments. The surgery was deductible under an obscure portion of the Internal Revenue Code (IRC), but because she could have had the procedure performed in Albuquerque, I disallowed her transportation, lodging and meal expenses. I also disallowed the clothing purchases as I felt she could go braless if she couldn't afford new clothing. Her boyfriend jumped in when I was finished and told her he thought I had been fair and she should pay the bill, which she did. Strange cases were not infrequent, and my co-workers and I often had good laughs discussing them at the end of the work day.

One afternoon after the last audit, the office gang got together to see if it could be determined who was the toughest auditor. The weak kneed auditors were dropped off the list without hesitation. After some more discussion, there were only two left; an elderly, no nonsense lady who had been an auditor for many years and me, a relative rookie. Everyone agreed that we were about equal in the way we protected the government's money, but finally, one of the auditors came up with a fine point that made me the toughest auditor in the place. That mean old lady always had a box of Kleenex on her desk for the taxpayers who cried, but because I refused to do that, I was awarded the honor as the toughest auditor in the office.

Chapter 4 – A New IRS Agent in Roswell, New Mexico

Because I had continued with my secondary education at night school, I qualified to attend the school that would certify me as an Internal Revenue Service Agent if I would accept a transfer to Roswell, New Mexico. The difference between an auditor and an agent is striking. Auditors, normally GS-7s, work in the office and taxpayers report to them to be audited. Agents, GS-9 and above, perform the audits at the taxpayers' businesses or at the offices of CPAs that represent them. I had taken a great number of accounting courses to prepare me for the position, so I readily accepted. I completed the agent school in Dallas and we moved to Roswell in the summer of 1978. We sold the house in Albuquerque and purchased another one in Roswell. Clay and Kelly had changed locations and schools so many times in their lives that they took this change in stride. They knew how to judge people and make friends in a hurry.

My supervisor in the Roswell office was a slow talking, bright, pragmatic man named Bobby French. He was from Eastern New Mexico, where people sound more like Texans than the people west of the mountain range that splits New Mexico. Bobby was a likable person whose hobby was bee keeping. He was patient with me during my break-in period and helped me succeed as an IRS Agent. After school started, Bobby asked me what my children thought of the high school. I replied that Clay had told me that it was really nice and that it must have been repainted during the summer. Bobby assured me that it hadn't been painted during the summer and that, if it had, he would have known about it because he was on the school board. When I related this conversion to Clay, he told me he just assumed it had been painted because there was no graffiti anywhere. Bobby laughed out loud when I told him what Clay had said. He said, "David, tell Clay that this is Roswell, not Albuquerque. Our kids know that if we ever caught one of them spray painting school property, we'd cut off a hand." It really was a redneck, conservative town at that time.

I don't know how he did it, but Clay landed his first job that summer in Roswell. He went to work at minimum wage for a plumbing contractor. His first assignment was to join a gang of men digging a long ditch for a water line He was not a very big sixteen year old, and when he came home exhausted that first evening, I asked him if he had learned anything about plumbing other than it was hard work. He said he didn't learn about plumbing but he learned how to "work like a Mexican." I ask what that meant and he explained that he started off wrong because he began digging really fast when the starting time arrived. The other guys, all Hispanic, stopped him and explained that he wouldn't last until the first break if he didn't work slower. One of the guys told him he had to learn to "work like a Mexican;" which meant, dig slow but steady and you can do it all day long. I agreed that he had gotten good advice but then he told me the rest of the story. During the ten o'clock break, the same man explained that it was time to sit and smoke a little marijuana to rebuild their stamina while they rested. I told him that was bad advice.

My audit cases were located in Roswell and the surrounding towns of Hagerman, Dexter, Hobbs, Artesia, Ruidoso, Portales, Clovis and Carlsbad. I spent a lot of time on the road and learned about the area and the populace. I would be away for about ten days out of every month, but we soon got used to the schedule. Sylvia found a job working for the Social Security Administration that was located in the same building as the IRS office. The people in the building started to call me Robin Hood. They liked to say that I would come back from being on the road on Friday afternoons with a bag full of money from my audits to turn in to the government, and on Monday mornings, Sylvia would dole it out to the poor.

There were the usual crazy audits. I audited extremely wealthy citizens who gave large enough sums to charities to warrant examination; some audits involved complex layers of companies owning other companies; and then we had the run of the mill tax cheaters. One of these was a used car dealership in one of the small towns. If there wasn't a Monday night football game on television, there wasn't anything else to do in the small town, so I usually worked on my audits in the motel. One evening when I was reviewing an inventory of used cars, I noticed there were two 1953 Jeeps listed among the hundreds of vehicles. It struck me as a rare vehicle, so I looked closer and noticed that the same Vehicle Identification Number (VIN) was listed for both Jeeps. This told me it had been entered into the inventory twice. By doing this, the dealership had inflated the cost of the vehicle to the point that, when it was sold, the transaction reflected a loss. Being a nice guy, I just assumed that a mistake had been made, but to meet the due diligence requirement, I probed further. I found that scores of vehicles had been entered into the inventory twice. The dealership had been selected for audit was because it had reported losses for the past six years on its tax returns; I then knew the reason for the reported losses. I broke off the audit and reported my findings to Bobby French. He arranged for the case to be assigned to the Special Agent Section that deals solely with fraud cases. I worked with them on the case for some months doing the grunt work. I don't know if the owner went to jail or not, but I did notice the dealership was out of business within a few months. I audited a number of cheaters who claimed to be, "just a country boy who don't know nothing about accounting." They knew plenty about accounting. Whenever a rancher lost a head of live stock to a predator, you can be sure it was the most expensive one in his inventory. It was like a game and I enjoyed it very much.

One evening, I received a call from the "Inspection" office in Denver. The Inspection people deal with auditing IRS employees, tax protesters and dangerous taxpayers. The voice on the telephone told me he was aware that I would be auditing a particular person in Clovis the next day and advised me there was a possibility of violence as the man had threatened agents in the past. The business owner scheduled for examination was a member of the Posse Comitatus, an anti-government group that was very active in those days. The group, which has since morphed into a white supremacist organization, taught members that the government had no constitutional right to levy taxes on its citizens. The caller advised me to record the interview and to terminate it immediately if tempers flared.

The man had filed a tax return to satisfy the filing requirement, but simply wrote in large letters across the first page, "Not required." This action was based on the advice of the leader of the Posse Comitatus who accepted contributions and fees from his followers for his advice. Unknown to them was the fact that their leader properly reported the fees in his annual tax returns. He advised others to break the law, but he wasn't about to go to jail for tax evasion. In my view, it was all a simple confidence game aimed at gullible people.

When the taxpayer arrived at the federal building in Clovis, he had three other people with him. I asked if any of them represented the taxpayer and was told that they were there as witnesses only. I told them they could stay, but could not interject comments or give advice. I set up my recorder in the center of the conference table and began the discussion. I had a very difficult time suppressing a laugh when I looked across the table. There sat a heavy set, sour faced, post fifty year old woman with a poorly disguised microphone protruding from a silly looking plastic flower in her lapel. A wire was plainly visible winding its way down the side of her jacket and into the purse she kept strapped to her shoulder. The whole interview was hilarious. I let him vent about the constitution, the government and the IRS for a while, and then I asked if he would sit there with me and fill out the proper tax return. He refused and I terminated the examination so the next step in the case could be taken.

Some months later, the tax protester was taken to court and I was called to testify. He represented himself in the proceedings and examined me on the witness stand. After reading the complicated excerpt from the Constitution that led him to conclude that federal income taxes are illegal, he asked me for a "yes" or "no" answer to a long, convoluted question on Constitutional Law. There was no way I could follow his rambling question, so I looked up at the judge and asked if I had to answer a question I could not understand. The judge smiled at me and said, "I'll tell you what; guess at an answer and I'll tell you if you are correct or not." When I replied to the question in the negative, the judge said, "Bingo! You got it right." Then the judge addressed the taxpayer, "You, mister taxpayer, have wasted enough of my time. Your application is denied." It really was fun being an Internal Revenue Service Agent.

There were just too many funny cases to cover in this book. Business owners tried everything they could think of to win the battle and very few of them realized it wasn't a good idea to irritate the examiner. I remember a meat packer who tried to give me a place in the freezer to work; a stock yard owner who gave me an office without screens so there were millions of flies to irritate me; a sheet metal manufacturer who gave me a place on the assembly floor where the noise was really loud; and a CPA who consistently did not have the books and records I requested ready for me upon my arrival. Regardless of their tactics, if taxes were owed, I was normally able to uncover the errors and obtain payment.

Those stories about my success as Robin Hood make me sound a little conceited and indomitable, which, of course, I am neither, as this little encounter will prove. It is easy meet people and make new friends in a small town, and Roswell was really a small town. Somewhere along the way, we met Renate and Bill and socialized with them on occasion. One evening at a dinner party, Renate, a reasonably attractive woman, engaged me in conversation while Sylvia was chatting with someone else. She asked if I had encountered any prostate problems in my life. I told her I was only forty-five and felt that was something I would have to deal with in the future. She responded that she and her husband had felt the same way, but that he had developed prostate cancer at a young age and his prostate had been removed. Renate went on to tell me how difficult it was to live with an impotent man at her age. She told me he understood her problem and even approved of her once a month visits to Albuquerque to spend a night with a special "friend." I praised her husband for being such a nice guy and she responded that the long, two hundred mile trip to and from Albuquerque was getting old and she wished there were another option. I broke off the conversation with the advice that she should be happy she had such a great husband and that the two hundred mile trip between Roswell and Albuquerque wasn't all that bad.

After we got home that evening, I related my conversation with Renate to Sylvia from the point of view that Bill was really a great guy. Sylvia said, "You've got to be kidding." I told her I wasn't kidding, and that if the same thing happened to me, I would understand her needs and probably be just like Bill. She responded, "I don't mean kidding about Bill. Don't you even know when some woman is hitting on you?" I told her I didn't take the conversation that way; I thought she just wanted to talk with someone about Bill's problem. Exasperated, Sylvia said, "I'm keeping a close eye on her from now on and you need to stay away from her. She's after a local replacement for her friend in

Albuquerque." I was a good Internal Revenue Service Agent but a lousy Romeo.

The children thrived in Roswell as they got older. Clay had girlfriends and even Kelly reached the age for boyfriends. They attended Goddard High School together and were both in the marching band. It was a healthy environment for teenagers. They didn't get into much trouble and did well in academics. Kelly came to me one day in a terrible state of despondence about her school grade record. In her entire life she had nothing but perfect grades until her final grade of "B" in driving class. She asked me if I could help because she didn't want her perfect record to be blemished. I told her I would try to help and made an appointment with the instructor.

When I discussed the matter with the instructor, it was a pleasant experience because he, like all of the other teachers in the school, really liked Kelly. He thought that a "B" grade, which represents above average work, was not a bad thing. He patiently listened to my explanation of her personality and history of perfect grades. He agreed she could retake the course, at our expense, during the coming summer to see if she could improve her grade. As I was leaving his office, he suggested I ask Kelly about her nicknames in the class.

Kelly's nicknames were "Hoppy" and "Killer." It seems she had a lot of trouble learning how to drive a car with a manual transmission. She had difficulty in keeping a vehicle from hopping forward when using a manual clutch. "Killer" came from her aggressive driving around in the mock up of a town where the students were taught to drive. Supervising via radio as he viewed the students from a tower, the instructor would normally call out the number on the roof of the vehicle to contact a student; everyone knew who he was speaking to when he gave instructions to "Killer" instead of calling out her number.

Kelly repeated the course in the summer and received an "A," which kept her record intact. It was during this period that I contacted her counselor at the high school to discuss Kelly's tremendous drive to be perfect. During our conversation, she told me that the need for perfection in all things was not an uncommon trait for people with extremely high IQ scores. I asked what Kelly's score was but the counselor felt she did not have the authority to release it to me. I persisted and she finally said it was in excess of 150 but would not tell me the exact score. We knew she was very bright but had associated her success in maintaining perfect grades with her hard work as much as with her natural ability. The counselor went on to say that Kelly had the perfect combination of traits. She had a high IQ, was attractive, was modest, had a strong work ethic, and had a personality that endeared her to students and teachers alike. We still didn't realize that a tremendous desire to be perfect in all things can be a disability regardless of other talents.

Clay had no trouble maintaining a "B" average with very little attention to home work. He and Kelly argued about how much work was necessary to be successful in school. She told him that if he didn't get 100% on test, he had not learned all of the material; he told her she should lighten up and enjoy school. Clay also had a high IQ and it showed when he took the Scholastic Aptitude Test (SAT) during his junior year in high school. The day he took the test, I had to be in Clovis for business and the test was to be administered at Eastern New Mexico State University at Portales, a town half way between Roswell and Clovis. We got up early and drove to Portales. I dropped him off at the college and promised to return by 12:30 P.M. because he had to be back in Roswell to participate in a marching band competition at 2:00 P.M. When I picked him up at 12:30 P.M. and asked how he did on the test, he responded, "A piece of cake, Dad. I think I aced it." It must have been one of his best days. He did so well on the test, he was selected as a National Merit Scholarship Semifinalist. The award was given to the top 1.2% of the 1.4 million students who took the test that year. In a few months, Clay received a letter from the University of New Mexico with the offer of full scholarship for tuition and books for four years. With a big grin, Clay said to Kelly, "You see, Kel, I did okay without being perfect."

Clay was less than perfect, as are all teenagers. He came home one evening seriously inebriated. In his fogged mind, he thought if he just came in the door and went to his room without saying anything, we wouldn't notice. We did notice and read the riot act to him. He swore that his girlfriend Loraine, who lived a few houses away, drove him home because he knew he was too impaired to drive. I still wonder about that. For his punishment, he couldn't drive for six weeks and his sister was to drive both of them to school each day in his vehicle. It was very many years later when Kelly told us he made her pull over once they were around the corner and he would drive the rest of the way to school. There was no way he was going show up in the high school parking lot with his little sister driving his car.

On another evening, during one of the weeks I stayed in Carlsbad to do audits, Clay came home, said he was tired and went directly to bed. Sylvia chalked it up as typical teenager behavior until later in the evening. At about 9:30 P.M. the doorbell rang and Sylvia found a police officer at the door. He was looking for Clay. Her heart sped up as she asked why he wanted to see Clay. The officer told her Clay had been involved in an automobile accident earlier in the day and that he wanted to interview him as to the facts of the case. The officer quickly told Sylvia that there were no charges; he only wanted to confirm some facts. After arousing Clay and listening to the interview, Sylvia learned that he had been a passenger in a high school friend's vehicle that had crashed into and destroyed a utility pole. The vehicle was still drivable, so they left the scene in hopes of avoiding scrutiny. Their escape was doomed; both boys suffered minor injuries and had gone to the hospital emergency room for care where Clay's seriously bruised ribs were bound and he was released. The hospital officials reported the injuries to the police who investigated the hit and run. Even the best teenagers can cause parents grief.

Clay turned seventeen while we were living in Roswell. We could see that he was rapidly moving from boyhood into manhood and wanted to give him a special present. Clay was a fantastic reader and lover of the written word. These traits probably developed because we did not have the availability of television during his early years; instead, we read books for entertainment. His favorite fiction author was J. R. R. Tolkien. His appreciation for Tolkien started when he read *The Hobbit* and then *The Lord of the Rings* trilogy. He eventually read everything Tolkien had written and anything he could find written about Tolkien. Because of his fixation on Tolkien's work, we settled on the perfect substitute for a class ring. Gold had risen in value during the late seventies, so we gathered our unimportant and seldom used gold jewelry and sold it to a jeweler. With part of the funds we purchased a wide gold ring. Kelly used the Rune alphabet found in *The Hobbit* to write, "The One Ring," and we sent the ring and the translation to an artist in Santa Fe to have it engraved with the Runes. Clay was nearly overcome when he received the present. Some years later, his ring, like the one in the book, was lost. He was at a University of New Mexico basketball game and removed the ring from his finger because it was uncomfortable when he clapped. After the game, as he ran through a snow storm to the unpaved student parking lot, the ring apparently popped out of his pocket and fell to the ground. When he realized where it might have been lost, he returned to search for it only to find that the lot had been paved. We hope that someday, when that parking lot is replaced, someone will find the ring and give it life again.

Chapter 5 - Back to Albuquerque

Sylvia and I still hadn't amassed any savings. We paid our bills on time and lived well for a family of four, but there was no way we could afford to send our children out of town to college. We had always told them that they would have to count on scholarships and work their way through school. They grew up aware that many of my days were spent at work in the day time and taking college classes during the evening and both internalized the idea that school didn't end until a Bachelor's Degree had been earned. We were wrestling with the problem of Clay attending college when two events overtook us.

The IRS hired two new Agents straight out of college for the Roswell office who started at the GS-11 level. I had worked my way up through auditing to Agent but was only a GS-9 because I still lacked two courses for my Bachelor's Degree. I stewed over this because, when I discussed it with Bobby, he told me he had already complained to the personnel manager in Albuquerque and they said they were bound by the rules; I couldn't be promoted until I had my Bachelor's Degree. The irony of the situation was that neither one of the new hires lasted more than a few months. They did not have the maturity to look cheaters in the eye and tell them that they owed back taxes, penalties and interest and were required to pay the bill on the spot or deal with the collection enforcement side of the organization. You had to believe in your work to be able to do that, and these kids were just too young to understand that tax cheaters are law breakers.

One evening while Sylvia and I discussed the problem with Clay's coming college year and my unhappiness with the IRS, I received a call from Ray Turnley. Ray attended IRS Agent School with me and at one time was my supervisor when I worked in the audit department in Albuquerque. He had accepted a position as the Director of the Tax Department at the Public Service Company of New Mexico (PNM). PNM is an investor-owned utility company that supplies electricity to most of New Mexico, and at that time, also provided water to the cities of Las Vegas and Santa Fe, New Mexico. He told me he wasn't quite sure he could handle the job without help from someone trained in taxation and wanted to hire me to work in the department. He said he was authorized to offer me whatever I was making with the IRS and pay any moving expenses. Sylvia and I discussed the offer, and never having been people who were afraid to move, accepted it and started making plans.

The house went on the market; we packed up our household goods and moved back to Albuquerque at the end of December, 1979. We purchased a home in a nice neighborhood in the Northeast Heights section of Albuquerque, even though the home in Roswell hadn't sold yet. We were able to make the deal by obtaining a bridge loan from our bank in Roswell based on our good credit rating. Clay handled the move well but Kelly was very upset with us. She had a boyfriend and many girlfriends she did not want to leave. I guess fifteen, going on sixteen, is a sensitive time in a young girl's life.

We weren't living in the new home very long, when Kelly came home from school one afternoon and told me she had had some trouble on the school bus. One of the boys from her school had reached over from the seat behind her and grabbed her breasts. She went on to say that he had done it to other girls and had been known to run his hands under the skirts of unsuspecting girls. I immediately called the boy's telephone number and his mother answered. After ascertaining I had reached the correct family, I told the woman that only out of the goodness of my heart, I was going to give her an opportunity to give her son a new start on life. I told her of the incident and the reputation her son had with other students and advised her that the boy was never to come near my daughter again. I went on to say that I would not allow any retaliation from him, so he was to turn and go in a different direction whenever he saw my daughter in the future. If she felt she could not agree to my terms, I intended to drive to the police station and file a sexual assault report against her son. With only the slightest hesitation, the woman said, "Mr. Joyce, my son will never ride the school bus again and your daughter will never see him again." I told her I could accept her decision and terminated the call. Kelly never saw the boy again. She also strongly internalized the fact that women do not have to put up with improper treatment from anyone. Perhaps that boy mended his ways, but somehow, I doubt that he did; sexual deviants have a very high recidivism rate.

Clay started school at the University of New Mexico (UNM) and found a part time job as a bus boy in a new restaurant in town; he wasn't old enough to serve liquor so he had to wait a while before moving up to waiter status. He absolutely loved going to college. He was a big supporter of the Lobos, the university's basketball team. As we discussed his future when he neared eighteen, I told him that when he reached that age he would be an adult and would not be getting any more unsolicited advice from me. He told me that he wanted to study Psychology. I cautioned him that he could never make a living in that field without a Ph.D. and he responded that he was well aware he would have to do post graduate work. He also reminded me that I had advised him to take courses that interested him if he wanted to do well in school. He was correct; I had taken many courses I thought were a waste of time only because they were required. My time would have been better spent studying subjects I enjoyed. He decided to concentrate on Psychology, Philosophy and History and did very well in all three subjects. Just before he turned eighteen, I asked him what he would like for a birthday present; he was ready with an idea.

When our children were very young and we lived overseas without television, I made up stories for entertainment. One of the farfetched stories I conjured up made a big impression on them. I went to great lengths to convince them I had been a bullfrog in a past life and that Sylvia had kissed me and turned me into the Prince that I am. It worked so well, I had to caution them when they started school that is wasn't really true; I didn't want them telling the story to teachers and other children. With that story in mind and the music from "Joy to the World" (Jeremiah was a bullfrog....) ringing in his ears, Clay said he wanted to have a tattoo of a bullfrog put on his shoulder. I agreed it was a good idea and we went in search of a tattoo artist. There weren't many in Albuquerque in 1980, but finally we found one in a part of town rarely frequented by middle class accountants. Clay had a great looking tattoo of a small bullfrog sitting on a Lilly pad etched into his upper right arm. We were in good spirits over the whole episode until we started to drive home; it struck us that we hadn't checked out our idea with Sylvia. At first, we, especially I, had strong emotions of trepidation and hesitated in returning home with Clay's birthday present so visible. Then an old piece of advice that I had kept from my children came to mind. I smiled as I told Clay, "Someone once told me that you are more likely to be successful if you ask for forgiveness rather than for permission. Let's look at it that way and take our medicine." Sylvia was not very happy with us at all when she found what we had done. She let Clay off the hook much sooner than she did me.

We got by some rough financial times because it took nine months to sell the house in Roswell and I finally earned enough credits for my Bachelor's Degree. I had attended night school for eighteen years and had credits from five different colleges, The University of Maryland, San Antonio Junior College, Victoria College, Eastern New Mexico State University and the University of Albuquerque. I had completed all of the requirements for a degree in accounting from the University of Albuquerque save a course in Statistics. They offered me a degree in University Studies, which is a generic Bachelor's Degree; I accepted it because I was really tired of going to college at night while working full time and more.

The work at PNM was hard; corporate taxation can be complicated but taxation of utility corporations can be staggeringly complex. The good thing was, PNM placed high emphasis on the well being of its employees. There were company sponsored sports teams, talent shows, picnics, bonuses at Christmas personally handed to employees by the company President and a generally felt sense that we were members of a family. It's not that way anymore and I can't really pinpoint exactly when it changed, but it was a great place to work until just before I left that company in 1988.

Ray Turnley, the man I worked for in the PNM Tax Department, is a very bright person. He and Kelly are a lot alike in that they have the ability to concentrate all of their brain power on any problem at hand to the exclusion of everything and everybody surrounding them. This trait helps in solving problems but can also be a detriment. In Ray's case, he was unable to deal with personnel matters and was an ineffective supervisor. It never entered his mind to go to bat for his people in the area of promotions or raises. He had difficulty dealing with people on a one-on-one basis. His process for decision making amounted to waiting for circumstances to dictate only one alternative.

After eighteen months in the Tax Department, I hadn't had a promotion, so I accepted a transfer and promotion to Supervisor of the Accounts Payable Department.

An example of Ray's supervisory style was displayed in a strange incident that occurred while I still worked for him. One of the employees in the tax department had been in an ill-fated love affair with a strong minded young lady in the accounting department, which was on the same floor of the building. He apparently was engaged in a telephone call with her late one afternoon and made a remark that riled her. She hung up the telephone, came over to the tax department, walked into his cubical, screamed, "No one talks to me like that," and slapped him across the face. The man was a classical Italian male who could not allow such a disgrace, so he got up and forcefully smacked her. The lady screamed again, "This man just struck me. I want him arrested for assault. Where is his supervisor? Who is his supervisor?" I came out of my cubicle and saw the two of them glaring at each other, ready to take more swings. I looked into Ray's office and didn't see him. I told the lady that the tax supervisor was gone for the afternoon and it would be better if she discussed the situation with her own supervisor. She agreed and went back to her office. The rest of us went to look for Ray to tell him what had happened. We didn't have to look far; we found him crawling out of the knee space under his desk. When he heard the outbreak of hostilities, he dove for cover. Ray told us his reaction to hide was because he was involved in an incident at the IRS when a taxpayer pulled a gun which made him overly cautious in volatile situations, but I don't buy that. I was happy to leave the Tax Department and start a new job.

There were twenty-three female, clerical employees in my new department and no male employees. When I took over from the former supervisor, the only thing he said was that I would find out that supervising that many women is next to impossible. As I look back at it now, I realize that with a wife, a daughter and twenty-three female employees, I never had a day when I wasn't dealing with someone who was suffering with PMS. I remember when a client of Middle Eastern origin visited me on business jokingly commented that I was a lucky man to have such a large harem. I let him know right away that it was not even near as nice as it seemed. I dealt with attempted suicides (two), broken hearts, abusive husbands and boyfriends, aggravating feminists and a few very nice, bright, hardworking women. It was an experience I never want to repeat.

My management training told me that the direct supervision of more than seven employees is ineffective. The way the Accounts Payable Department was organized, I was the direct supervisor of all the employees. I obtained permission from my supervisor to break up the department along naturally occurring job subcategories and promoted three of the ladies to supervisory level. The change was welcomed by all of the employees, relieved me of many routine duties, and allowed the department to function more effectively. The new organizational structure also facilitated the subsequent change from a manual operation to a computerized system. Within a year, I had things running smoother than ever before.

During this period, Kelly graduated from Eldorado High School with honors and perfect grades. The teachers voted her as their favorite pupil and she was elected as the Prom Queen. By working after school during earlier years, Kelly was able to save enough money to finance a trip to Europe during her senior year. While she was a senior, the Dean of Students at the University of New Mexico asked for an opportunity to speak with her about attending UNM. Of course, we agreed, and he came by our home one evening. He told Kelly that her achievements in high school had been made known to him and he wanted to offer her a Presidential Scholarship (which amounted to four years of tuition and books) if she would attend UNM. We thought she wanted to attend the New Mexico Institute of Mining and Technology, a school in Socorro that specializes in science and engineering, or New Mexico State College in Las Cruces. Our funds were still limited and Kelly knew that, so she told the Dean she would accept his offer. She concentrated on Chemistry, Biology and Mathematics while attending UNM; choices quite different from those of her brother. As students, Both Kelly and Clay made us proud. They each earned a Bachelor's Degree from the University of New Mexico in four years without any monetary support from us. They both held part time jobs during the school years and full time jobs during the summer breaks

When we first returned from Roswell, Sylvia met a friend from Sandia National Laboratories in a grocery store one evening who told her they were still looking for good people, so she applied, had her clearance reinstated and went back to work for them. We all had workplace and school friends which lead to many enjoyable times. We even had a swimming pool installed in the back yard of our home on Noreen Northeast. Life was good for all of us. I had continued my jogging routine that I started back in 1972 in Germany and was in pretty good shape. I would get up early in the morning and jog on the dark streets for four miles before returning to wake up the family. On one of the weekend days, I would jog ten miles. I regularly entered the annual run up the La Luz Trail that winds up the steep, west face of Sandia Mountain, which has a crest at 10,600 feet and borders Albuquerque on the east side of town. My best time up the nine mile trail that starts at 6,000 feet above sea level, where the air is already thin, to the crest of the mountain where the air is really thin, was two hours and thirty-two minutes. Things were going smoothly in our lives, so I decided to go back to school.

One afternoon, PNM allowed a representative from the Anderson School of Business at UNM to address a group of employees. The school was recruiting applicants for a Master's Degree program in Management tailored for personnel already engaged in business. PNM agreed to allow participants every other Friday afternoon off to attend classes if an applicant were to be accepted. Ray Turnley and I applied and for the next two years we attended school from 1:00 P.M. to 6:00 P.M. every other Friday and from 8:00 A.M. to 1:00 P.M. every other Saturday to earn the advanced degree. I'm not sure if I knew any more about business or management after I graduated or not, but I am sure holding a Master's Degree was an asset when looking for employment or promotions.

It was great that Clay was attending UNM at the same time I was. We would often meet for lunch on the Fridays when I attended classes. Death touched Clay again while we were at the university. During his sophomore year, one of his classmates, a beautiful, full of life young lady, was abducted from the driveway in front of her home by a group of four sociopaths. She was held captive for several days, drugged, brutally raped and murdered. The manner in which the case was solved soured Clay on our criminal justice system. As one of the perpetrators sensed the authorities were closing in on him, he contacted a lawyer and arranged to surrender. He made a deal with the District Attorney to testify against the other three and tell where the young woman's body had been hidden in exchange for not serving any time in jail. The arrangement was disgusting to the law enforcement personnel involved in the case, as well as the citizens of the city. The deal was made to mitigate the pain of the grieving parents by providing them with the remains of their daughter. I am certain from our discussion of the case that it had the effect of pushing Clay's political orientation to the right while he was attending classes in the normal sea of liberalism found at the university.

Chapter 6 - Near Death Experience

It was nearing 5:30 P.M. on May 30, 1983. I had recently returned to Albuquerque from a trip of several weeks to Japan to study Japanese management as part of the Master's Degree program and Sylvia had arranged a coming home party. The return flight was a difficult one because I couldn't get any sleep, and I was suffering from a serious case of jet lag. There were about twenty-five guests, including children, enjoying the fine weather and our swimming pool. I was sitting on the edge of the pool at the shallow end talking with one of Sylvia's friends from the office where she worked. Janie and I were discussing our tattoos; I had the panther on my upper arm and she had a butterfly just above her bikini line. Sylvia walked over and said, "You better get those Bar-B-Que grills started up so we can get the steaks on."

I was sitting in direct sun light and sweating a little bit. I replied, "Okay. Just let me cool off a little and I'll light them." I pushed myself forward off the edge into three feet of water. The last thing I saw before I died was Janie's tattoo. For some reason, probably a result of the jet lag, I didn't get my hands in front of my head and my forehead hit squarely on the bottom of the pool. The blow fractured the fifth vertebrae in my neck and crushed the sixth; and I had severely bruised my spinal cord. As hosts of a swimming party, Sylvia and I were acutely aware of our water safety responsibilities concerning our guests and had agreed not to consume any alcoholic beverages, so alcohol was not involved in the accident.

There was no pain when I hit the bottom of the pool; only an explosion of stars in my mind's eye. Although my body was floating face down in the water, my mind felt as if it were floating in the air. I could not see the water, my body or any of the other people. I did see a tunnel with indefinable walls and a light at the end. The light was not necessarily bright, but bright enough to contrast with the tunnel walls. As I hung there suspended in the tunnel, not going forward toward the light but staring at it, I sensed I was laughing. I said to myself, "Man! This is funny. I'm dead and I don't feel bad. I ought to feel bad for Sylvia and Clay and Kelly who won't have me anymore and are probably going to feel really sad, but I feel too good to feel bad for them. This is really great. I don't have anything to worry about; I don't have any pain."

I can describe this feeling of well being as being incomparable to any pleasure you could ever imagine. It was as if the complete weight of the world had been lifted from my shoulders. My inability to feel bad about the devastation I knew Sylvia and the children were to endure when they realized I was dead convinced me I had truly passed over to the other side. The four of us were as close to a single island of beings in a huge ocean of humanity as one could possibly imagine. We had traveled the world together and adapted to all sorts of situations with little help from anyone but each other. Because we had moved so often, the children had learned to make friends quickly but were solidly aware that the most important thing in the world was our family. As for me, there was nothing else in the world of importance other than Sylvia, Clay and Kelly. My own life came far, far behind their safety and care. I continue to be astonished that death feels so good that I didn't feel bad for them.

The underwater sounds of children at play filtered through to my brain and I thought, "Maybe if I stay where I am and don't go through the tunnel, someone will pull me back to the other side." The out of body experience ended as suddenly as it had begun with Sylvia looking at me and asking, "Are you alright?"

Ray Turnley had noticed me hanging face down in the water and asked Sylvia, "What is he doing down there?"

Sylvia had replied, "I don't know, but he never fools around in the water." She got up and went to the side of the pool where she could lean over and reach me. She grabbed my hair and pulled my head up so she could see my face. According to Sylvia, I had a silly grin on my face and just stared at her. To her question as to if I was alright, I calmly responded, "No." The weight of my body and the thinness of my hair caused her to let me slide back under the water but I don't remember that. She called to Ray for help and he and another friend, Steve Breeze, jumped into the pool. As Sylvia held my face out of the water by hanging on to my hair, Ray and Steve got their hands under me, lifted my body out of the pool and laid me on my stomach.

I couldn't feel anything at first. Then, Steve, who was still standing in the pool and was looking right into my eyes, asked, "Are you alright, Guy?"

I said, "I don't know. My right leg feels really cold but I can't move it. Take it out of the water will you, Steve?"

A few seconds went by and Steve said, "I hate to be the one to tell you this, David, but your leg isn't in the water."

I said, "I guess I have a problem."

I could only see Steve because I couldn't move and no one else was in my line of sight. As they were lifting me out of the pool, Clay happened to be looking out of the bay window at the end of the kitchen and clearly observed the scene. He immediately dialed 911 and requested help. When the dispatcher wanted to know if it was a life threatening situation, Clay responded, "I think it must be. They just pulled my father out of the swimming pool. He has either drowned or had a heart attack."

The next thing I remember about that day is the arrival of the Emergency Medical Technicians. One of them asked "How are you feeling, sir?"

I told him, "I can't feel anything and I can't move." They told me they were going to put me on a stretcher and take me inside to get me out of the sun. I agreed to this after letting them know I wanted them to be careful not to drop me back into the pool. One of them laughed and let me know that he had picked up thousands of stretchers and had never dropped a patient.

As I lay on the stretcher in the living room and listened to the technician providing my vital signs to someone at the other end of his radio, the pain hit me. The best and only way I can describe it is to say it felt as if my forearms and hands were being held in a roaring campfire. The pain was absolutely overwhelming. I was given an injection of something on the advice of a faceless person on the radio speaking with the technician. The medication reduced the pain to some degree. All of this time, I couldn't see or hear anyone except the technicians working on me; I could only look straight up. The pain in my arms and the shock to my body were so severe I didn't reflect on my out of body experience until later that evening as I lay in a hospital bed with fifteen pounds of weights hooked up to my skull with screws and pulleys to relieve the pressure on my spinal cord.

It was about 11:30 P.M. The nurses on the acute care ward had made me as comfortable as possible and I had been given some strong medicine for the pain. At this point I couldn't move anything but my mouth. I was in a private room next to the nurses' station so I could call if I needed help. They had put the remote control for the television set, which was high up in one corner of the room, in my hand but I was unable to press the buttons to change the channels. One of the nurses put CNN Headline News on the television set for me just before the shift change.

The night nurse came in to check my vital signs and started a routine which was to happen many times. As she checked my pulse, I sensed excitement in her voice when she asked how I felt while she repeated the procedure. I told her I didn't feel anything and that she shouldn't panic because my pulse was so low. I explained that I was a La Luz Trail runner and that my pulse was normally below fifty when lying down. When I told Doctor Kaplan, the Neurosurgeon who cared for me, that I was a La Luz trail runner, he told me with a grin that I received all of my dividends for all of that training in one split second when I hit the bottom of the pool. He felt that anyone who was not in such fine physical shape couldn't possibly have survived the shock. The way he put it was, "You are not a doctor. You have no idea what horrendous damage you did to yourself. I have no idea why you are alive." That was true; I was alive, but I couldn't move. My natural defenses took over and the thought of not ever getting out of the bed never entered my mind.

After the night nurse finished checking on me and I settled down to watch the news again, the smiling face of a beautiful young woman with long red hair came into my view. She was wearing a flowered smock instead of the plain hospital white. She leaned over so I could see her face and asked, "How are you doing?"

I wondered who she was for a few seconds and then asked, "Who are you? Are you a candy striper or what?"

She smiled and said, "No. In fact, I'm the head nurse for this shift and I always check on my new patients." She said, "I came in to make sure you have everything you need. Is there anything I can do to make you feel better?"

I sensed she really wanted to know how I felt inside, not just how my body felt, but how I felt in my mind. I told her, "I'm very afraid. I died this afternoon and it's a good feeling to die, but I came back and I want to stay here now. I'm afraid if I go to sleep I'll die again." She looked at my charts and told me that she felt certain I'd be alright if I went to sleep. It was good to hear but I was still nervous. I asked her if she would stay and talk with me for a while and she did. Her reassurance allowed me to drift off, and get a few hours of sleep.

Although I resisted falling asleep that night, there came a time when I welcomed the drift into unconsciousness. The next day, after the effect of the medication had dissipated, the pain in my arms and hands returned. Doctor Kaplan explained that we had to find a balance between the level of pain I could endure and the strength of the medication he wanted to administer. Before many hours had passed, the combination of the pain, the depressing effect of the pain medication, and my realization that I couldn't move my legs and had only minimal movement of my arms took a toll on my psyche. Depending on my level of depression at the time, I often wished that I would die as I drifted off into short naps during the days and nights; it seemed to me to be the best answer to my problem. I didn't mention these feelings to Sylvia; she already had enough worry etched on her face.

Kelly had been out of town when the accident happened and didn't see me until the next morning. As she approached my room, Sylvia stopped her and said, "Kel, your father doesn't look good at all. He is pale and he has some contraption screwed into the sides of his head to manipulate the weights pulling on his vertebrae. The last thing he needs is to see you upset. Control yourself when you see him." When Kelly walked up to the side of my bed, I thought for sure I was going to die. Her face registered shock and tears started to roll down her face. The doctor had placed my left hand into a removable cast to force the fingers that had been clasped into a fist into a more functional position in the event I was never to move them again. I guess I really looked like a basket case. Sylvia reassured Kelly and me that Doctor Kaplan had said the outlook for some degree of recovery was good and that we shouldn't worry. I was worried about Kelly.

For the next ten days, Sylvia, Clay, or Kelly would be with me in my room. Normally, Sylvia would spend the evening and sleep all night on a couch brought in for her, and Clay would come in the morning and spend the day with me. I told them both in detail about my near death experience. The discussion of the incident was of particular interest to Clay who was between his third and fourth year at the University of New Mexico with Psychology as his major.

On the morning of the third day when Clay arrived to relieve Sylvia, I was in low spirits. The intravenously administered medication to alleviate the pain in my arms made me feel nauseous. This feeling frightened me because I was flat on my back with the weights forcing my head into a chin up position. I saw Clay's face as he came through the doorway and knew he would come directly to my side. As he approached, he asked, "How you doing, Dad?" At the same time I had the overwhelming need to regurgitate.

I said, "Stay back!"

"What for?" he asked as he stopped at the foot of the bed.

Trying to resurrect my humor, I said, "For a couple of seconds," and then spewed a greenish, thin liquid out of my mouth with surprising velocity. There was mass confusion as Clay went for a nurse and Sylvia tried to assure herself I was not going to choke to death. After considerable effort on the part of the nurses to ensure I didn't choke to death and to clean up the mess, things calmed down. Clay stopped one of the nurses as she was leaving and brought her back to my bed side. He had seen her reach for a suction mechanism attached to the wall at the head of my bed as soon as she approached me. If I had been choking, she was prepared to clear my airway. Clay wanted to know how to operate the mechanism.

He said, "Look, my Dad could have choked to death when he threw up. I want you to teach me how to operate this thing in case that happens again." The nurse was happy to teach him how the suction pump worked and told him she was glad to have his help. I felt a lot better, too, knowing he would be there if I needed help.

During the fourth day after my accident, I felt a sensation in my left wrist. It was like the twitch one feels from time to time in an eye but the eye really isn't moving. Clay was reading the local newspaper to me when I felt the twitching. I said, "Clay! Do you remember our deal?" I had made him promise many years earlier that if I ever got to the point where I couldn't take care of myself, he would help me commit suicide. He acknowledged he hadn't forgotten and I said, "I just felt something in my left wrist. I think my feeling is coming back. You better give me a few more days to see if things get better."

He said, "Okay, Dad. We've got lots of time. Let's read some more until the doctor comes to check you." The doctor was happy to hear about the feeling coming back and continued with his wait and see policy.

About five days later, I experienced what I thought was another close encounter with death. The tongs which had been screwed into my head had been removed and I had been placed into a two piece plastic brace. The pieces of the brace were held together with Velcro straps. The doctor had instructed Sylvia on how to remove the front half of the brace while I laid flat on my back so she could shave and bathe me once I was released from the hospital. During the practice session, he failed to warn her not to make the straps overly tight. Sylvia wanted to make sure my head remained immobile so she adjusted the straps as tightly as possible without either of us realizing the brace was restricting my breathing. At about eight o'clock in the evening I felt a very sharp pain in my chest and assumed it was caused by a heart attack. I calmly said to Sylvia, "Sylvia, I just had a heart attack. It feels like the big one. You better call a nurse in here so she'll be here when I die."

"What are you saying? Are you kidding?" she shouted as she approached the side of the high, hospital bed.

"No. I'm not kidding," I replied, "I just had a heart attack and I guess I'm going to die." She ran out of the room to the nearby nurse's station to get help. She doesn't remember what she said to the nurse that evening but she definitely got her attention. As soon as the nurse reached my bed side, she reached over and loosened the Velcro straps holding my brace together. I took in a deep breath and almost immediately started to feel better.

With a barely detectable smile on her lips, she said, "You were not having a heart attack, Mr. Joyce, you were suffocating. The straps were too tight on your brace and your breathing has been too shallow to support your system. You'll be okay now." Sylvia was crushed. She thought she had almost killed me, which, of course, wasn't true. Then she couldn't understand how I could face what I assumed was my death so calmly. I tried to explain why I had no fear of death but she probably thought I was hallucinating.

The time in the hospital was very difficult. Every twenty-four hours, around six in the evening, someone administered a shot of the blood thinner Heparin into my abdomen. At the opposite side of the day, every twenty-four hours at about six in the morning, someone would remove the old catheter and insert a new one into my bladder. For me, that procedure was uncomfortable at best and downright breathtaking at worst. I began to feel like a large piece of meat being poked at all day long. Little by little, I began to get feelings in different parts of my body. By the morning of the eleventh day, although in a brace that I was required to wear for the next three months, the physical therapist had me on my feet, tied to her with straps, and I was taking tiny little shuffling steps.

Kelly was able to get over her initial shock and visited me when she could. Below is a photograph taken by her mother as she was giving physical therapy to the fingers on my left hand which tended to ball into a fist if not in the cast. At the time the picture was taken, the weight mechanism was still screwed into my skull.

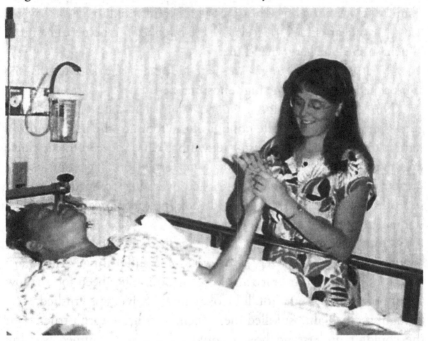

Kelly guaranteed she would get my fingers working again.
(Courtesy: Sylvia Joyce)

Although severe pain in my arms and hands persisted for the first six months, within a year I was ninety-five percent recovered. When Doctor Kaplan released me he told me again that I should have died that day, and then he added, "Even worse, you should be in a wheel chair." When I asked him why he hadn't shared that feeling with me, he pointed out that I had never asked him for a prognosis in that area. He was right of course. For me there was never any doubt; I would walk or I would die. When Clay and Kelly were small children, I once told them that given enough time and enough shovels, I could have dug the Panama Canal by myself. When I taught them that lesson on perseverance, I didn't realize I would have to follow my own advice when it came to recovering from such a devastating injury.

Before I could earn my Master's Degree, I had a few more courses to take at graduate school that late summer and early fall. Sylvia drove me to the Anderson School of Management on the UNM campus, helped me to the classroom and picked me up after class. The other students also did what they could to help me. By the time we graduated, I was getting around very well. Several of the students hosted graduation parties, but one was especially memorable. Sylvia and one of my classmates, Findlay Edwards, planned and pulled off a great charade. I had no idea what was planned and was completely surprised and amused by their skit.

There were at least fifty guests milling around the yard and swimming pool at the home of one of the students when Sylvia and Findlay started the show. They waited for me to head to the bathroom before starting a loud, lengthy argument at pool side. As I was returning, I heard a few insults being shouted just before Findlay shoved fully clothed Sylvia into the pool. Everyone was shocked into silence, and the echo of their shouts floated on the air above the pool. Then the guests broke into laughter as they saw Sylvia, the only person in the pool, shed her dress to reveal she was wearing a bikini underneath. She is a great swimmer and it posed no problem for her to disrobe while treading water. Sylvia had stored a change of clothes in the trunk of the car without my knowledge and had them available after the swimming party ended. Sylvia and Findlay had pulled of a joke that brought tears of laughter to the eyes of many of the guests. That may have been the turning point in my fight with depression caused by worrying if I would ever completely recover.

One evening, about a year later, as we sat around the table after supper having a second glass of wine, I retold the swimming pool party joke to our guests. As I smiled across the table at Clay, I said, "It's a good thing I told you to wait a few days back there when I was in the hospital and couldn't move anything but felt that twitching in my wrist; I'd have missed a lot of fun."

Clay looked at me and said, "I couldn't have done it, Dad." I couldn't believe what I heard. The deal wasn't between a father and son. It was an arrangement between two people who were closer than friends, closer than brothers. We were like two halves of one personality.

I said, "Clay, I can't believe that. We have a deal. I've always counted on that. How can you say you wouldn't have helped me?"

He said very clearly and confidently, "Dad, you can't kill someone you love. Maybe someday you'll be able to understand. But our deal is off." We argued good naturedly over the point for many years.

Chapter 7 - Clay's Police Work

At the end of the 1983/1984 school year, Clay graduated from UNM with a Bachelor's Degree in Psychology. He came to me and said that he was tired of going to school and wanted to start life on his own. I reminded him of my comment about a Ph.D. and he said he would go back to school after a break. Then he told me he wanted to become a police officer and had filled out an application with the Albuquerque Police Department (APD). I didn't want him to become a police officer for many reasons, but I didn't say that, and I do not think he sensed my displeasure. I concluded that Clay had the "Blue Knight" syndrome; he really thought he could help the citizenry by working for the police department.

Clay went through all of the physical, academic and psychological testing for the position without a hitch. The last hurdle was a personal appearance in front of a board of APD Officers. I assumed he would be selected and would be part of the next Police Academy class. I was shocked when he called to tell me his application had been denied. When I asked if he knew why, he told me what had transpired. The Personnel Officer for the APD asked him why a young man with a Bachelor's Degree wanted to be a police officer and Clay replied that he wanted to be able to help people. The man then asked if he was considering long term employment with the APD. Clay told him that as long as promotions came along at reasonable intervals, he planned to stay on the police force; but if his career stagnated, it would be reasonable for him to look elsewhere. The Personnel Officer told Clay he didn't believe that a college graduate would stay in the job long enough for the department to benefit from investing in the training he would receive and cast the negative vote that prevented Clay's selection.

I could tell Clay was crushed as he related the interview to me. I told him to relax and follow my advice. I suggested that he call the Police Chief and insist on being allowed to speak with him about a personal matter. Albuquerque was still a small enough town in 1984 that he didn't have a problem getting to tell his story to the Chief. Per my instructions, he suggested to the Chief that the Personnel Officer's job should be to enhance the education level of men and women on the force rather than to prevent a fully qualified applicant from being selected for the academy because he had a college degree. Without consultation or delay, the Chief told Clay he would see that an extra spot in the next academy class was created for him. Clay attended the academy, graduated close to the top of the class and became an APD Officer.

Of course, as a police officer, he was to be associated with death many more times. The new officers, most often by request, staffed the beats in what is known in all cities as the "war zone." It is the part of town where there is the most criminal activity. He told me about some unspeakable things done to each other by the drug addicted dregs of our society which I choose not to discuss here. There was one fatal accident he investigated that I will mention.

One evening, as Clay parked to write a report on his last call, he noticed a column of smoke coming from a block away. Clay's friend, Jerry Roach, was riding with him because Jerry's patrol car was in the shop for maintenance. They quickly drove around the corner and came upon a major vehicular accident. As Jerry called for backup police officers and emergency medical personnel, Clay ran to the nearest victim to see what he could do. A suspected drunk driver in a pickup truck had ignored a stop sign and crashed broadside into a motorcycle ridden by a high school student and his teenage girlfriend. The fuel tank of the motorcycle had ruptured and the gasoline was burning on the pavement. Jerry went to help the girl while Clay gave the young man mouth-to-mouth resuscitation and CPR. He told me he remembered the medical technician coming to him and saying, "Joyce! What are you doing? Can't you see he gone? He was probably gone when you started."

Clay was not out of control when he told me about the accident but I could see he was upset. He described the school books laying all over the intersection; the smoke and burning fuel; and the heartbreak of seeing two young people - their entire adult lives in front of them - mangled and killed in just a few seconds. What he didn't tell me was how much it affected him at the time. His friend, Jerry, spoke about this incident when I asked him about it later. He said, "You know, Mr. Joyce, some of us never felt Clay should have been a police officer. He was just too sensitive. The night those two kids got killed he was really shaken. After the 'Fatal Team' took over and we got back into his unit, he looked over at me and said, 'You better drive, Jerry. I'm shaking too much.'"

"I can believe that." I replied.

"But you don't understand, Mr. Joyce. The one thing a police officer just doesn't do is let someone else drive his vehicle. He was so upset he wasn't able to function. We always worried about him because he tended to give the low life people out there an extra half second to do what he said. We worried about him getting hurt some night because he was just too nice." A dozen years later, Jerry witnessed a fatal shooting and chased the killer into a blind alley. As the killer turned to face him, Jerry fired his service weapon first and took down the culprit. It was a classical case of justified self defense; he did not give the man the extra half of a second that might have changed the outcome. I had discussed this tendency to be overly tolerant with Clay because I was worried, too. Clay had responded by saying, "Dad, I've had to pull and aim my gun at someone four times. I'm alive and the other guys are alive, so I guess I'm doing everything right." I didn't argue with him about it anymore, but I still worried.

It doesn't happen often in Albuquerque, but there were two police officers killed in the line of duty while Clay was on the force. One of them, Shawn McWethy, a young police officer, had responded to a robbery in progress call in one of our less densely populated areas. Shawn followed procedures precisely. He pulled up near the scene and tried to evaluate the situation as he waited for the backup officer. The robbery suspect had already fled the scene of the robbery and was hiding behind a hedge right where Shawn had stopped. As Shawn was calling in his location, the killer crept up to the driver's side of the police car and emptied a nine shot magazine from a .22 caliber hand gun into Shawn's side. Shawn was wearing a protective vest but several of the bullets found their way through the gap where the vest came together at his side. The killer escaped the scene and an extensive hunt failed to locate him. Everyone on the streets and the police investigators knew who had killed Shawn but there was not enough evidence to convict him. As happens more times than not, the killer was arrested and convicted of other crimes not long after the shooting and is still incarcerated.

After the shooting, I kept wondering what it would be like to be Shawn's father. I told myself that, had it been Clay who had been killed, I would have gone to the top of the highest building in Albuquerque and shouted to all who could hear that my son was dead and the killer would pay with his life. I know that I would have found a way to make him pay. Shawn's father had spent his life in law enforcement, which perhaps gave him more control of his emotions than I would have had and his experience allowed him to let the system take care of punishment. This killing stayed on my mind all the while Clay was a police officer.

John Carrillo was the second officer who died while Clay was on the force. Carrillo and his back up officer, John Messimer, had responded to what was originally reported as a domestic dispute. In reality, it was a dispute between a well-to-do citizen and a prostitute he had hired for the evening. The woman had left the home before the officers arrived but they were not aware of that fact. The home owner invited them in to look around the house. While they were in an upstairs bedroom, the man asked if he could use the bathroom. The officers agreed, but as the man entered the bathroom, one of them noticed there was another door at the other end of the room. John Carrillo went to the other side of the bedroom to make sure the man didn't leave through the second door.

They didn't notice him pick up his brief case as he entered the bathroom. Some words were exchanged between John Carrillo and the man concerning privacy and then the killer opened fire with an automatic hand gun that had been hidden in his briefcase. All of the conversation and the shooting were recorded on a small tape recorder John had in his shirt pocket. After the first shots were fired, a loud scream is heard and Carrillo shouts out to his partner, "John, I'm shot! I'm dying." For one reason or another, he was not wearing a protective vest and one of the bullets severed the main artery from his heart. The wound rendered him unconscious in seconds and he died soon after. Many more shots were recorded on the tape as John Messimer exchanged fire with the killer while he tried to protect himself and pull his dying friend to safety. The tape was played over and over again on radio and television news programs as well as at the trial. Each time I heard it played I identified with the young man who was dying because I've been there, and I know that you are aware of your death when it comes. But I also identified with the father of young John Carrillo because my son was a police officer.

Clay and I discussed these police shootings several times. He seemed to be able to deal with them on a professional basis and was convinced the odds of becoming involved in a shooting were very low. He continually reminded me he was young, quick, strong and well trained. He felt he had the edge on anyone who would try to do him harm, and that if he were not to survive, it was just meant to be that way.

While Clay was working on the streets, Kelly continued her classes at UNM and graduated with a double major, Chemistry and Biology, with a 4. 0 grade point average. Her streak of straight "A" grades was unblemished. She started working on a graduate degree in Cell Biology but hit a stumbling block in a related class. A professor felt her work in his graduate level Inorganic Chemistry course was only worth a "B." Kelly felt crushed, but finally accepted the setback when the professor told her that employers are wary of graduates with perfect grades and that a 3. 99 would be a good thing. Not long after this blow to her ego, she decided to interrupt her education and find a job in the world outside of academia. She went to work in the APD laboratory as a Criminalist with a specialty as a Serologist. Now we had both of our children working in law enforcement.

Chapter 8 - Kelly's Struggles

We all have demons in our minds. Some of us recognize them, some don't and some misidentify them, which often leads to compounding our struggles in life. Kelly's demon was an uncontrollable urge to be perfect in everything she attempted in life. My high IQ friend, Ray Turnley, could solve complex problems through his ability to focus completely on the task at hand while he ignored everything around him; but he was unable to keep his office, home or life organized. Kelly, on the other hand, could concentrate completely on any task at hand, but every moment away from the particular problem was used to concentrate on every other aspect of her life. Her attention to detail in every aspect in life was brought home to me one day when I noticed the pencils in her desk draw as she reached for a replacement. The pencils were stored side by side in order of length. Every other item in the drawer was also placed in a specific position according to size. I should have recognized this strange drive as a problem, but I didn't. I assumed it was an offshoot of the neat and orderly way Sylvia and I kept our home and belongings.

Kelly was much different than Clay was as a child. She did not speak clearly until she was almost four years old. Because she was our child, we could understand her, but others had a difficulty understanding her speech. I remember overhearing a relative comment that is was so sad that she was retarded in her mental development. It never entered our minds that she might be mentally challenged; we assumed she would catch up later, which she did with gusto. From an early age she showed some unique abilities. When she received her first tricycle, she first learned to ride it backwards as if that were the normal thing to do. She was able to operate that three wheeler equally well in either direction. It was at about that time when Kelly began to have episodes that in layman's terms would be called seizures. If scolded or if frustrated with trying to accomplish a task beyond her ability, she would break out in tears, fall down, her eyes would roll back in her head and she would become clammy and semiconscious. Although they lasted only minutes, these episodes were frightening to us and we sought medical help.

Among many other tests, the doctors at the hospital on Lackland Air Force Base did a brainwave study which suggested the possibility of epilepsy but added the caveat that their diagnosis was tenuous. They prescribed a daily dose of Phenobarbital, a barbiturate used to treat epilepsy, which we administered for two years. The seizures ceased and she returned to normal; well, almost normal. As she progressed through elementary school, Kelly developed a strange talent. If she could spell a word, she could also spell it backwards. Then she showed us that she could write backwards. I asked her if she were imagining the word in her mind and then using the picture to write the word, but she said she wasn't doing that. She told us she wasn't practicing how to spell and write backwards; she said it just happened. Kelly came to me one day and said, "Watch this, Dad, I can write upside down." As she sat across the table from me, she started to write words upside down from her right to left. We never investigated the root of this skill; to us, it was just something she could do. When telling a guest about her ability one evening, I asked Kelly to show him how she could write upside down and backwards. Without any prompting from me, she took her pencil and wrote the word "backwards" upside down in both cursive and printing and from her left to right and right to left. She had a big smile on her face when she finished as if she had pulled a joke on us. With no sound reason to maintain the strange skill of writing upside down, her ability eventually faded.

As a serologist in the police laboratory, she knew that every bit of work she did had to be perfect because it had great impact on trials. Fortunately, the other Criminalists assigned to the laboratory felt the same way and she interacted well with them. The pressures of the job did have an adverse effect on her. She began to be afflicted with various minor illnesses that affected her attendance. When counseled about this by her supervisor, the result was added pressure. She also mentioned to me that she found it difficult to work every day with the blood stained instruments of pain used in assaults and the blood stained items of victims' clothing. The importance and seriousness of her position as a serologist was brought home to her after she testified in a rape case. The rape had occurred on Kirtland Air Force Base and the perpetrator was prosecuted by the Air Force. Although Kelly's testimony was purely technical, it was an important part of the prosecution's case. At the end of the Court Martial proceedings, the man was found guilty and sentenced to fifty years in the federal penal system. Kelly told me that after the sentence was pronounced, she had a sinking, almost guilty, feeling about being instrumental in sending someone to prison for such a long time. She acknowledged that he was guilty and deserved to be punished, yet she internalized what she thought he must have felt when the sentence was read. I never gave her advice as to what she should do about those feelings, but soon afterward she resigned from the police department. She went to work for a group of Cardiologists to work in the field of double blind drug trials that were part of a national study administered by Duke University.

Kelly's specific position at her new place of employment was as a Research Coordinator. She worked only with seriously ill heart patients who had agreed to participate in the studies of new medications. Working with the patients or the Cardiologists posed no problems, but she began to have difficulties with some coworkers who did not possess the intense work ethic and extraordinary attention to detail that she did. They felt she was trying to show them up as less skilled or less dedicated then she was. I did counsel her on this subject and my advice was simple. I told her there was no way she could ever purposely do less than her best at whatever she attempted and to ignore coworkers who couldn't keep up with her pace and skill. Eventually, her new co-workers came to accept her style, but only a few became friends.

Chapter 9 - Troubles at Work

As soon as I could after the swimming pool accident, I returned to my job at PNM as the Accounts Payable Supervisor. I was able to work four hours, then six hours a day, and eventually full time. I was very busy as we had to switch from manual processing of paper work to a computerized system. The operation of a company with 2,700 employees and several electric generating stations entails thousands of requests for payment for goods or services received each year. Each invoice must be associated with an original purchase order and a receiving report to ensure that the product or service was legally ordered and satisfactorily provided. Invoices cannot be paid without this three way match of paperwork. It sounds simple enough until the human element is considered. Not often, but occasionally, the purchase order was not delivered to Accounts Payable. Very often, the end users of the product or service failed to send receiving reports to Accounts Payable. Many employees, once they received the product or service, forgot about the paper work and moved on with their work. When vendors are not paid on time, they do two things. They complain to the Accounts Payable department and they withhold services or products until they are paid for overdue invoices. When I assumed control of the department, it had a bad reputation with vendors and there were many problems in obtaining critical products and services. As the supervisor, I met with personnel in every department at headquarters, and also our outlying areas such as Las Vegas, Deming, Roswell and Santa Fe. During these visits, I explained the importance of the receiving report to the accounts payable process. The program worked and processing of invoices improved to the point that there were very few complaints.

I thought I had done a fine job in solving the payment problems and in implementing the computerization of the department and expected to be rewarded for my efforts. When my immediate supervisor was selected for a promotion, I felt I was qualified to replace him and hoped to be promoted. Another accountant was selected to replace my supervisor and I felt disappointed. Shortly thereafter, a position as an Assistant Director in the Stockholder Services Department opened and I was promoted to serve in that capacity. I was unable to tell going through the interview and selection process that I would be working for a tyrant.

My new job was to manage the Employee 401(k) plan, the Employee Stock Option Plan and the investors' Dividend Reinvestment Plan. The governmental rules and regulations regarding these plans alone produce enough work to keep plenty of employees busy. Hard work never bothered me so I jumped right in and started managing. Karin, my new supervisor, was happy with my work and gave me a glowing evaluation after the first year; things seemed to be going smoothly. I was a little annoyed that she wanted to be involved in the minutest details of what I was doing every day, but considered it a minor problem. I felt I was being paid as an Assistant Director to make decisions, so I often didn't consult with her until afterward, which seemed to aggravate her. My counterpart in the department, a young lady named Yvonne, managed the accounts of company shareholders; she never made the smallest decision without first obtaining Karin's approval. I didn't realize it, but a sore spot from my independent manner of operating my department festered under the surface with Karin. I was in the midst of integrating the employee plans of the Gas Company of New Mexico, a company acquired by PNM, into our system when she became more abrasive in our employer/employee relationship.

At about the same time, I encountered a personnel problem with one of my employees in that she was taking advantage of the company's unlimited sick day policy. The employee had been out sick for 42 days during the most recent twelve month period. I did further research and found that, almost without exception, the sick days taken were Fridays or Mondays. To me this meant the employee had a drug problem, an alcohol abuse problem or was just a simple opportunist who chose to take advantage of a lenient company policy. I called her to my office and presented the problem in those terms. She denied all three scenarios and claimed that it was a coincidence that she became ill on Fridays and Mondays. I dismissed her while I contemplated further action.

I didn't have long to contemplate. The next day I was summoned to Karin's office and received a dressing down for accusing one of her favorite employees of nefarious acts. I didn't know the woman was the teacher's pet. Karin was well aware that the woman had been abusing the system for years and had allowed it to continue.

At this point, it became more and more distasteful to deal with Karin. I was told that she had developed her hatred of men when her husband left her after she had worked to put him through medical school. Her dislike of me was enhanced when she learned that my son was a police officer, because her two sons had a history of problems with the police and the legal system. My employees liked and respected me but my supervisor harbored ill feelings.

One day, Karin informed me that she wanted me to provide a written report of anything I had to say at the weekly staff meetings. I assumed it was a new policy and complied even though I felt it was a waste of my time. At the first staff meeting after her request, it became obvious that I was the only one of the six member staff who had been charged with submitting a written report. I realized then that the situation was deteriorating.

When it came time for my second yearly evaluation, Karin, as many lazy supervisors do, told me to fill out the evaluation form and write a narrative to support each entry. I did as she requested and sent it to her office. A few days later, I received it back from her with some minor changes and a note asking if I agreed with her modifications. I sent it back noting that I had no problem with her changes. The following Monday morning, I was called to Karin's office. I assumed it was for the formal signing of the evaluation by both of us and thought the meeting was to be routine. I was met by Karin with a scowl on her face and a document she wanted me to read. As she handed it to me, she told me she had changed her mind about the annual evaluation report and was putting me on notice that if I didn't change my style of supervision, she would terminate my employment. The document she handed me said the same thing and had a place for my signature. I thought she had gone crazy. To this day, I have no idea what might have been the catalyst that prompted her to put me into a difficult position with regard to my employment. Perhaps I had offended another of her pets, but I don't recall any incidents of that nature. I knew she was on thin ice with her threat, so I signed the document and asked to be excused for the rest of the day to contemplate the situation. Karin authorized the absence and I made my plans. I had kept a copy of her tentatively approved annual evaluation and took that, her evaluation from the prior year and her letter of admonishment to a lawyer who specialized in employer/employee relations, and told him my story.

The lawyer advised me that based on the evaluations and the lack of any specific violation of company policies, any termination of employment instituted by Karin would be illegal and the company would be subject to suit. He had his secretary write up a summation of his opinion and told me to give it to the Human Resources department at PNM. He also advised me that, if I were terminated, he would be happy to represent me in a suit. I delivered the opinion to the Personnel Officer the first thing in the morning and returned to my office. By mid afternoon, I was summoned to a meeting with a representative from Human Resources and Karin. The HR representative tried to talk me out of dealing with a lawyer and to let him resolve the problem. I politely told him he was ill armed if he thought he could force me to let the fox guard the hen house. My next step was to make an appointment with the Vice President responsible for Stockholder Services.

The next morning, I gave the Vice President the opinion from my lawyer and a typed report of everything that had transpired. He was the first person I had encountered who seemed genuinely friendly toward me. He told me he was aware of Karin's unorthodox style of management and asked me to give him a day to solve the problem. I would have given him however much time he asked for as long as I felt he was working on my behalf. The next day, I was transferred to fill an open position as a senior auditor in the Internal Audit Department. The pay was the same, I did not have to deal with the problems attendant with being a supervisor, and my skills learned as an IRS Auditor and Agent dovetailed perfectly with the challenges in the Audit Department. The person selected to fill my position in Karin's department was a malcontent who gave her grief for as long as he worked there, but the company didn't get sued because of her actions so she got away cheap.

Chapter 10 - Life Goes On

While I was struggling on the job with my tyrannical supervisor, the important part of my life, enjoying family and friends, continued. In late 1983, Sylvia decided she did not want to live in the house where I broke my neck, so we sold the place on Noreen NE and purchased a new patio home on the outskirts of Albuquerque. Both of the children were living in their own apartments and we felt we didn't need the larger home. The new home on Tramway Terrace Loop Northeast was a two bedroom, 1,500 square foot building in a very nice neighborhood. While living in the patio home, I hit another low spot in life.

It was about 5:30 P.M. on a dark winter evening when, as I approached the left turn from Tramway Boulevard on to Tramway Terrace Loop, my vehicle was slammed into by a pickup truck driven by an impaired or inattentive driver. As I slowed to a stop to allow oncoming traffic to pass before making the left turn, I noticed in the rearview mirror that the vehicle was approaching at a high rate of speed. I tapped my brakes several times to get the driver's attention but it was to no avail. Many years ago when I was only sixteen, my father had taught me never to turn the wheels for a left turn until any oncoming traffic cleared. That lesson probably saved my life. When the truck hit the rear of my vehicle, it was pushed forward about fifty feet but remained in the proper lane. The pickup, its rear axle and wheels separated from its frame, ended up off the road on the right. My car was demolished but, thanks to the seat belt, I was only slightly bruised and did not need medical attention; however, the event took a toll on my psyche.

After surviving a broken neck less than a year earlier and then surviving what easily could have been a disastrous motor vehicle accident, I became seriously paranoid about my safety, especially with regard to driving. As with most people who are paranoid, I was completely unaware I was suffering from a mental illness. After some months, Sylvia convinced me to see a Psychologist because I was driving my family and friends to distraction. I made an appointment with Dr. Gail Feldman, a therapist recommended by my general practitioner. After a number of therapy sessions, Gail arrived at a diagnosis of Post Traumatic Stress Disorder (PTSD). She told me it was due to an accumulation of stress from my service in Vietnam, the swimming pool accident and the motor vehicle accident. When she eventually discharged me from her care, her last words, with a big smile, were, "Everyone out there in the world is not out to get you, only about ten percent of them, so relax." Sylvia told me I was much easier to live with after the therapy but I don't think there ever was anything seriously wrong with me.

After living in the patio home for a while, we concluded it was too small for us. I guess I must be hard to live with, and any cohabitant of mine needs a fair amount of personal space. On a Sunday afternoon, about a year later, when I returned from some morning skiing, Sylvia told me she wanted to look at a home she had found advertized in the newspaper. We visited the 2,400 square foot home on Bauer Northeast, which was closer in to the city and her place of work, and decided it was what we wanted.

We listed and sold our patio home and on April 15, 1985, we moved into the house on Bauer Northeast. Clay lived there with us for some months when he was in between apartments. He had been living with his long time lady friend, Loraine, but that romance cooled. One summer day, as Clay and I were running up the La Luz trail to the top of Sandia Crest while training for the annual race, he told me he had decided to marry Jane Brueggemann, a woman who was seven and a half years his senior. When I asked him if he had carefully considered the complexity of marrying an older woman, his response was that he didn't think he could live with an immature woman. Perhaps his experiences on the streets had made him far more mature than his actual age and he felt that he was not compatible with younger women. Clay had previously told me that Jane was diagnosed with a "Manic Depressive Personality Disorder" and I asked him about that risk. He said he felt confident that with medication to keep her malady under control and his education in Psychology there would be no problem. Jane had an ex husband who caused problems for her and Clay while they were dating and there was a three year old son, Carl, whose custody they shared. I felt he was getting himself into a complicated situation that could develop into unhappiness. Again, I sensed he was making a mistake but covered my feelings and went along with his decision. They were married on October 11, 1986.

About eighteen months later, Kelly and her fiancé, Rod Heimgartner, were married in our home on Bauer Northeast; it was a great affair with many guests. The judge who was to perform the ceremony was delayed and unable to call to give a time of arrival so Kelly, with her penchant for perfection, really became upset, but was kept under control by Clay with his laid back personality. At about the time Clay was to lose control of Kelly, Rod said, "I've got an idea! Let's start the reception while we wait for the judge." How could anyone not like a guy like that? We started the reception and everyone was in a great mood when the judge arrived. The reception was interrupted for a few minutes for the wedding and then continued far into the evening. Her happiness with Rod had calmed her to a great degree and life was good for them. They sold Rod's townhome and, with both of them employed, had no problem qualifying for a mortgage on a nice home in the far northeast heights of Albuquerque. It was a happy time.

One day in mid 1987, Clay came to me and told me that his name was going to be in an issue of *National Geographic*, a magazine I had subscribed to since 1972. When I asked how that could be possible, he told me that he met a *National Geographic* reporter doing an article on Albuquerque who had participated in a citizen ride along with one of the police officers during the graveyard shift. When they met at a crime scene, Clay told the writer that his father had a copy of every *National Geographic* ever issued (he tended to exaggerate somewhat) and that the reporter just had to mention his name to make me proud. The writer agreed and, in the November 1987 issue, wrote, "Officer Clay Joyce remarks, 'I haven't had dinner.' Nor have we, and it's past midnight. We carefully select a restaurant where no cook has been arrested." Sylvia was doubly pleased with the overall treatment of Albuquerque in the magazine. The article included information on J. Pace Van Devender, the scientist at Sandia National Laboratory for whom she was the administrative assistant. Pace is an internationally known physicist who managed the Particle Beam Fusion Accelerator project. She figured it had to be fairly rare for a person to have her son and her employer quoted in the same issue of *National Geographic*.

In the middle of 1988, Clay came to me to say that he was going to leave the police department and join the United States Air Force. I thought he had lost his mind until he told me they had offered him a commission as a Second Lieutenant. Without confiding in me, he had gone through the application process and testing, and had been accepted to the Officer Training School at Medina Air Base in San Antonio, Texas. He had never participated in any ROTC programs in high school or college, so I was surprised that he was selected for a coveted slot in the training program. The recruiter told him it was rare but his high grades in college, and the results of the Air Force academic and sociological testing combined with his street experience, made him a prime applicant for an Air Force Military Police career. I was pleased with his initiative and success. Clay completed his initial training and in late summer and we traveled to San Antonio to attend his graduation. He then attended the military police training school located on Lackland Air Force Base in San Antonio and eventually he, Jane, Carl and their son, Danny, who had been born on July 29, 1987, moved to his first assignment at Minot Air Force Base in Minot, North Dakota; he was a brand new Second Lieutenant. Their daughter, Rachael, was born on October 16, 1989 and Clay was promoted to First Lieutenant soon after that. We spoke often on the telephone and he assured me he was enjoying his work, they were financially secure (even with only one wage earner), and he looked forward to a great career in the Air force.

In November of 1988, PNM went through a corporate downsizing and gave me an early retirement package. I was only fifty-four and they agreed to pay me almost a thousand dollars a month for the rest of my life not to come into work. I thought it was a great deal. I didn't realize that most companies in town were not likely to hire anyone in their fifties until I started to look for a replacement job. Sylvia was working and I had my Air Force and PNM retirement income so we got by okay. I decided to take over the running of the household to include the cooking and cleaning. I became a stay at home dad without children. Sylvia threatened to rent a couple of children to live with us so I could see how it really is to run a household, but she never did.

Running the household was a pleasure. When Sylvia's lady friends found out about the arrangement, several of them jokingly offered to rent me from her. After a while, the large house with its half acre yard became a pain to maintain, so in February of 1990, we sold it and moved into an apartment while we waited for a new home to be constructed. During the construction, we had a disagreement with the builder regarding the quality of some of the work and terminated our contract. After a little hesitation, the builder returned our down payment and we purchased an existing townhouse on Denali Street in northeast Albuquerque. Soon after this move, our lives changed forever.

Chapter 11 - Clay's Death

If you have lived very many years at all, you have heard the adage that the worse loss of all is the loss of a child. It is, of course, true, but even that loss has degrees of devastation. In my case, the anguish was overwhelming. This photograph was taken by Clay's maternal grandmother about a year before his death.

He had an engaging smile. (Courtesy: Margaret Stamps)

On July 12, 1990, Clay had the day off and went out for an exercise run. After he returned, he took a shower and sat down at his desk to take care of some paper work. It was near noon time and as Jane went up the stairs to put nine month old Rachel down for a nap, she asked him to go outside and call Danny to come in for lunch. Carl, who was seven years old at the time, was spending the summer with his biological father in Idaho. Jane heard Clay call to Danny to come in for lunch but then nothing more. A few minutes later, Danny came upstairs and told Jane, "Daddy's taking a nap on the floor and he won't wake up." She ran down the stairs and found Clay lying on his back, half on the porch and half on the entry way floor. He was not breathing and his eyes were fixed and dilated. Jane used the telephone which was on a table in the hallway to call the base emergency number and the rescue squad arrived within minutes. They worked for forty-five minutes to resuscitate him but were unsuccessful.

Because the rescue crew found a dark substance in the mask used in their unsuccessful resuscitation attempt and there was a Snickers candy bar wrapper in the waste basket in the office, it was assumed he choked to death on chocolate. At autopsy, a bruise was found on his right shoulder and the back of his head which raised questions as to the cause of death. Clay was in his stocking feet and the entry way had a hard wood floor. The doctor who performed the autopsy reported that he may have fallen, and hit his head, which caused him to regurgitate the chocolate that he aspirated, or the very last bite of the candy bar had lodged in his trachea. Whichever was the case, he choked to death. A son most men would kill to have was gone forever.

Jane's first thought after recovering from the initial shock of losing her husband was of the effect his death would have on me. She insisted that the fatality notification team at Kirtland Air Force Base refrain from informing me of Clay's death until they could locate his best friend on the Albuquerque Police Department, Jerry Roach, to accompany them to our home. She also arranged for the team to wait outside of our residence until she could call me and personally inform me of Clay's death.

When I received her call, I immediately accepted the veracity of the information because she never called us; all of the calls we had received from them were initiated by Clay, so when I heard her voice, I knew there would be tragic news. My first reaction was to ask what I could do to help her. Maybe that was a defense mechanism, maybe not; it is typical of me to be proactive in all situations, whether inconsequential or dire. When our call ended, the notification team received a signal from Minot AFB and came to the front door. Jerry was with them and his presence did indeed make the process a bit less devastating. It was near the time when Sylvia would return from work, so after the formalities, I asked the Air Force team to leave; I didn't want Sylvia to see their blue Air Force vehicle. It was not unusual for Jerry to visit us, so I didn't worry about her noticing his police vehicle. In fact, the first thing she said as she came through the door was, "I'm home! Is that Jerry's car out there?"

With the knowledge that I would have to be the one to tell Sylvia and Kelly of our loss, I was able to hold myself together although I think I was operating on automatic pilot. I told Sylvia of the tragedy and with Jerry's support got through the next few minutes. Then I called Kelly's home and told her. She was seven months pregnant with their first child, Samantha, so I hesitated, not knowing what the effect might be, but I had to tell her. I trace Kelly's decent into a long period of illness to the day I told her of Clay's death.

The painful details of what transpired over the next ten days were covered in a previous book and will not be repeated here. Suffice it to say, the loss of my son was a blow that knocked me into a state of depression that would last nearly two full years. My friends and family, especially Sylvia, endured my madness until my psychological ship was righted in the early summer of 1992. My grief, though mitigated by the passage of time, remains. The ordeal convinced me that women are stronger than men in these circumstances. Sylvia had to deal with her own grief, the loss of her husband's sanity, and still participate in the planning of her son's funeral; a daunting task for anyone.

The Air Force and the Albuquerque Police Department worked together to provide a fine military funeral with all of the prescribed formal activities. Family came from San Antonio and whatever help was needed was provided by friends. I moved through the proceedings in a fog. Jane was also in a fog and Danny was so struck by events that he ceased to talk for almost a week. His first words, the evening before the funeral, were addressed to no one as he sat alone in the kitchen of Jane's parents' home. He simply blurted out, "My Daddy died. They took him away in a big truck [the military ambulance]."

After the funeral, Sylvia returned to work and I returned to my full time job of running the household. I didn't know I was in a daze, but I was. I was going through the motions of living but was only partially functional. On one occasion I found myself wandering through a shopping mall when I felt I was having a heart attack. I located a bench and sat until I could catch my breath and the tightness in my chest subsided. Then I drove from one drug store to another to use the free blood pressure check machines because I refused to believe my blood pressure was as high as indicated on successive machines. I called Kelly at the cardiologic practice where she worked and asked for advice. She insisted I check in to the hospital for an examination. The bottom line was that I wasn't having a heart attack; I was having an anxiety attack. The Cardiologist who examined me, Doctor Kathleen Blake, one of the best in the country, said to me, "Mr. Joyce, your heart is not sick; your heart is broken over the loss of your son." I was glad to hear I didn't have a heart problem but I still felt miserable.

In the fall of 1990, Jane decided she didn't want to live in Albuquerque and contacted a privately owned and supported housing facility on Lackland Air Force Base in San Antonio, Texas. The facility was established in the 1960s to provide housing for Air Force widows of the Vietnam War and continues to offer accommodations. She made all of the moving arrangements herself. On moving day, I drove one of our vehicles with Carl and she drove her car with Danny to San Antonio with an overnight stop along the way. Sylvia flew from Albuquerque to San Antonio with eleven month old Rachael and met us there. As I look back on the trip, I probably shouldn't have been on the road as detached from reality as I was. Jane was probably in worse shape than I was. At about a hundred miles east of Albuquerque when we stopped for fuel, she locked the keys in her car and it took several hours to get a police officer to come by the gas station with a "Slim Jim" to open the vehicle. That incident put us behind schedule and aggravated me. I never knew what was going in Jane's mind. She never spoke much so it was hard to realize what she was thinking.

We eventually got Jane and the children moved into their apartment and used the opportunity to visit family while we were in the San Antonio area. Clay had been wise enough to have a second life insurance policy in force, so in addition to the standard government policy for $50,000, Jane received $50,000 more from the second policy. I helped her set up accounts at my credit union in San Antonio and gave her my best advice regarding finances. Some months after we returned to Albuquerque,

Jane decided to purchase a new house that was near the boys' school and Lackland Air Force Base where she had some military benefits as Clay's widow. She also received monetary compensation as a widow and income to help raise the children until they reached the age of twenty-three as long as they were students, so she was reasonably secure.

Clay's cremated remains had been interred in a cemetery in Albuquerque which was his adopted home town. After moving to San Antonio, Jane had his remains moved to Texas and reinterred in the national cemetery at Fort Sam Houston in San Antonio. In support of the theory that death is the ultimate equalizer, burial plots are assigned by lottery. The remains of sergeants, privates and generals from many periods and services are intermingled there. The luck of the draw gave Clay an easily accessible, very attractive plot. Just before we returned to Albuquerque in April of 2006, I drove from New Braunfels to San Antonio early on a Sunday morning and took a photograph of his tombstone. Every once in a while, it flashes up on my computer screen as part of my screen saver program and makes me feel close to him.

Clay's final resting place at Fort Sam Houston National Cemetery.

One night, in the spring of 1991, I had a dream that almost convinced me there is an afterlife and that spirits of deceased people do roam around the earth. I dreamed that a noise awakened me and I heard Clay's voice. I saw a milk carton sized lantern hanging in the air with four glass sides, but instead of a light inside, I could only see swirling mist. From the lantern, I heard Clay calling to me. He said, "Dad! Dad! Come over to my side. It's time to come to my side." I told him I couldn't do that because I still had things to do, but he insisted and said again, "It's okay, Dad, it good over here. Come on over." I reiterated that I couldn't do that, and he replied, "Okay, Dad. I've got to go now." And the lantern floated away into the dark. When I told this story to Sylvia in the morning, I didn't say I dreamed about Clay, I told her that Clay had visited me the night before and tried to get me to go over to his side. I'm sure she thought I was on the edge of losing my mind and was very worried. We discussed this incident and many other things until one of us suggested that perhaps we would feel better if we left Albuquerque where we saw the specter of Clay on every corner and in every police vehicle we saw.

We were both familiar with the advice that no one should make any life changing decisions within a year of losing a loved one but didn't think the decision to move to another city fell into a life changing act for us. We had moved so many times and lived in so many places, it was a routine decision for us. We decided to move to San Antonio and be closer to Sylvia's family. The place on Denali went on the market and by June it had sold and closed. I flew over to San Antonio to rent a place for us to live while we looked for a new home, and found a rental house for a reasonable price. We packed our belongings, hired a moving company and started off on another adventure.

Chapter 12 - San Antonio in 1991

The rental home I found in the northwest part of town was about forty-five minutes away from Jane's place in southwest San Antonio and about the same distance from Sylvia's parents in the southeast part of town. The distances meant there were no unannounced visits from relatives which is the way I like to live. We purchased a half acre lot in a nice housing development in Northeast San Antonio and made plans to build a home. Not long after moving to San Antonio, we took a previously planned trip to Europe to visit with our friends, the Zahns. Peter and Uschi were wonderful hosts. They had planned an automobile trip from Berlin, through France to the French Rivera, the northern part of Italy, Austria and southern Germany before our return to Berlin. It was a much needed trip for both of us and we still reminisce about that time in our lives. As pleasant as the trip to Europe was, I went deeper into depression after we returned. Sylvia found employment and I resumed my duties as the home husband, but I was barely functional. I continued to be out of touch with the world but went through the motions of studying floor plans, selecting tile and carpet for the new house and visiting with family over the next few months. Jane too, was suffering from grief and her underlying mental illness of manic depression. She was seeing a Psychiatrist on a regular basis but we couldn't see any improvement. She couldn't keep an appointment and would show up for family events from an hour to a day late. On occasion, we would have harsh words because she was afraid we had moved to San Antonio to steal Clay's children from her. The news from Albuquerque was that Kelly was having a terrible time dealing with Clay's death and was continually ill with various minor maladies. It was not a happy time.

By early fall, Sylvia had determined that I was in worse mental condition than when we were living in Albuquerque and suggested that we terminate the contract with our builder regardless of cost and return to New Mexico. Her theory was that we should be where we might be

284

able to help Kelly and be around our circle of long time friends to help me recover. We lost a few thousand dollars on account with the builder and a few more thousand when we sold the lot, but money was not as important as healing our spirits. Sylvia called her previous employer, the Sandia National Laboratories and asked if her clearance could be reinstated. They told her that as long as no more than six months had elapsed, her clearance could be reinstated. They also told her they would be happy to rehire her. We packed our belongings and moved back to Albuquerque in December of 1991.

Chapter 13 – Back to Albuquerque and a New Job

After a few months in an apartment, we purchased a townhouse in Northeast Albuquerque and moved again. The townhouse needed some repairs so I went to work to bring it up to our standards. The work kept me busy and helped keep my mind off of my grief, but I was still dysfunctional. On Sylvia's urging, I returned to therapy with Gail Feldman but could not make any progress. She tried everything she knew including Past Life Regression Therapy through hypnosis. Finally, she recommended I see a Psychiatrist, who would have the option of prescribing medication, and recommended Dr. Ronald Romanik.

I called Dr. Romanik and made an appointment. The first thing he did was have a Psychologist administer a battery of tests which revealed some mental strengths and weaknesses that are probably normal in most people. During the fifth therapy session, Dr. Romanik stumbled upon the reason I was having such a difficult time dealing with Clay's death. He concluded that I had been vicariously living a parallel life as I watched Clay proceed through his life. His attendance of college right after high school, his success on the police force and his earning a commission as an Air Force Officer, something I had tried to do many times without success, represented an extension of my psyche. When I lost my son, who I loved and held in such high esteem, I also lost my parallel life that gave me so much happiness. His analysis struck such a chord of truth, I knew he was right. What I thought was pride in my son's accomplishments was also pride in my imaginary self moving through life in Clay. When I left therapy that day, I told Dr. Romanik I was cured and did not need any more appointments. When I related the session to Sylvia, she agreed that it was a sound theory and that I should think about it for a while before deciding I was over my problem. I agreed with her and promised to make a better effort deal with my grief.

In the fall of 1992, Sylvia's vehicle needed replacement and we purchased a new Infinity from the local dealership. A few weeks later, Betty Rivera, the owner of the agency and a businesswoman we knew from social gatherings, called to thank me for the purchase. She explained she had been out of town when we visited the dealership or she would have dealt with us personally. I told her we didn't go there looking for a favor from her; we went there because she sold the product we wanted to buy. Betty asked if I were working, and when I told her I wasn't, she told me of an opportunity to return to work if I so chose. I told her I would consider working if the job were right for me and she agreed to have Al Robinson, an executive who had worked at PNM when I was an employee there, call me.

Al was managing an automobile tire recapping business. He invited me to an interview with him for the position of controller of Acutred Incorporated. We hit it off and he offered me a reasonable salary to return to work, which I accepted. The company purchased used tires from several tire collection centers in the western part of the country and recapped them for resale. It is an interesting process and we manufactured a good product that was sold at a reasonable price, but there were risks. Every once in a while, a tread on one of our tires would break loose and damage the wheel well of a vehicle. These product failures, though rare, cost us an average of $5,000 per incident. We had to sell a lot of tires to make up for one failure. Another problem was the availability of tire carcasses for our highest selling tires. Cash flow was also a problem because our salesmen, eager to make sales, often made large sales to customers that were not creditworthy. We had orders we could not fill because we couldn't find enough used tires of the proper size and we filled orders from customers with large Accounts Receivable balances. Al was a real wheeler – dealer type and I couldn't get him interested in considering the financial weakness of the endeavor. He made advertisement commitments without checking the expenditures with me beforehand and approved sales to people who already owed us large sums. The parent company kept pumping cash into our company to pay our bills but I could see that the business was bound to fail.

After a staff meeting one evening, I told Al that I couldn't bring myself to continue in my position if he wouldn't take action on some of my recommendations to keep us afloat. He carried on that he couldn't afford to lose me and even offered a generous raise if I would stay on board. The salary had nothing to do with my decision and Al made it clear he would continue to run the company the way he felt was the best way for survival. I quit that evening and within three months the company went into bankruptcy. The work at the tire company took my mind off of my grief and further helped in my recovery.

The help from Dr. Romanik and the effort I put in while working for Al Robinson combined to help me return to normal. On a June morning in 1992, after finishing breakfast, I suddenly had an awakening. My mind cleared of a fog that had kept me from being normal. I looked across the table at my wife and said, "Sylvia, I feel like I just woke up from a bad dream."

Sylvia stared across the table and said, "If you think you have been having a bad dream, think about me. I lost my son and then, essentially, lost you for these past twenty-three months." She suddenly realized she had sounded harsh and got up from her chair to come around the table to hug me and said, "Welcome back." I guess I had been worse than I imagined over the almost two years since Clay's death. Wherever my mind went for such a long time was a place it needed to be to keep me from dying from grief.

In February of 1994, we had an opportunity to sell the townhouse we purchased in 1992 and accepted the offer. We purchased another townhouse in Tanoan, a gated, country club community. It was during this period that I lost my favorite brother, Bobby. He had been diagnosed with a fast growing, inoperable cancer of the prostate gland. In my conversations with him over the telephone, he sounded very serene in his acceptance of his fate. We decided to take some time and visit with him at his home in Florida before it was too late.

We flew to Florida in the spring of 1994 and had a very nice visit with Bobby before he became bedridden. We talked about old times and he gave me a lot of advice on prostate cancer. He was still able to get around, so we were able to go out to dinner, which he insisted on paying for because, as he said, "I won't need money much longer." He was well known for his dry humor. Before we left to return to Albuquerque, Bobby went into a closet and brought out the antique, front loading, cap and ball shot gun that was owned by our grandfather. In the family it was always referred to as the "duck gun" because of the duck hunting scene carved into the stock. Bobby handed me the gun and said he wanted me to have it on one condition. The condition was that it never fall into the hands of our brother, Buddy. There was bad blood between Buddy and me but I was not aware of any problem between Buddy and Bobby. My major problem with Buddy started at the same time Bobby's problem did. It was shortly after my father's death when Buddy took it upon himself to confiscate the family's gun collection. Buddy was very wealthy at the time and had a large collection of expensive guns of his own. At my mother's ninetieth birthday party held in Dover, Delaware, I had asked him what the source of his wealth was since I didn't know what he did for a living. He reached into his pocket and produced a medallion identical to the one I had seen in Vietnam displayed by the Green Beret trooper who claimed to be an assassin. He asked me if I knew what the medallion represented. I told him that, oddly enough, I had seen one before and I knew what it represented. He asked, "Do you remember when I was missing for eight years?" Before I could respond, he continued, "That's what I was doing for a living and it paid pretty good." Apparently, Buddy was hired by the CIA to participate in the Phoenix Project.[29]

The guns in the family collection were not unusually valuable but held sentimental value for Bobby and me. I thought it was singularly sad that a man facing certain death was so annoyed with a sibling that he wanted to ensure a family heirloom would not end up in his hands.

After settling the disposition of the antique shotgun, Bobby took out a second family treasure he did not want to fall into the hands of his older brother. He handed me an eight by ten inch frame that held a severely faded, handwritten letter secured between two pieces of clear glass. It was the one my grandfather brought with him when he emigrated from Ireland in 1872. Bobby reiterated his desire that I ensure the document be handed down to a family member other than Buddy's offspring. After well over a hundred and twenty years, the ink had faded to a nearly unreadable level, but I was able to decipher most of what was written. On personalized stationery, it read: *Bearer Richard Joice, I have known from his childhood. He has also, for a long time, been in my employment as an assistant groom and I have no hesitation in stating*

29   A program managed by the CIA engaged in the assassination of thousands of government officials supporting the Viet Cong and the North Vietnamese.

that a better, competent young man could not be had in every respect. The document was signed with an illegible signature and dated May 16, 1872.

Bobby died an uncomfortable death in July of 1995 and I, of course, honored his requests. The shotgun is in my possession and I have chosen my grandson, Lucas Heimgartner to receive it upon my demise. My grandfather's letter has been delivered to my niece, Denise Connolly Kearns, who has a keen interest and expertise in restoring antique documents.

Some years later, when Buddy was facing certain death from throat cancer, I wrote to him and asked that he send my father's portion of his gun collection to me to be handed down to family members. He not only refused, he became incensed that I would even ask for the guns. I was nice enough not to tell him about Bobby's dying wish, but he and I never spoke again. When Buddy died in December of 1999, the collection disappeared and no one in the family knows of its location.

Living in Tanoan was quiet, safe and interesting but the bug to move was again soon to bite. On one of our visits to San Antonio we spent a few days in the town of Kerrville, Texas, and looked for land purchase opportunities. We found a great deal on a seven and a half acre piece of land on Tierra Linda Ranch, a community a few miles from Kerrville. An elderly couple had purchased the land many years before but never built their retirement home there because of medical problems. The couple had passed on and the heirs had priced the land forty percent below market to make a quick sale. The reduction in price made it affordable for us. Each time we went to San Antonio for a visit we stopped by our land to dream of our retirement home. We sold the townhome on the golf course in June of 1996 and moved into a rental unit in Kerrville where we lived while our retirement home was under construction.

Chapter 14 - Tierra Linda Ranch in Texas

The Tierra Linda Ranch, located about ten miles northeast of Kerrville, Texas, is a unique experiment that allows owners to enjoy attractive country living. It is a 3,000 acre working cattle ranch operated by a homeowners association. Each member of the association owns at least five acres on the ranch and many members own considerably more land than that. Quarterly dues paid to the association are based on the number of acres owned. The funds pay for the maintenance of the roads, fence construction and repair, feed for 100 head of cattle and 50 to 60 calves each year, and other necessary facilities. Dues also pay the salaries for an office manager, a ranch manager, a wrangler and a few ranch hands.

When we lived on the ranch, there were approximately 250 owners who paid roughly $358,000 in dues per year to subsidize the operation. Electricity is provided by a local cooperative and telephone service is available through the local telephone company. Each home there has its own water well and septic system. Owners are only allowed to fence off twenty percent of their property so most of the land remains available for the cattle to graze and for the benefit of horseback riders. There are many acres on the ranch that fall into the category of common land. The common land is used for cattle and horse grazing and for facilities available to the owners, such as a club house, horse stables, tennis courts and swimming pool. A year round stream meanders through the ranch which provides replenishment water for the ranch's two lakes. Roaming free on the ranch are white tail deer, mouflon sheep, black buck antelope, turkey and many other forms of Texas wildlife. It is an idyllic life and a wonderful place for all of the men and women who wanted to be cowboys and cowgirls as children, which is probably most of us. Following is a photograph of yours truly doing his cowboy impersonation.

There is not much better than enjoying nature on a fine horse.
(Courtesy: Marian F. Turner)

There are opportunities to work as "gentleman ranchers" if one is so inclined. I was inclined in that direction when I lived there and thoroughly enjoyed riding around the ranch on horseback while sporting my cowboy boots and straw hat. For some reason, most of the men on the ranch had little interest in using the string of fine riding horses owned by the association. On the other hand, many of the ladies learned to ride and often frequented the stables. I took riding lessons from Buffey, the ranch wrangler, and met a number of riding buddies. Two close friends were Gina Rolfes, who was in her thirties and took riding lessons with me, and Marian Turner, a lady in her forties who helped Gina and me with our training and turned us into advanced riders. Because the rules based on safety and insurance liability did not allow single riders roaming around the ranch, it meant that I had many riding partners of the opposite sex. I have fond memories of long rides over those 3,000 acres with Linda, Marian, Loretta, Gina, Rebecca and many others who occasionally joined us. Although we were not supposed to "run" the horses, some of those ladies just had to test my abilities from time to time and we had some exhilarating rides. I remember an accident that caused Marian to need eight stitches in her ear, and one that left me with cuts and bruises on my head and legs from haphazardly running our horses through the underbrush. On one ride I came close to getting seriously hurt.

In the process of what we jokingly called an "unauthorized dismount," I was knocked silly during an otherwise gentle trail ride. As qualified advanced riders, Marian and I often escorted less experienced riders on trail rides. To enhance safety, Marian, who was a better rider than I and was more familiar with the area, would normally take the lead and I would bring up the rear. As we rode through a forested area on a winding trail with Marian out of my site around a bend, I heard her shout, "Fire Ants!" Her horse had bolted and was stomping its front feet which led Marian to believe it had stepped into a fire ant mound, but she was mistaken. The foot falls from her horse had stirred up a nest of yellow jacket bees. She and the other riders passed the hive before they came out in mass. By the time I reached the area, the yellow jackets had swarmed and went after my horse's nose and eyes and he reared in fear. I tried to hang on but when he came down on his front legs, he bucked hard and I went up into the air. I remember looking at nothing but blue sky for a second and thinking, "These old bones of mine are brittle; something is bound to break when I hit the ground."

When I landed square on the upper part of my shoulders, my head snapped back onto the rocky ground and I bit my tongue. The blow to my head made me semiconscious and I wasn't aware of what had happened for a short period. The first thing I remember seeing when I regained my senses was a pretty blond woman leaning over me and slapping at my chest. I recognized Marian, and for a second, I thought she was making a very weak attempt at CPR. When I asked her what she was doing, she said, "I'm trying to get the bees off of you! Are you okay?" As any normal male would do in the situation, I told her I was fine. She said, "You don't look fine. Your head is bleeding and your mouth is bleeding." I tasted the blood then and checked for missing teeth with my tongue, but didn't find any damage. In a few minutes, I was on my feet and gathering up my horse that had returned to the scene on his own; we decided to call off the rest of the ride and walked back to the stable. We laughed about the scene of Marian beating the bees off of my chest, but she says she was really worried when she saw me on the ground. She said she heard the loud thump when my body hit the ground and when she saw me lying still with blood on my face, she thought, "How are we going to tell Sylvia that we killed David on a trail ride."

There was a serious incident when loose dogs spooked Gina's mount into bucking her high into the air and she landed face down on the rock strewn ground. I had a clear view of her as she flew through the air and landed with a sickening thump. I dismounted, tied my horse and ran through the brush to help her. She had been knocked senseless but as I rolled her over on her back and pulled her up to sitting position I could see she was breathing and was blinking her eyes as she looked into my face. I couldn't think of anything to do but hug her. When she came to her senses she told me she thought she was alright and got to her feet to look for her horse. Some weeks later, she told us she remembered flying through the air and then wondering why I was hugging her. She also told us her breasts were so bruised it looked like she was wearing a black bra when she was naked. Because that was such a serious incident, we contacted the ranch manager and asked that he track down the dogs. He quickly discovered they had come from an abandoned residence. The dogs were dispatched by the ranch manager but, as far as anyone knew, they were last seen running down a road that bordered the ranch, and were never seen again. My riding buddies and I must have been quite a site to passersby. We ranged in age from thirty to sixty-five, some of us wore wide brimmed cowboy hats, some baseball caps and Marian, especially after the eight stitches, always wore a riding helmet. Following is a photograph taken in 2001, before one of our rides. From left to right are: Rebecca Bowman, Linda Laird, yours truly, Marian Turner and Gina Rolfes.

I had plenty of great riding buddies on the ranch. (Courtesy: Sylvia Joyce)

We didn't realize it when we purchased the land, but an overwhelming number of the residents on Tierra Linda Ranch were very wealthy; a station in life that did not apply to us. Most of the men were former leaders in the oil, manufacturing and financial industries, and each one of them was sure he knew the best way to manage the ranch. Not many of them wanted to donate their time to participate in governing but almost all of them made their opinions known. I was to encounter many of these men after I volunteered my time to help manage the ranch.

After our home was completed and we moved onto the ranch in January of 1997, Sylvia found a job she enjoyed with the local Chamber of Commerce in Kerrville and I had some time on my hands. I wandered into the ranch office one morning and asked the man I found there if my skill as an accountant could be of use to the association. The man was Larry Higgins and he was then serving on the ranch Board of Directors as the Treasurer. He greeted me with a big smile and explained that, when his time on the Board was finished at the end of the year, they would be looking for someone who could function as Treasurer and I should plan on running for election to the post. He suggested that in the meantime, if I volunteered as the chairman of the Facilities Committee, I would become familiar with running the ranch. This would give me exposure to the owners that would help in the election process. I agreed and was appointed by the Board as the Chairman of the Facilities Committee. The other two members were women of about my age and we got along fine.

Construction of a new home for the Ranch Manager was already underway when I assumed the responsibilities as the Chairman of the Facilities Committee, but I had other projects as well. During that year, covered bulletin boards were installed, extensive renovations on the club house were completed, new pool furniture was purchased and a new tack room at the stable was constructed with the help of owners skilled in architectural design and the building trades. It was a fun filled year for me. There were fences to be built on our place and cedar trees to be cut and burned. Marian, an active member of the Riders Advisory Group, worked with me on the construction of the new tack room so we became well acquainted. At the end of the year, I was elected to the Board to fill the treasurer's position for the next two years and Marian was elected to fill the secretary's position.

Working on the Board of Directors, supervising the operation of the ranch and managing the funds provided by so many people were enlightening and challenging tasks. Just about everyone had an opinion as to solving the problem of the overabundance of white tail deer. Opinions ran from leaving the deer alone to removing all but a few. By Texas law, all of the deer in the state belong to all of the people, so killing cannot be done without permission from the State Game Department. After conducting a survey, the state representative told us we had at least 500 more deer than the land could support due to the depletion of the natural foliage, and gave us permission to remove them in any way we desired. Attempts were made to capture them with nets but that was unsuccessful. Getting permission of home owners to allow the ranch hands to shoot the deer was iffy at best. Many did not approve of the program. In addition, the deer tend to congregate near residences where home owners feed them which added to the danger. Some wanted to erect a ten foot tall deer fence around the ranch; that was nowhere near cost effective. The bottom line is, the association members are still squabbling today about managing the deer population. With so many deer trying to survive on the meager foliage, they have become much smaller in stature than the normal Texas white tail deer population.

When the ranch was developed as a residential project, the association built an airstrip and ten hangars. Leases for the hangars were offered at a ridiculously low price as an incentive to lure new, wealthy residents. The leases were for twenty years and at the end of that time, the rent would revert to market price. During my tenure on the Board, some of the leases were about to expire and those using the hangars wanted the leases to be extended ten years longer at the original rate. To me, that would represent an economic loss to the ranch and increase the value of the lessee's property should a sale occur. There was a huge battle between the pilot's association and their backers and other groups on the ranch. Even within the pilot's association there were hard feelings. Some of the pilots constructed hangars at their own expense and resented those with the inexpensive leases. We were unable to resolve the issue while I was on the Board and it probably persists today.

There were problems with dog lovers who let their dogs run loose which was contrary to the rules and regulations of the ranch. The dogs harassed the cattle and frightened horses being ridden by association members. Dealing with people who prefer dogs to people can become exasperating.

Larry Higgins quit speaking to me when he found out that I had changed the books to comply with the Generally Accepted Accounting Principles (GAAP). The ranch borrowed $70,000 from a bank to build the new Ranch Manager's home and Larry had entered the funds on the books as income and then accounted for the repayment of principle and interest as an expense. The proper treatment was to list the debt as a liability and the cash from the bank as an asset. As the loan is paid off, the interest is treated as an expense and the principle payment is assigned to the value of the house. Larry was a very successful economist, but he did not understand accounting.

There came a time when Elsie Downey, the office manager who had been in the position for many years, accepted a job at the nearby school district office and left before we could find a replacement. There was no one on the ranch who knew anything about the billing for dues, accounts payable, preparing financial reports, paying taxes, preparing the annual budget and dealing with the day-to-day aspects of running the office. It fell to me, as Treasurer, to run the office. Marian, who had worked in a bank as a young woman understood debits and credits, offered to help me. The first thing we did was to close the service window at the office for a few days until we could get a handle on the operation. Being computer literate, we were able to work our way through the morass of programs and paperwork and got the office working again. Marian and I ran the office while we tried to find a capable office manager, which was no small task. Eventually, after a few false starts, we found a young lady to replace Elsie. I wrote a desk manual for her to use that covered every aspect of the office operations and after several weeks, was finally able to get back to my real life.

While on the Board of Directors, Marian and I were required to spend a great deal of time working together on various projects. Add to that contact our once weekly horseback ride, albeit with other participants, and we were fodder for rumor mongers. One evening I received a telephone call from Loretta Weinstock, who was one of my regular riding companions. She called to tell me there was a rumor circulating on the ranch that Marian and I were engaged in a love affair. My emotions went from anger, to giddiness and then to pride. My anger came from the realization that someone would make up a story and put it into the rumor mill. My giddiness came from thinking how stupid people must be to believe that we were having an affair. Pride entered into the picture when I thought about what those gullible people must be thinking. They had to accept the fact that a sixty-five year old, five foot, eight inch, balding, grey bearded man was irresistibly attractive to a tall, beautiful, forty-two year old, blond woman who could have had her pick of the men on the ranch if she wanted to have an affair. That puffed me up a little bit, but not for long. I called Marian and let her know about Loretta's call. She laughed and said she would take care of it the next day.

We had a Board meeting the next afternoon and Marian chose that forum to make a preemptive strike. After the meeting was called to order, she requested the floor and announced that she had heard rumors that not only were she and I engaged in an extramarital love affair, but that she was also engaged in a lesbian affair with Buffey, the ranch's female wrangler. To the shocked listeners, she gave assurance that neither story was true. After a few uncomfortable chuckles by the other Board members, I chimed in and told them as far as I knew I wasn't having an affair with Marian, but was sure that my reputation with the ladies was enhanced by the rumor. The Board members knew both of us and our spouses well and took us at our word. Marian's way of dealing with the situation was very effective; I never heard either rumor after that day. Loretta was nice enough to tell me who had started the rumor. He was an individual who liked to sit on his front porch with a view of the main road through the ranch. Apparently, he didn't have much to do except watch traffic to see who was riding with whom and fertilize his imagination with meanness and envy.

While I was on the Board, a law suit was filed by an association member against past and present Board members. When the previous Board decided to remove the dilapidated home provided to the ranch manager and replace it with a new building, it was necessary to borrow the $70,000 dollars mentioned earlier. It was also determined that major improvements to other assets were necessary, so the quarterly dues were slightly increased to repay the loan and provide funds for the additional planned improvements. William Barber, a man who had only been on the ranch for a few months, and his neighbor had taken issue with the way a "horse trap" fence had been constructed on common land that boarded their property. They had no legal standing in the dispute and the ranch manager had explained why the fence had been constructed in that particular configuration. Mr. Barber could not be satisfied and decided to vent his anger by filing suit against the previous and current Board members for approving and implementing the dues increase. His point was that the increase was a special assessment to pay for the new ranch house which required a vote by the entire membership. The position of the Board was that it was a regular increase dictated by the overall need to improve many ranch assets. I just laughed at the situation and never thought it would ever go to trial. It was a good thing we had insurance to protect Board members, because it did go to trial.

Many months later and after many meetings with our lawyer and much research into sources and uses of funds during the history of the ranch, a trial was held at Gillespie County Courthouse in Fredericksburg, Texas. It was like something from an old western movie. We had record heat during that period and the refrigerated air conditioner was unable to completely handle the cooling demand. Everyone in the courtroom was uncomfortably warm and used whatever was available for fans. One of the largest brush fires in the area in many years was in progress, which prevented many homeowners who were members of the Tierra Linda Ranch Volunteer Fire Department from attending. The trial was a two and a half day affair well attended by ranch owners who were not fighting the fire.

Those supporting the Board sat on the left side of the courtroom and those who supported Mr. Barber sat on the right side. The only people I ever saw on the right side were Mrs. Barber and the neighbor who was unhappy about the horse trap fence. The verbal dissecting of every aspect of the accounting actions and the rules and regulations that governed the operation of the ranch was mind numbing. The eyes of jury members were often glazed over during presentations. I was intimately involved with the material and it came close to putting me to sleep. On the third day, after several hours of contemplation, the jury returned a verdict. After they filed into the courtroom and were seated in the jury box, the judge asked, "Has the jury reached a verdict?"

The foreman stood up and uttered one word, "Regular." The judge thanked the jury and dismissed them. It took me some time to absorb the verdict. When the foreman said, "Regular," it meant that we had won; but it was stated so quickly and succinctly, I couldn't grasp the moment until the association members in the courtroom started expressing their approval. Some months later after relating this story to a family member, who practiced courtroom law, she smiled and said, "You experienced something that few citizens ever do. That moment in the courtroom when you win or lose is a special moment you will never forget." She knew what she was talking about; it was a thrilling moment. The insurance company that had paid for our defense took the action one step further and offered to pay Mr. Barber's legal expenses if he would sign a document stating he would not appeal the decision. He accepted and the issue was put behind us forever. Shortly thereafter, the Barbers sold their property and moved away.

Eventually, my two years on the Board of Directors came to an end and I enjoyed ridding myself of the responsibilities almost as much as I enjoyed the challenging work. I spent the bulk of my time improving our acreage and continued my riding activities. I worried every time Kelly and her family drove the seven hundred plus miles to visit us but was always happy to see them. After their Christmas visit in December of 2000, we decided we might like living closer to them and elected to return to Albuquerque. We sold our property on Tierra Linda Ranch on May 1, 2001 and headed back to the high desert of New Mexico.

Chapter 15 – Another Move to Albuquerque

We purchased a townhouse in the Northeast Heights of Albuquerque and set up housekeeping again. Sylvia was rehired by Sandia National Laboratories and I resumed my position as male homemaker. I reconnected with my golf buddies yet again and fell into a nice routine, but life was not perfect.

All the while we were living on Tierra Linda Ranch, Kelly had been struggling with her health but kept her problems private to keep from causing any stress in our lives. She suffered from migraine headaches and was often debilitated. Based on my father's history of migraines, I felt guilty because I assumed she had inherited that condition through me. For many years she also had mysterious symptoms of many kinds of illnesses that left her only partially functional. Her irritable bowel syndrome was particularly debilitating. One doctor felt she had Chrome's disease. Severe pain in various parts of her body, extended periods of fatigue and general ill feelings were suggested to be symptoms of several autoimmune diseases such as Lupus Erythematosus, Sjogren Syndrome, Lime disease, Myasthenia Gravis and Rheumatoid Arthritis. Her doctors had performed countless invasive and noninvasive tests to confirm or eliminate particular diseases with no firm results. She was sent to the Mayo Clinic facility in Phoenix, Arizona, for a week of testing. The results of the tests suggested there were no underlying autoimmune diseases present. Over the years of her illness, her local doctors had continued to prescribe pain relief medication without noticing that she had developed a tolerance for, and a dependence on, addictive drugs. The doctors simply increased dosages each time Kelly reported she was not getting the expected pain relief. Because of her penchant for keeping records, Kelly was able to provide a list of medications prescribed over a two year period. The list contains no less than twenty-three different medications. At the level of her most serious addiction, she was taking high dosages of Oxycontin and Vicodin, two very dangerous drugs.

Sylvia and I anguished over her condition and felt helpless as months went by and Kelly became more and more dysfunctional. I suggested to Sylvia that it could be psychosomatic because I remembered her problems when Clay died. I surmised that the stress of her unattainable need for perfection in everything she attempted collided with the tremendous feeling of loss when Clay died and had rendered her unable to cope with life. I explained that it reminded me of the symptoms of combat fatigue, a psychological event that causes combat troops to become unable to continue fighting. On a smaller scale, I pointed out that while in Vietnam, it was normal for us to develop diarrhea and headaches after a close encounter with death simply because of the associated stress. I felt the stress she had placed on herself for so many years was the root cause of her overall problems.

One summer afternoon in 2002, Kelly asked me to take her to a medical appointment as she did not think it would be safe for her to drive. As we were driving back from the appointment, I told her I had an opinion on her illness and asked if she wanted to hear my thoughts. She replied that she did and I explained my feelings as I had explained them to Sylvia. I didn't suggest she was a hypochondriac or that her pains were completely psychosomatic, but I told her I understood what stress can do to a mind and body and she should seriously consider my thoughts. She agreed to do some research on my theory but told me she knew enough about chemistry, biology and the pain she had endured to convince herself that I had it wrong. I felt better after I had made my feelings known.

Sylvia was not happy when I told her how direct I had been with my opinion, but the die had been cast so she started researching my theory. Although there was a great deal of information available that presented examples of stress causing all sorts of problems, we were unable to pinpoint the true root of her ailments. Kelly's research also left us with no answers. It was breaking our hearts to know she was in pain most of the time and medical treatment offered her little relief. I told her again of my father's addiction to doctor prescribed morphine and how whenever he felt the need for the drug, his migraine headaches would become more severe. I suggested she may be addicted to some of the pain killers and her body was fooling her into obtaining drugs by mimicking pain. Eventually, in late summer of 2003, she decided to purge herself of the addiction and, under her doctor's supervision, ceased taking all medication. One discussion with her that sticks in my mind was the time she discovered why it is called "kicking the habit." As my father had learned so many years before in Narco, Kelly had to go through that period when an addict looses leg control as the body is demanding a fix.

Cleansing her system of drugs had a tremendous beneficial effect on her systems. Whereas she is still not free of all of the symptoms for which she had been treated with so many drugs, they are vastly diminished and she is able to function more like a completely healthy person. As a professional who tested drugs on volunteers, she is very cognizant of placebo effects and the existence of psychosomatic illness and is certain that her illness and ailments are real but in remission at the moment.

Chapter 16 - Back to Texas

Kelly's recovery coincided with that point in the lives of Sylvia's parents when they were approaching ninety years of age. Sylvia had retired from the Sandia National Laboratory and wanted to live closer to her parents for a change. The housing market was good, so we listed and sold our townhouse and moved to New Braunfels, Texas, a town about thirty-five miles northeast of San Antonio and about thirty minutes driving time from Sylvia's two sisters' homes near Seguin, Texas. We moved into a rental home and contracted to have a home built on an acre of land we had purchased during a previous visit. The land was about six miles outside of New Braunfels in a beautiful part of the area. There were many oak trees on our one acre of Texas and it was on the top of a hill, which provided us the cooling, southern breezes. Earlier in my life I had convinced myself that if I were to live in hot, humid, Texas, it would have to be in the Kerrville region that was about 2,000 feet above sea level; but I changed my mind when I saw the New Braunfels area. Although it was only a little higher in altitude than San Antonio, it seemed cooler. There is a strong German influence in the local architecture and a strong conservative leaning in the political system. The Guadalupe River flows through New Braunfels adding to the beauty of the area and drawing thousands of visitors, which encourages an overall feeling of a holiday season for most of the year.

By February of 2002, the construction was completed and we moved into yet another new home. There was plenty of land clearing to be done and many rocks to be removed to allow lawn mower clearance. Sylvia and I had a great time working outside on our little piece of property, even if we did have to fight chiggers, fire ants, armadillos, snakes, scorpions, skunks, wild turkeys, the occasional raccoon and white tail deer who believed the land belonged to them. The oak leaf rollers, a tenacious breed of moth that begins life as a caterpillar in oak trees, were really difficult to manage. In the spring, they drop down in the millions from the trees on strong silky threads making it difficult to walk anywhere near an oak tree without becoming entangled with them. I was wise enough to insist on a screened-in back porch so we were able to enjoy the outdoors protected from the mosquitoes, but there wasn't very much we could do about the scorpions that liked to come into our house to live. There were so many scorpions, I regularly caught them and placed them in a terrarium in my office. I even had an encounter with a snake while living in New Braunfels.

Sylvia came in from working in the front yard one afternoon and told me she had discovered a snake in her flower bed. A harmless rat snake had gotten tangled in netting Sylvia had placed over some delicate plants to discourage the deer from eating them. I had accidentally killed one a week earlier while mowing the back lawn on my John Deere lawn tractor and felt I should make up for that by freeing this one. I grabbed the snake by the tail and dislodged the netting from the plants while Sylvia went to get some scissors to cut away the tangled material. Holding the snake with my left hand and with Sylvia putting tension on the netting, I proceeded to snip the tangled mess around its head. With the final snip, the snake's head turned toward my hand with lightning like speed and latched onto my fingers. I yanked him off and he hit the ground running. My fingers were bleeding and a few snake teeth remained imbedded in one of them. I was certain it was not a poisonous snake and planned to cover the wound with band aids once I stopped the bleeding but Sylvia insisted I go to the Emergency Room; she worried about what bacteria or germs might have been in the snake's mouth. I argued with her but finally gave in and we drove to town.

The day before the snake bit me, I had a spot of skin cancer removed from my nose that required a large incision and twelve stitches, so there was a prominent bandage on my face at that time. When our time came to see the nurse at the Emergency Room, she asked, "What seems to be your problem this evening, young man?" When I innocently replied that I had been bitten by a snake, she sat back in her chair and with wide eyes replied, "You got bit on the nose by a snake?" I had completely forgotten about the bandage on my nose and was not trying to fool her. When I showed her my fingers, she relaxed and arranged for the necessary treatment which was cleansing and a prescription for ointment. Nothing ever developed from the bite and I paid back nature for accidentally killing a harmless, beneficial snake.

My mother died while we were living in New Braunfels. I had long ago told my remaining siblings, the five sisters, that I did not intend to attend the funeral when she passed. Since my father had died almost forty years earlier, there was no one there for me to comfort. We did travel to Delaware twice to help her celebrate her ninetieth and one hundredth birthdays. My mother must have had some really good genes. She had a hard life, bore nine children, had a few miscarriages and lived to be almost one hundred and four. Maybe she passed on some of those genes on to me. I've already lived more years than any of the male members of my immediate family. Although I could easily be found guilty of misspending my youth, partying too hard during my middle age and not exercising enough as I enter the winter of my life, I am as healthy as the Euro Dollar. Below are photographs of Sylvia and me working on our place in New Braunfels when I was seventy and she was sixty-two. She got tired of my telling her how to dig the holes for the oleander plants and tried to kill me.

Swinging a Pick at Seventy. (Courtesy: Sylvia Joyce)

She tired of hearing me say "Dig faster."
(Courtesy: Alexander Heimgartner)

Chapter 17 – The Final Move to New Mexico

Margaret, Sylvia's mother, was a very active woman even as she neared her ninetieth birthday. She was still driving, and from time to time, she and Clayton would make the forty-five mile trip from San Antonio to New Braunfels and spend the night with us. On one of those visits, Clayton fell and fractured his hip. Remarkably, he came through the surgical procedure and subsequent rehabilitation but the family decided they would not be able to live alone in their home of fifty years any longer.

Sylvia's sister, Penny, and her husband Frank, owned about nine acres near Seguin. Her other sister, Nancy, and her husband, Ben, owned a thirty-five acre place about fifteen minutes driving time away from Penny. Nancy had a relatively new single wide mobile home on her property that they used while building their retirement home. Because Nancy's property was somewhat remote, the decision was made to move the mobile home to Penny's place to be used by their parents and for the original home in San Antonio to be sold. The home sold and Margaret and Clayton insisted on paying off the mortgage on the single wide, and obtain formal ownership. Penny and Frank sold a half acre of their land to Margaret and Clayton for the home and allowed them to hook up to the water and septic systems. Margaret often told me how happy she was to be living in the country where she could see the wildlife, cattle and horses on adjoining ranches.

We lived in New Braunfels for about a year after Margaret and Clayton moved to Seguin. Nancy was still teaching school in San Antonio but was able to help her parents by running errands when she could. Sylvia drove to Sequin at least once a week to maintain their financial records, help around the house and take them to medical appointments as well as just sit and visit with them. Penny provided the lion's share of assistance. Sylvia's brother, Jack, who lived and worked in Austin about an hour away, visited as often as he could. The siblings felt these arrangements were the best way to keep their parents out of an assisted living home and allow them to continue their relative independence.

With Sylvia's parents settled and getting the assistance they needed, we started to think about our own family. We realized that Kelly's three children were growing up and missed being near them during their development. We decided to sell our place and move back to the Albuquerque area to enjoy life with our only remaining child and our grandchildren.

Our home sold on the second day it was on the market and we arranged a closing date for thirty days later. Not expecting such a quick sale, we hadn't told the family of our plans, so it was a surprise to everyone when we announced that we wanted to live closer to Kelly and had sold our home. Sylvia's family understood our desires and expressed sadness that we were to leave, but happiness that we would be near Kelly and our grandchildren.

Sylvia and Nancy drove to Albuquerque to locate interim housing for us until we decided where we wanted to live. While there, they found a housing development in Rio Rancho (a suburb of Albuquerque) that seemed satisfactory to both of us. They found a half acre lot with a view and Sylvia signed a contract for the land. To say that we had a disagreement with yet another building contractor makes me sound like a difficult customer. I like to think that after purchasing so many homes during our married life, I've developed a reasonable sense of caution. In May of 2006, we contracted for a home to be constructed on the half acre of land. Before too long, we discovered that the contractor's salesman had used the bait and switch ploy with regard to the type of residential roads to be provided. We did not want to spend the rest of our lives driving on gravel roads and complained to the builder. I offered them the choice of providing a similar home in a development with hard top streets or a refund of our good faith money; they chose to refund our down payment and we separated on good terms. Eventually, we purchased a suitable existing home in Rio Rancho and have now lived here for two years. We are less than fifteen minutes from Kelly's home and only five minutes from the high school attended by our grandchildren. Jane and her children live in the small town of Bosque Farms, which is about a forty-five minute drive from

Rio Rancho. Living near the grandchildren is wonderful; we are having great times together.

Clayton's health vacillated during the period we lived in New Braunfels. Eventually, the years took their toll and it became necessary for him to return to the nursing home. Margaret is a tiny lady who weighs less than a hundred pounds and was physically overwhelmed with his care. Late in June of 2007, Kelly decided she wanted to visit her grandparents and drove with her family to Seguin. After visiting her grandfather, she called Sylvia and told her she felt the end was near and suggested Sylvia fly over to San Antonio. Sylvia took Kelly's advice and was there when her ninety-four old father died on July 1, 2007. At the funeral, Margaret amazed me with her ability to deal with the death of her husband of seventy years. Perhaps her strength was rooted in her strong religious beliefs.

Not yet ready for full retirement, Sylvia took advantage of an opportunity to return to work. A friend and previous employer offered to hire her on a part time basis as an office manager. Her schedule is flexible and she only works four hours a day, three days a week. She enjoys the challenges of the job and getting out of the house. I reconnected once more with my old golf buddies and I play at that game once a week. Except for a few minor aches and pains that come with aging, we are in fine health and feel like we are looking at the world through thirty year old eyes. So far, with the sad exception of losing Clay, life has been wonderful.

I have to stop writing now; Sylvia just said she wants to go look at some model homes in a new area under development.

AFTERWORD

In case you weren't counting, I've had forty-two major moves since I left home including thirty-two during our forty-seven years of marriage. Looking at moves in a positive manner made each of them an adventure rather than something to approach with dread. Even now, when the Albuquerque winter seems too long or the spring winds last until early summer, we wonder if there is a better place to live. The emotional tug of being near our grandchildren makes it harder and harder to consider another move, but who knows? Many times in the past, after moving into a new home, I have been heard to say, "This is it. I'm going to live in this place until I die!" That statement has long since become a joke with friends and family.

I have always been one to plan for the future. Sometimes I plan too far ahead which has taught me the future is indeed unknown. Still, it makes me feel secure to have plans. I have planned to never allow myself to become dependent upon others for my physical care. I have asked my wife to arrange for the least expensive cremation procedure once my body reaches its biological limit and I breathe no more. If the currently empty grave site next to Clay at Fort Sam Houston Cemetery is no longer available when I check out, I want Sylvia to simply scatter my ashes over his grave.

I do not fear death or any hereafter. I have lived a good and honorable life. I have had human failings but kept them to a minimum. I could cease to exist today and would have had a better life than ninety-nine percent of the people on earth. I have lived the American dream. From a poor beginning with hand-me-down clothes, I struggled through my formal and informal education and succeeded through hard work and determination. I met the love of my life, known the exhilaration of being a father and suffered the pain of losing a child. I've experienced the joy of happily roaming when I chose, and the stark reality of warfare. I've been financially devastated and worked my way back to financial security. Most of the credit for that good life can

311

be traced to being born in the United States of America. I also credit my wife who stood with me through the good and the bad decisions I made, and my parents who provided me with an excellent work ethic, a drive to become financially independent and a strong sense of fair play.

A person only gets to go through life once; it should be done with gusto and honor.

Appendix A – Aircraft losses

My twenty years in the United States Air Force were spent in training for, or actively involved in, operations of the United States Air Force Security Service. During that period, we lost several reconnaissance aircraft associated with our intelligence collection activity. It was during the height of the cold war and although several other serious air incidents occurred, I will list here only our *reconnaissance* aircraft loses from the time I entered the service in 1953 through my retirement at the end of 1973. The list does not include our reconnaissance losses in the Vietnam Theater of Operations during that war. There were many other losses before my enlistment and more after I retired from the Air Force.

July 29, 1953
Soviet fighters shot down an Air Force RB-50 over the Sea of Japan. The record lists three killed in action and thirteen missing in action.

September 4, 1954
A United States Navy P2V was shot down by Soviet fighters off the coast of Siberia. The record lists one killed in action and nine rescued.

April 18, 1955
Soviet fighters shot down an Air Force RB-47 over the Pacific Ocean off the coast of the Kamchatka Peninsula. The record lists three missing in action.

August 22, 1956
A United States Navy P4M on an intelligence collection mission was shot down over the East China Sea by Chinese fighters. The record lists four killed in action and twelve missing in action.

September 10, 1956
An Air Force RB-50 disappeared on an intelligence gathering mission over the Sea of Japan. The record lists sixteen missing in action. This loss could have been weather related.

September 2, 1958
An Air Force RC-130 was shot down by Soviet fighters near the city of Yerevan, Armenia. The record lists six killed in action and eleven missing in action.

May 1, 1960
A U-2 reconnaissance aircraft was brought down over the Central Soviet Union by a surface to air missile after the engine failed and the pilot was forced to descend to an altitude that allowed the successful shoot down. The pilot, Francis G. Powers, bailed out and was captured. He was eventually exchanged for a Soviet spy, Rudolf Able, held by the United States. During the attack on the U-2, the Soviets fired missiles that unintentionally destroyed one of their own fighter aircraft.

July 1, 1960
An Air Force RB-47 was shot down by Soviet fighters over the Barents Sea. The record reveals that two men, the co-pilot and the navigator were captured. They were eventually released but the other four crewmembers perished. There is an unconfirmed report that the pilot was able to activate the remotely controlled gun in the tail section and shot down one of the attacking Mig-17s. According to the report, as the American survivors floated down to the sea in their parachutes, they observed the pilot of the Mig-17 descending using his distinctive, Soviet style, black parachute. The fate of the Soviet pilot is unknown.

October 27, 1962
A U-2 reconnaissance aircraft was brought down by a surface to air missile over Cuba. The pilot perished.

March 10, 1964
An Air Force RB-66 strayed across the East German border and was shot down by Soviet fighters. The three crewmen survived and were eventually returned to friendly forces.

December 14, 1965
An Air Force RB-47 disappeared over the Black Sea. This loss may have been mechanical or weather related but enemy fire has not been ruled out as the cause. The record lists two missing in action. There was one report that suggested a Soviet submarine was observed recovering some of the electronic equipment from the aircraft before it disappeared beneath the surface of the sea.

April 15, 1969
A United States Navy EC-121 on an intelligence collection mission over the Sea of Japan was shot down by North Korean Mig-21 fighters. The record lists two killed in action and twenty-nine missing in action.

July 5, 1969
An Air Force RC-135 disappeared over the Bearing Sea. This loss may have been related to mechanical problems. The record lists nineteen missing in action.

These operations and losses were generally unknown to the American public. Many Air Force, Navy and Army personnel have put their lives on the line for many years in the pursuit of intelligence gathering to protect the country.

Appendix B – Military Assignments

1. I enlisted in the USAF on July 8, 1953 and was sent to Sampson AFB in New York for basic training.

2. In November of 1953, I was selected for Radio Operator training and was sent to Keesler AFB, Mississippi.

3. By August of 1954, I completed Morse code training, a typewriting course and Intercept Operator training. I was sent to the 3rd Radio Squadron Mobile in Anchorage, Alaska and subsequently to a small detachment at Naknek, Alaska, a remote village on Bristol Bay.

4. After I completed my service in Alaska, I was sent to Intelligence Analyst School at March AFB at Riverside, California in January of 1956.

5. I completed the Analyst School in California and was transferred to USAFSS Headquarters in San Antonio, Texas in May of 1956.

6. I was discharged from the USAF on July 7, 1957 and reenlisted in California on September 17, 1957. I was assigned to TUSLOG (Turkish-United States Logistics) Detachment 3-1 at Trabzon, Turkey as an Intelligence Analyst Supervisor in November of 1957.

7. After completion of the Turkey assignment, I transferred to the 6913 RSM in Bremerhaven, Germany for a one year assignment in November of 1958 where I was assigned as the Assistant Surveillance and Warning Center Supervisor.

8. After completion of the Bremerhaven assignment, I transferred

to the USAFSS Headquarters in San Antonio, Texas where I served as an Intelligence Analyst.

9. I was transferred to the 6912TH RSM, Berlin, Germany as an Intelligence Analyst Supervisor in October of 1962.

10. After completion of the Berlin assignment, I returned to the USAFSS Headquarters in San Antonio, Texas in October of 1965 where I worked as an Intelligence Analyst.

11. I was assigned to Detachment 1 of the 6994 RSM at Nha Trang, South Vietnam as an Airborne Intelligence Analyst in September of 1967.

12. After completion of my Vietnam assignment in August of 1968, I transferred to the 6917 RSM at San Vito de Normani (Brindisi) Italy where I was assigned as a Surveillance and Warning Center Supervisor and subsequently served as the Base Plans Writer/Supervisor.

13. After completion of the Italy assignment in February of 1971, I transferred to the 6910 RGM at Darmstadt, Germany and served as a Surveillance and Warning Center Supervisor.

14. I remained with the 6910th when it moved to Augsburg, Germany in June of 1972. I completed my service there as a Surveillance and Warning Center Supervisor in October of 1973 and retired from the USAF upon arrival at McGuire AFB in New Jersey on October 31, 1973.

Appendix C – Life Time Moves

Basic training at Sampson AFB in upstate New York.	July of 1953
Transferred to Keesler AFB in Biloxi, Mississippi	November of 1953
Transferred to Alaska (Anchorage and Aleutian Islands)	Summer of 1954
Transferred to Riverside, California	Spring of 1956
Transferred to San Antonio, Texas	Summer of 1956
Discharged and moved to California	July of 1957
Reenlisted and transferred to Trabzon, Turkey	September of 1957
Transferred to Bremerhaven, Germany	November of 1958
Transferred to San Antonio, Texas	December of 1959
Married – moved into on base apartment	August of 1961
Transferred to Berlin, Germany (Marien Str.)	October of 1962
Moved to Government Quarters in Berlin	August of 1963
Transferred to San Antonio, Texas. (Paradise Valley)	October of 1965
Transferred to Nha Trang, South Vietnam	September of 1967
Transferred to Brindisi, Italy	August of 1968
Moved within Brindisi, Italy	Spring of 1969
Moved into Government Quarters	Spring of 1970
Transferred to Darmstadt, Germany	February of 1971
Moved within Darmstadt	Fall of 1971
Transferred to Augsburg, Germany	Summer of 1972
Retired at McGuire AFB, New Jersey	January 2, 1974
Moved to San Antonio, Texas (La Barca)	January 1974
Moved to Victoria, Texas (Antitem)	September of 1974
Moved to Albuquerque, New Mexico (Apartment)	August of 1976
Moved within Albuquerque (Otero)	December of 1976
Moved to Roswell, New Mexico (Twin Diamond)	June of 1978
Moved to Albuquerque, New Mexico (Noreen)	December of 1979
Moved within Albuquerque (Tramway Terrace)	December of 1983
Moved within Albuquerque (Bauer)	April of 1985
Moved to an apartment for three months	February of 1990
Moved within Albuquerque (Denali)	May of 1990
Moved to San Antonio, Texas (Country Field)	May of 1991

Moved to Albuquerque, New Mexico (Verbena)	November of 1991
Moved to an apartment in Albuquerque	February of 1994
Moved within Albuquerque (Merion Circle)	May of 1994
Moved to Kerrville, Texas (Apartment)	July of 1996
Moved to Tierra Linda Ranch in Kerrville	December of 1996
Moved to Albuquerque, New Mexico (Cambridge)	May of 2001
Moved to apartment in New Braunfels, Texas	September of 2002
Moved within New Braunfels, Texas (North Ridge)	February of 2003
Moved to rental house in Albuquerque	April of 2006
Moved to Rio Rancho, New Mexico (Nicklaus)	December of 2006